IN MY TIME

By the same author

LITTLE PETER VACUUM
THE ELDER BROTHER
HIGH ENDEAVOUR
ENTER A GREEK
HEYDAY
THE DRAMATIST
YOUNG APOLLO
THE NEW CRUSADE
LONDON SYMPHONY
ROYAL EXCHANGE
RESTORATION COMEDY
HERE LIES TOMORROW
GIBBS AND A PHONEY WAR

In My Time

ANTHONY GIBBS

PETER DAVIES : LONDON

Printed in Great Britain by
The Camelot Press Ltd., London and Southampton

Illustrations

1. THE AUTHOR, AGED NINE   *Facing page* 90

2. (*a*) THE AUTHOR'S WIFE, MAISIE, AND   91
        HER FATHER, SIR CHARLES MARTIN
     (*b*) MAISIE AND THE TWO CHILDREN   91

3. FOUR GENERATIONS OF GIBBSES   122

4. CHARLES FRY   123

Author's Note

This book has been pieced together entirely from scraps of memory without benefit of notes.

It may well be that, over the years, inaccuracies have crept in, and statements are made here which might unintentionally cause irritation or even pain to certain persons.

If this is so, it is to be greatly regretted, but the author has attempted to record events to the best of his own recollection, and apologises in advance if in doing so he has caused any offence.

In case there should be any misunderstanding from a statement made on page 239, he would like also to allude to an earlier reference on page 227, and record the fact that he appreciates that Mr. Howard Samuel did not purchase the Cresset Press.

ANTHONY GIBBS

I

Where does one begin a thing like this? Certainly not at the beginning.

'I was born in Bolton.'

When I showed this manuscript to a friend of mine who is also a publisher, he suggested that an appropriate title might be 'Diary of a Middle Class Snob'. So you may as well have it.

My father was born in Kensington, which was a bit better. His father was born in Windsor Castle, which was better still. *His* father was a Queen's Messenger which is how the Castle came about, and *his* father was what used to be known as a 'horse-leech', at a place called Bramshaw, in the New Forest. He was born, possibly on the wrong side of the blanket, at Clyst St George, in Devonshire, where all the better Gibbses have been born since the year eleven hundred and something. That makes me a fifth cousin of Sir Humphrey in Rhodesia, for instance, hastily removed.

On the distaff side, things are rather more aristocratic—or, at least, *upper* middle class. One of my grandmothers was an Irish Hamilton. The other was a Domville, and she, bless her heart, was descended, by courtesy of his children's nurse, from Henry II. This made her a rather irregular Plantagenet, but not more irregular, I fancy, than the present lot.

There was an Irish title in that family which would have descended upon me in a circumlocutory motion via two uncles. It is a pity that my great-grandfather shot his butler dead for bringing up the wrong bottle of vintage port at dinner one day. The deed was heavily frowned upon and the title put into abeyance.

As a matter of fact—it's something I've always kept from my dearest friends—I *was* born in Bolton. My parents were passing at the time. My father, not yet in the least distinguished, had a job with something called Tillotson's Literary Syndicate. It still exists, distributing articles and features in the North.

One hot summer day, when I myself had notched up a few weeks, my father was sitting in the sunshine on the front steps of Tillotson's during the lunch hour. He was wearing a top-hat and was reading Goethe in the original German.

As he read a bulky shadow fell across the pages and a slightly flutey voice said, 'Young man, can you understand that stuff?'

My father said he could.

'Come and see me on Monday,' said the voice. 'I'll make you Literary Editor of the *Daily Mail*.'

It was Alfred Harmsworth, Lord Northcliffe.

So we shook the dust of Bolton from our feet, and, on Monday morning, my father presented himself at Carmelite House and told the commissionaire, 'I'm the new Literary Editor of the *Daily Mail*.'

'That's all right, sir,' said the commissionaire. 'Third floor, right at the end of the passage, last door on the left.'

My father went up in the lift, found the passage, found the door marked Literary Editor, and went in.

There was a man sitting at the desk.

He said, 'Who the hell are you?'

'My name's Philip Gibbs,' my father told him. 'I'm the Literary Editor of the *Daily Mail*. Who the hell are you?'

'That's funny,' the man said, 'my name's Filson Young, and I'm the Literary Editor of the *Daily Mail*.'

So they made a pact. It was eighteen months before Lord Northcliffe discovered he had two Literary Editors, and was paying both of them.

My father held the job and Filson Young went away and

2

wrote a brilliant and sensitive life of Christopher Columbus in two volumes.

The result was that when I really came to, at about the age of six, my father had already written *The Street of Adventure* and some other novels and was well on the way to literary and journalistic success. We lived at No. 36 Holland Street, Kensington. I went to have a look at it the other day. It was exactly the same.

It was the ordinary small London terrace house built, I suppose, in about the year 1830, still retaining the graceful Georgian proportions. Opposite lived Mr Cotton the tailor and Mr Osborn the painter. Two doors away was a public house, and on Saturday nights half a dozen men could generally be stepped over, flat out on the pavement outside. By Sunday morning they were always gone.

On Thursday mornings a German band played outside Mr Osborn's. There was a gigantic euphonium that went oomp-pom oomph-pom oomph-pom, and a variety of trumpets, with of course a big bass drum. The man who played this wore a peaked cap placed quite flat on his dirty white hair and had a large, curly meerschaum in his mouth. The man with the euphonium wore a walrus moustache. They were wonderfully shabby and ill-kempt but their music was lively and their rheumy old eyes twinkled with human kindness. They disappeared for ever on 4 August 1914.

Apart from this the noise of London was the noise of horses. I often wonder what the horse population was in, say, 1910. A million? Their excrement was pervasive. A series of little men with shovel hats and wide shovels spent many hours a day pushing it about, but they never caught up with it. It lay about in great steaming heaps that disintegrated in the process of time into straw-like wisps which the wind lifted and blew into the eyes of pretty ladies.

Nobody seemed to mind or even to notice. There could, of course, be a world of elegance about the horse. To go to Hyde Park on a fine May afternoon and to lean on those iron railings near the statue of Achilles was to be translated. The sun glinted on the spokes of the wheels. The harness shone, the water-carts had laid the dust and left a comforting aroma of dung and asphalt and leather and perspiration. There were cockades of gold braid on the silk hats of the coachmen and the footmen, and the smart clop of hooves, and the jingle of harness, and parasols and gracious inclinations of the head and little boys sitting up behind with toppers and leggings and punctiliously folded arms.

Yet those same fashionable and aristocratic ladies, eternally occupied with the rigorous protocol of calling, and returning calls, and leaving cards—you generally sent the footman in with one of your own large ones and a lot of little ones of your husband's for every member of the family, all dog-eared to show you had arrived personally at the door—those same ladies would be completely unabashed when a horse, at a few inches' distance from their faces, would lift its well-cut tail, extrude a little premonitory sphinctum, and utter a colossal fart that could be heard as far as Belgrave Square, and overwhelming in its concentration of sulphuretted hydrogen.

Every horse and every sort, shape and size of vehicle had its own sound. If you had chicken-pox and lay in bed you could hear them all go down Holland Street and recognize them as they went. A four-wheeler cab had a completely different sound from a hansom. The hansom flitted by with a swish and a jingle of trotting hooves. The four-wheeler plodded humbly and quietly by. The delivery vans had no rubber tyres, so their wheels crunched in the roadway, and their horses' feet fell at second intervals. The carriage and pair had a complicated, asynchronous and immediately recognizable rhythm which generally sent one bounding to the be-curtained window. The pantechnicon groaned and strained and creaked and the iron shoes of the horses skidded and dug into the road and skidded again.

Sometimes, but very, very occasionally, there was a new sound in the land. It went 'toofle toofle toofle toof toof toofle toofle' and there was a great clatter of lamps and metal furniture and the clank of chains.

Before leaving the park I must just mention my uncle. I had a very splendid uncle. His name was Cosmo Hamilton and he had friends like Victor Gordon-Lennox. He was always beautifully dressed. Suits by Hooper. Shirts by Izzard. Shoes by Lobb. You know the sort of thing. He wore a monocle and smoked cigarettes through a long tortoiseshell holder. His hair was always beautifully strained back over a rather fine head (the Gibbs family is noticeably good-looking) so that it showed the comb marks; and he wrote the words of all the successful pre-first-war musical comedies like *The Belle of Mayfair* and *The Girl from This* and *The Girl from That*. All of them, that is, except the ones that were written by Adrian Ross. You only had to look at him to see he was tremendously well off.

He married a wonderful lady called Beryl Faber who was reputed to be the most beautiful woman in London. She was a sister of C. Aubrey Smith, who kept Englishry alive for fifty years in Hollywood, and wasn't a bad-looking old thing himself.

Cosmo had a curricle, a most elegant equipage with two horses which he drove himself from inside, if you follow me. (This reminds me that my cousin Charlie used to drive a coach and six in a state of high inebriation playing a banjo on the box.)

Imagine my uncle with the most beautiful woman in London beside him, two spanking bays in front, and the monocle in his eye. Just as he was passing the French Embassy gate in very good order a beastly Lean-Bollee backfired. The horses leaped in the air, pawed the sky for a few agonizing seconds, and set off at forty miles an hour with their ears cocked and their tails up.

Cosmo stood up and put all his weight into tugging at the reins. My aunt was screaming at the top of her voice. Men shouted and ran. The pavement was strewn into patterns with fainting women. Cosmo threw away the reins, climbed over the curly footboard and began to make his way along the shaft between the two terrified horses. The curricle bucked and bounded. Horses were standing on two feet all over the place as coachmen and riders reined to make a path. My uncle got to the horses' heads, seized a bridle in each hand and by a process of pulling their heads together with all his strength managed to confuse them sufficiently to bring them to a halt. Hundreds of people rushed to pat the horses, to pat Cosmo on the back, and to comfort the lovely Beryl. They were the heroes of the week.

Looking back, although I don't want to sound too elderly about it, this really was more picturesque than the usual slightly battered Jaguar facing the wrong way on the grass beside the Kingston by-pass.

[2]

Of course I went to school, but as the whole process of education is so peculiarly unpleasant I prefer not to dwell upon it. First, a lady called Miss Wallick, in Kensington Square. She wore half-moon pince-nez. And afterwards to a Catholic institution called Stonyhurst College. But enough of that.

One could walk one way down Holland Street, cross Church Street, and cut through a passage to sail boats on the Round Pond; or one could walk straight opposite the house down another passage to the Kensington Public Library, to get another book by Jules Verne, to whose novels I was already greatly devoted.

Encouraged by the master, who always used the longest possible words, due largely to bad translation from the French, I produced my first novel at the age of seven. It contained only four pages, of which the first carried the title, and the other three the single sentence which comprised the total opus.

It was called *The Mechanical Detective*, and the sentence was: 'The mechanical detective precipitated himself downstairs with the utmost velocity.

6

We authors, naturally, all knew one another. E. W. Hornung, who was making a fortune out of the Raffles books, lived just round the corner in Hornton Street, in a very superior house with a red moto-rcar standing in front of it. He was a nice man, not altogether English, in spite of his worship of cricket and Sullivan cigarettes. In fact he was a Hungarian, like Robert Donat and Leslie Howard. He was also a cousin of Conan Doyle.

My mother was at home on Thursdays. Doesn't that sound extraordinary? There would be tea going in the drawing-room, with little sandwiches and those rather jolly spherical wafers with soft chocolate insides. Galsworthy often came. I remember him as quite impossibly patrician. He had a beautiful domelike cranium and was very tall—or perhaps he only seemed so to me. He always stood up, with a cup of tea in one hand, in such a way that by bending slightly over some seated female he presented that splendid profile to the best advantage.

Another was Wells. Always piping like one of his own Selenites. And there was Bennett. Mathematically symmetrical. Also I suppose there must have been Barrie, though I confess I have no recollection of him whatsoever. He was the one who discovered my father in the Royal Societies Club about to attack a kedgeree and said, 'Good God, Gibbs, are you going to eat that? Or have you done so?'

And, of course, there was Chesterton and there was Belloc. Truly an age of giants.

Chesterton was a huge man, full of whimsy and port. There was a time when he lived near enough to us to be seen out of the window. He had a tiny wife. He used to order a hansom at the same time each day to take him to Fleet Street. Every morning he boarded the hansom first, a vast flapping figure with a broad-brimmed hat and a flamboyant cloak. The horse reared in its shafts. When the commotion was over and the horse and the wheels and the springs had subsided Mrs Chesterton would get in. If she had done so first he would undoubtedly have killed her.

Of all these people there was one man, and he was the smallest, who towered head and shoulders above the rest. Wells. It is a curious thing that Wells is now remembered largely for the youthful extravaganzas which first made me, as a small boy, his most devoted slave. The reason, I imagine, is that films were made of *The Invisible Man*, *The War of the Worlds*, *The Man Who Could Work Miracles* and *The Shape of Things to Come*. Like all the small boys of the period, I lapped these up, together with *The Food of the Gods* and *The First Men in the Moon*. In my humble opinion they are still the best science fiction, written with an economy of words, a sharpness of imagination, a dramatic deftness, and an awareness of the absurdity and littleness of man against the vast background of creation, which spell the one word 'genius'.

I can still see Wells very clearly, strutting in our drawing-room like a cock-sparrow, with a negligible chin, watched always by the adoring eyes of his wife, and fluting querulously in that extra-terrestrial voice.

Now I come to think of it, it was that curious quality of extra-terrestriality which made Wells great. He took an absurdly God-like view of humanity, and its little struggles. He could come down upon this planet with all the superior intelligence of an older civilization in Another Place, and pin-point a young chemist's assistant in a country town at the beginning of this century, or a draper in his shop, and study his excited frustrations as if he were an ant in a formicarium.

You may laugh at me, I know, but to my dying day I shall do battle for *The Outline of History*, which Wells tossed off as a sort of journalistic job to be published in fortnightly parts, as his greatest book, to be set on the same pedestal as the immortal formula of Einstein: $E = MC^2$. And for this same reason: passing historians, intent upon the Kings and Queens of England, and the date of the Norman Conquest, dismiss it as 'inaccurate'. Who cares?

8

For the first and only time in the history of human consciousness, an intellect was born great enough to put the whole story, from the moment of creation to the idiocies of the Versailles Peace Conference, into a single volume.

[3]

First and foremost my father was a journalist, and this was enormous fun for me.

Exactly twenty-five years older than myself, my father had the gift of youth. So that when I grew to be ten and he was still only thirty-five, he treated me with an affectionate equality very different from the traditional 'father figure' of the period. I think he really enjoyed taking me about with him on his journalistic trips, and for me, of course, they spelled high adventure.

Looking backwards in time, I now see that the rather extraordinary relationship he and I developed made me a very abnormal and probably rather priggish small boy. I always felt enormously older than my contemporaries. Linked like this, with the events that made the daily headlines in the newspapers, I simply could not be bothered with tin soldiers, football, wrestling matches on the floor, and the other pursuits of infantilism. In a way this was a pity. It is a fact that, except for my father, I have never really made a friend.

We set off for instance in a second-class carriage to Windsor, where the paper had hired a window suitably draped in black, for the funeral of King Edward. As I remember it this was a jolly sort of public holiday, with thousands of people milling about in the narrow streets, and rows of raucous hawkers doing a roaring trade in souvenirs, time-tables of the procession, black rosettes, cream horns, mineral waters and funeral mugs. I had a new pair of field-glasses which had cost my father sixpence and which I was very anxious to try.

When the slow, musical procession finally arrived from

the station in the nether regions and turned the corner by the Castle Wall, the man who dominated the entire occasion and remained fixed in the mind of the crowd—for ever in mine—was, of course, the Kaiser, in a magnificent cloak, with a fantastic golden eagle on top of his helmet, reining a curvetting horse with one hand and darting his imperial glances over the waxed tips of his imperial moustaches. He really was a splendid figure, and the crowd rose to him. The field-glasses had a magnification of one. Two wars later I used to hear a lot about the Kaiser from his cousin Princess Marie Louise, who was the 'spitting' image of him, but without the moustaches. Did he know? Prancing about on the cobblestones of the old town behind the laborious catafalque of his uncle and watching the English eyes light up at his appearance, did he know that England had taken the other side? Did he realize that his uncle's visits to Paris meant exactly that? Did he know about the Schlieffen Plan, and the invasion of Belgium, in exactly four years' time?

I went for a ride on one of the very first London electric trams. It ran somewhere in Lambeth, and you sat on a long seat running up either side with a pattern of holes in it, while you swanned along with the driver lurching to the strange movement and stamping on a bell. Now, when I commute to London, I pass the Chessington Zoo which keeps a tram in its car park labelled 'London's last electric tram'.

One day a man called Latham took off from Dover in an aeroplane and tried to fly the Channel. The newspapers were in a state of high excitement. This was the time when Northcliffe, in order to push his sales, was offering cash prizes of a thousand pounds, and even ten thousand pounds, for the first man who could fly from England to France, or from London to Manchester.

Latham failed. His plane fell into the sea. It was a very shapely machine he had christened the 'Antoinette', and my father who was not, of course, in the middle of the Channel, wrote an imaginative piece built up from the stories of the men who were, describing how 'the intrepid aviator was discovered calmly smoking a cigarette'.

All London flocked to see his machine when they put it on exhibition at Barker's, spreading its vast wings over the provision department. And Latham tried again. I've no idea how many times he tried and failed. At least three. And on every occasion the intrepid aviator was discovered calmly smoking a cigarette. The phrase suddenly struck the public as funny. It appeared in *Punch*, and for a time it found its way into the language.

Then word came that something really epoch-making was afoot. My father and I got into a third-class smoker of the London, Brighton & South Coast Railway and made our way in a 'growler' to a hotel, on the top of a cliff over-looking the sea. I am not sure, now, precisely where this was, but I do remember that it was set rather apart, so that there was a large area of soft downland turf all about it, with a path crossing it, a road, and suddenly, the cliff. At night you could look out of the bedroom window and see the lights of France, shining at the further edge of the sea.

We stayed there several days. I believe Latham tried again and failed. It was a curious feeling that the eyes of the world were focused on this spot, for this business of flying the Channel was the most important and dramatic step mankind had taken since the invention of the wheel. It was the conquest of a new element, and every bit as up-lifting to the thoughts with its promise of triumph and freedom as the exploration of outer space.

One morning I woke early. It was difficult to sleep. I looked out of the window, and there, sitting just on the edge of the cliff with something wrong about one of its wheels, was a tiny aeroplane.

It was facing inwards! Three people were gathered round it, a policeman, a Boy Scout, and a corpulent gesticulating figure with a cap set the wrong way on his head, looking exactly like the plump characters you see writing with scratchy pens in the 'Café du Commerce' in any hotel in France.

For a minute I was arrested by the static quality of the scene. Then the policeman waved his arms at the Boy Scout, who suddenly started running like a mad thing down the path in the general direction of the town. I jumped and shouted to my father in a shrill voice. He bounded out of bed, took one look out of the window, flung clothes on and was running down the path before the Boy Scout was out of sight.

Monsieur Bleriot had done it while the world still waited for Mr Latham. I can supply you with the details. It was a victory for the Gnome engine, an astounding contrivance with a fixed crankshaft and the most complicated conceivable battery of con-rods, so that the cylinders with their pistons reciprocating inside them revolved about a single bearing, with an attached propeller.

Don't ask me how the little matter of conveying mixture to those revolving cylinders was arranged. The whole affair was implausible, but it worked, with absolute reliability, so that the French Air Force were still using it with complete success in the First World War.

Suddenly it was the age of flight.

[4]

One of the people my father got to know was Shackleton. The history has been told so many times of the American called Dr Cook who returned to Norway one day and announced that he had been to the North Pole that I haven't the heart to repeat it. My father managed to get hold of the ship's log book and found that the critical four pages were missing. The whole world was applauding the doctor, but my father sent a long cable to the *Daily Chronicle* challenging his claim, and the *Daily Chronicle*, staking its reputation, backed him and printed the dispatch. It was one of the greatest scoops in the history of journalism.

Shackleton was one of those quiet, almost contemplative people, whose *daimon* was quite unapparent to the outside world. Just like Scott, he was a square-jawed, handsome naval officer with his hair parted in the middle. I went to a lecture he gave. It must have been a very early film, but he had in fact a thrilling and lovely record of the ice parting before the bows of the ships and all that world of whiteness which I have never forgotten.

The little girl in Chelsea, whom I succeeded in marrying some years later, used to see Peter Scott at about this time, going down the Royal Hospital Road in his pram. He was something of a pioneer and was wheeled about in a loin-cloth; this, at a period when nakedness was disgusting and children who were not dressed as for the Antarctic caught their deaths of cold. All the other Chelsea mothers clucked in little groups. I am leading up to Commander Bernacchi who went, as a biologist, on one Scott and two Shackleton expeditions. He was the greatest living expert on the Emperor Penguin, and his house, near Barrie's on the north side of the Park, had penguins all up the stairs, in glass cases.

He swore that penguins used to talk, and described how he and Shackleton landed on Penguin Island. With infinite slowness and great dignity a dozen penguins in full evening dress detached themselves from the rest and held a conversation in measured tones lasting half an hour.

Then a welcoming party of three advanced solemnly on Shackleton and Bernacchi, halted at a few paces' distance and bowed with the utmost gravity. Shackleton and Bernacchi bowed back. Then a spokesman for the inner cabinet bent down, picked up a rounded stone with its beak and, mistaking Bernacchi for the leader of the expedition, laid it ceremoniously at his feet. Bernacchi told me that this gesture was the male penguin's customary proposal of marriage. To deposit an egg-shaped stone at the feet of his adored was a hint no lady penguin would be likely to misinterpret.

Between these long expeditions to the Antarctic Bernacchi was an inconsolable explorer. He became fascinated with the Mayan civilization and, having a year to spend while a new

13

expedition was being fitted out, he took a boat across the Southern Atlantic, a voyage of nine and a half days. Then he spent two weeks on a river steamer. When the river steamer could go no further he took to a canoe and penetrated deeper and deeper into the forests of Yucatan. When the canoe was bogged down among the roots of gigantic trees he hired twelve porters and a head-man and set forth on foot. He was looking for a legendary step-pyramid which was once the centre of a thriving hieratic city but was now engulfed in jungle.

'And did you find it?' I asked, a very fascinated small boy.

'Well,' said Bernacchi, 'we walked for days and days and days. There was always a sort of path but we had to hack our way along it most of the time, but I had an idea we were getting somewhere, because the bearers kept on disappearing. At the end of the first walk there were still twelve. Next day two of them disappeared. Just vanished like smoke, leaving their apple barrel where they'd been standing.'

'Apple barrel?' I asked.

'Fond of apples,' said Bernacchi. 'Best thing on a long march. Good as water and not so heavy. Had a big barrel of apples with poles sticking out at either end so two men could carry it. At the beginning of the fourteenth day we came down to five. And suddenly there it was. And every one of the damn bearers fled, all except the head-man.'

There it was. A step pyramid with each step four feet high, towering up above the tall trees, and at the very top, high in the sun, a carved stone trellis like a New York penthouse, with a tiled roof.

Bernacchi said he was going up. The head-man, as pale as a ghost, performed the Mayan equivalent of crossing himself and utterly refused. But he promised by the sun and the serpent to stay at the bottom. So Bernacchi started. It was a hell of a job, Bernacchi said, going up. The four-foot steps were quite impossible to climb in the ordinary way. Bernacchi tried everything. He tried muscling up with his hands, and getting one knee over. He tried sitting on each step with a little jump and a push with his arms and then half-turning to get his feet round. At the end of half an hour he had got almost half-way up and he was exhausted. The sun became high overhead and the air was thin.

He smoked a cigarette, flung the butt at a lizard, and went on. At the end of an hour, panting but not perspiring, he got one hand level with the stone trellis and pulled his head up.

The trellis was an intricately carved thing, a twined mass of serpents, and he couldn't see through it. He got his feet on the topmost step and stood up. The trellis was six feet high, and then there was a gap of three feet or so before the roof started. The whole thing seemed to be about eighteen feet square.

Bernacchi made a terrific effort, got his hands over the edge of the trellis, got his stomach over it, scrabbled with his feet, and tumbled over.

He was not alone.

There were eight of them up there, Bernacchi said. There was a marble table in the centre, and a marble bench ran round the inside of the trellis. And on the marble bench sat eight naked men.

'Sun-dried', said Bernacchi. 'Dead four hundred years, but sun-dried. Perfectly preserved, with all their flesh and all their hair. Something to do with the climate. Height. Astonishing.'

Bernacchi said he thought he had probably made one of the most startling finds in the history of anthropology. Every pore. Every eyelash. He had obviously stumbled on the hieratic council. The last hieratic council ever held. But what killed them? Why did they sit on and die and sit on for four hundred years?

He decided that somehow or other he had to get one of these people back to civilization. The sun was past its zenith. At the foot of the pyramid, infinitely far below, he could see his faithful head bearer, waiting. He knew now why the place was tabu. He chose a young man, picked him lightly up, dropped him over the rail, climbed over himself, and started down.

'Going down was easy,' Bernacchi told me, 'even holding the chap. We just slithered.'

Down below the head bearer shaded his eyes with his hand, took one look at what was happening, and bounded into the jungle.

Bernacchi lost his temper. The whole blessed lot of them could desert him, but he was damned well going to get this chap back, if he had to carry him alone. He reached the ground in this mood. There was no sign of the porter. He got hold of the apple barrel, prised off its lid, and tipped away all of the apples. Then he started trying to fold his young man. He was in a sitting position, and Bernacchi had the idea that if he could fold him so that his knees came up to his chin he would fit in the barrel quite nicely. But it was a difficult thing to do. Bernacchi didn't care a damn how difficult it was. With a great deal of struggling, trying it from the back, trying it on the ground, Bernacchi finally got him in, with the lid on. The moment he did so the head-man reappeared.

Bernacchi was much too tired to give the man the hell he thought he deserved. They loaded themselves up with as much of their stores as they could carry, slung the apple barrel on its two poles across their shoulders, loaded some more stuff across the poles, and set off down the jungle path.

They walked for ten days, and one by one the shamefaced porters reappeared. Bernacchi and the head-man always carried the apple barrel between them. They found the canoe where they had left it, renewed provisions and paddled back to the steamer.

Bernacchi said good-bye to everybody and climbed the gangplank with two suitcases and an apple barrel. Two weeks later a man slapped a label on it which said 'Southampton'. Two weeks more and Bernacchi arrived at Waterloo station, waved an arm at a growler, and told the man to drive to the Royal Geographical Society in Kensington Gore. They

16

arrived and the driver got down the apple barrel while
Bernacchi rang the bell.

'Good afternoon,' said Commander Bernacchi. 'I'm
Commander Bernacchi. I'm just back from Yucatan and
I'd like to present the Royal Geographical Society with a
sun-dried man. He's in here.'

'Well that's really exceedingly kind of you, Commander
Bernacchi,' said the secretary of the Royal Geographical
Society who had opened the door. 'Thank you very much
indeed. We'll let you know how he gets on.'

So Commander Bernacchi went back to Bayswater.

The next morning his telephone rang.

'Is that Commander Bernacchi? Well, this is the Royal
Geographical Society. Would you be so very kind as to
remove your sun-dried man?'

'Remove him?' Bernacchi repeated.

'Yes, please, Commander,' said the voice.

'Why? That's a pretty outrageous suggestion, isn't it?
For God's sake why?'

'Well the truth is,' said the voice apologetically, 'he
moves in the night.'

Bernacchi's temper began to go.

Moves in the night?

'Yes, Commander.'

'But, good God,' shouted Bernacchi. 'You're supposed to
be the Royal Geographical Society and a scientific institution! D'you mean to tell me you really believe this pre-
posterous story?'

'I can't help it,' the voice said. 'He moves.'

Bernacchi slammed down his receiver, bundled into his
overcoat, opened the front door of his house, saw a hansom,
yelled 'Cab!', stopped it, and climbed in.

The trap above his head opened, 'Where to, sir?'

'Royal Geographical Society.'

They cantered off, crossed the Serpentine Bridge and
arrived.

Bernacchi, by now, was speechless. When the door was

opened he just made a gesture with his fingers which meant 'give'.

'He's locked in here at the moment,' said the young man. 'I'll fetch him out.'

Half a minute later he re-appeared, carrying the naked figure in his arms.

Bernacchi exploded again.

'Where's my apple barrel?'

'Apple barrel?'

'Apple barrel, apple barrel, apple barrel!' roared Bernacchi. 'I brought him in an apple barrel and I'll take him away in an apple barrel.'

'Oh, you mean the thing he came in! I'm afraid that er— I'm afraid that got broken up. It's been thrown away.'

Bernacchi's silence was terrible. He took the naked young man in his arms and carried him across to the cab. A young lady said 'O-o-oh,' and went flat over on the pavement. Bernacchi propped his man in the seat and sat down beside him.

'South Kensington Museum,' he ordered.

The cabbie whipped up his horse.

At the top of Exhibition Road, where they were stopped by a policeman, two ladies fainted. Another who was just about to cross the street, let out a piercing yell and corkscrewed to the ground. The policeman blew a blast on his whistle. Bernacchi passed a pound up through the trap.

They arrived, in a cavalcade of whistling errand-boys on bicycles, a policeman puffing three hundred yards behind and a man on a horse who kept repeating, 'I say, you know!'

Bernacchi carried in his figure, asked to see somebody in authority and said, 'Good morning, I'm Commander Bernacchi—I'd like to present the museum with a sundried man.'

They were delighted, and let him out of the entrance in Queen's Gate.

The next morning the telephone rang.

'Commander Bernacchi? The South Kensington Museum.'

Bernacchi knew what they were going to say.

'We don't know how to explain it, but your man moved in the night.'

'How far?' asked Bernacchi.

'We put him on the top floor. This morning he was in the basement.'

'I'm coming round.'

He went round. And there was the sun-dried youth, lying quietly on his side with his knees drawn up to his chin. Three or four of them were standing there. They looked up the great well of the staircase to the topmost floor.

'He must have climbed over the balustrade and jumped all the way down here,' they said.

This time they kept him in a basement under lock and key.

He is still there, Bernacchi told me.

'If you want to see him they'll show him to you. But you have to ask.'

He evolved a theory. I am not sure that it makes sense. He thought perhaps, that the man's seated position, which had lasted for four hundred years, was his habitual one, and that his unnatural position when folded into the apple barrel might, in certain conditions of humidity or central heating, suddenly revert, with a galvanic action of the limbs.

It is a queer story. All I know is that Bernacchi had had three drinks when he told it to me, the day the German Band went.

My father went the day after the German Band, and for the same reason. There was going to be a war.

II

[1]

Twenty-five years later, when I was a war correspondent myself, I flew down from the coast at Dieppe to the Swiss border, along the line of the war cemeteries. Along that line were eight million graves. *Eight million!*

In Verdun alone there was a French Memorial to that famous battle. It simply said, 'Aux 400,000 morts.' Those were just the French casualties in that one place.

It must have been a funny war. For four solid years the armies faced each other, four million men on either side, in their system of trenches, killing one another in millions and never moving more than a few hundred yards. I saw the trenches. They were still there at Vimy Ridge in 1939, and you could wander about below ground in that horrible place where everybody died. I found one of my old class-pictures at school the other day. Rather more than half of them were killed. And here, with a candle still stuck in a bottle, and a tin hat still hanging on a nail where someone had put it more than twenty years before, was the place.

Fifty feet away—I said fifty feet—were the German trenches.

Why didn't somebody break it up? All you had to do to get the Germans out of their trenches was not to attack them across the bloodbath of No Man's Land but to retreat twenty or a hundred miles. That would have fetched them all right, and you could have had a war of movement. In the end, of course, that is exactly what happened, except that the retreat was involuntary.

Why didn't somebody do it on purpose? I have asked my father this, who was there every day of the war except for a week or two, from the day it started to the day it finished. He always said the same. 'The brains of canaries, and the manners of Potsdam.' He meant Haig, of course.

And why didn't we make peace with the wretched Germans when they tried for it in 1916 and Lord Lansdowne wrote his letter to *The Times*? I only ask.

Well, they won it, those dead men in their graves. And having won it they left us younger ones with a brand-new world to play in, full of hope, with the absolute knowledge that never, never, never again would the same thing happen. We had a brand-new world and a brand-new generation with arms and legs and eyes. Weren't we the lucky ones?

When I went to Oxford I was at a very low-class college. At this Oxford College there was a tutor called Cruttwell. There was nothing remarkable about him. He was a tall man with untidy trousers and a black moustache, but in some indefinable way he lent himself. I mean he lent himself to those deft touches of caricature. So it was almost inevitable that when I came down from Oxford, also rather suddenly, I wrote a brilliant first novel. It was really extremely good. The young master has never done anything better and it was called *Little Peter Vacuum* and was an uproarious success. Counting both sides of the Atlantic, it ran into twenty-seven editions. In it there was a butler called Cruttwell.

Evelyn Waugh took over my rooms. I have always wondered how *he* managed—about being seen going in at that gate, I mean. For a great aristocrat like that. And of course, when he came down, he wrote his brilliant first novel *Vile Bodies*. It was much more brilliant than mine. There was a chauffeur called Cruttwell in it.

I never met this Waugh, though I count his brother Alec among my friends. I wrote another book. This time Cruttwell was a policeman, Sergeant Cruttwell. Evelyn came right back with, if I remember, a window-cleaner. We kept this up for years. In the end Mr Cruttwell, I was told, went mad and died; so naturally when a new novel by

Evelyn Waugh was announced, I rushed to borrow it at Harrods and pawed through the pages. There was a gardener called Gibbs.

[2]

In my second term at that Oxford College I went to Cruttwell, told him I was a bit dissatisfied with the place, and asked if it would be all right if I moved out and took rooms at a convenient distance. He was quite decent about it, so a friend of mine and I went into a most agreeable spot at the corner of King Edward and Oriel Streets with red window boxes, where we were waited upon by men in striped waistcoats and life suddenly became comfortable.

As a matter of fact, life was becoming quite comfortable all round. I went along to Buckingham Palace to see my father collect a knighthood. King George's job was to hang a gigantic pendant round his neck on a piece of thick blue ribbon, to pin something on his breast, and then to add a piece of jewellery about five times the size of the Star of India to a place low down on the left-hand side, where a large iron hook had been fixed in position to receive it.

I was wearing my first pot hat. I still have the same one. I had to go to a wedding last year; I could just decipher the word 'Scott's' inside the lining, so I took it round there and placed it on the counter. All the assistants dived for cover underneath.

You never saw such a scene at an investiture. The King managed the first two parts all right, but my father was very tense, and clutched his top hat ever tighter to his stomach as he realized that some sort of hitch seemed to be occurring over the great climax of the ceremony.

From all sides came frenzied whispers.

'Hook!'

At last the King gently took hold of the hat, tugged it towards him and managed to insert the decoration before it sprang back into position.

22

We went straight on from there to the French Embassy where M. Jules Cambon added the Legion of Honour and kissed my father on both cheeks. It was quite a day.

This was the golden period of the Gibbs family. My Uncle Cosmo had moved to New York, set up an establishment at 1000 Park Avenue, and was universally respected, not only as a witty and successful dramatist, but as the most English thing that ever hit 59th Street. Another uncle, Arthur Hamilton, wrote a book called *Soundings*, found he had a bestseller, married a highly intelligent American lady from Boston and went to live in New England on thousands of acres. And I was given an A.V. Monocar.

They tell me that one of these still exists in Lord Montagu's museum at Beaulieu. In the language of the period it was absolutely priceless. It was about eighteen feet long and two feet wide, bright scarlet, cylindrical, and sharply pointed in front. Sticking out of the back, naked and unashamed, was a large V-twin aircooled engine.

You started it by putting your foot on a neat step provided for the purpose and pulling about three feet of chain out of its inside. It had a deep and splendid rhythm of suppressed power. You vaulted in, settled yourself behind a tiny aeroplane screen, gave it a bit of juice on the hand throttle and spat your way forward.

The performance of that machine was fantastic. I doubt if it weighed more than the modern scooter. You could lift the front of it easily with one hand. Indeed there was one place on the road between Oxford and Henley where, at any speed above sixty, I used to become airborne for, I should think, fifteen or twenty yards.

A really fast single-seater motor car is something which everybody ought to have, and I cannot imagine why somebody doesn't manufacture the thing today and sell it in millions. It cost a hundred and fifteen pounds, and the 'A.V.' referred of course to that A. V. Roe who was a pioneer of triplanes, and all the other Avro machines, up to the Hovercraft of today.

23

We were not supposed to keep mechanical contrivances in our first year at university, so I persuaded a sweet shop to let me lodge it in their passage. I used to go in and buy a packet of acid drops, slip through the side door, pull out the chain, fill up at Mr Morris's garage, and heigh-ho for the 'Riviera' at Maidenhead where there was always a chance of seeing Gladys Cooper.

[3]

Mr Morris had just assembled the first of his bull-nosed 'Oxfords' and 'Cowleys'. I say 'assembled', because this is exactly what he did. He bought the engines from Hotchkiss in Paris, the gear boxes here, the back axles there, ran the whole thing together and sold it in the neighbourhood of a hundred and seventy-five pounds.

In those days, if I may be forgiven for saying so, the cars were not conspicuous for elegance and refinement. 'Cheap' and 'sturdy' were the operative words. But like Henry Ford he altered civilization.

Before the first war, and immediately after it, the motor-car had not really come into its own, despite all the nostalgia of the Brighton Run, and 'Genevieve' and the bandying of words like 'veteran' and 'vintage'.

I'm afraid I can remember when the streets of London were suddenly running with little Renault taxis imported from Paris. They were painted scarlet, and seemed enormously exciting and up to date. I can remember, too, when the third horse which used to stand at the end of Holland Street to give the buses an extra tug up the incline of Church Street to Notting Hill, was displaced by the snorting steam chariots, painted white and with the word 'National' on their sides.

Very soon the whole of London went over to taxis and buses, the Vanguard, the General; and the horse only survived in the dray, lumbering along with a creaking cart, and a line of snorting hooting motor-cars behind it.

As I remember, there were no really *good* cars in the early

24

days. Sir Thomas Lipton had a pair of gigantic Mercedes, chain-driven monsters. Every Sunday he set out in one of those devilish machines from his house in Southgate and distributed Lipton's chocolates to all the little children who knew about it and waited in knots at every gate and alleyway. Their tyres were constantly collapsing. The chains stretched and came off. My future father-in-law had a Panhard. The only way he could get up the hill from Grosvenor Gardens into Hyde Park was to take it backwards.

One of my many amusing uncles possessed a very odd conveyance which he called 'The Jigger'. It was very like the machines with which superior shops were beginning to motorize their errand boys. The conductor sat on a saddle above a single wheel at the back which in turn motivated a single cylinder suitably attached with balls and chains. In my uncle's case, instead of the square box in front labelled 'Worth' there was a wicker basket containing two apprehensive passengers in goggles and veils, and he steered the whole contraption by pointing the passengers in the direction in which he wished to go.

Another of my uncles, who had married a 'rather close relative' of the Duke of Richmond, was the proud owner of a very gentlemanly, not to say ducal, carriage called an Argyll. This was quite a car. You entered the conveyance through a door at the back at the top of a small flight of stairs. When you were about eight feet in the air, you found yourself in a padded enclosure known as 'the tonneau'. I think it had a windscreen, zig-zagging up at right angles, any one of which could be altered by undoing a large brass wheel, rather like the things they use for opening lock-gates. When this equipage was in motion it went very well, with its oil dripping visibly in eight glass tubes, and a wonderful cloud of dust rising behind its towering rear. Most of the time it was stationary. My uncle never moved an inch without the gardener's boy, whom he would send forth in search of rescue, so that I associate the vehicle most with the 'silence' of the countryside, with the cawing of rooks and the babble

25

of brooks and the song of the thrush and the quiet gathering of the dust on the blackberries in the hedge, while the gardener's boy did his customary three miles, to come back with a horse. In many ways this provided me with the most peaceful motoring I remember. You've no idea how quiet and empty and unspoilt the English countryside was. There was absolutely nothing there at all.

Another car was, of course, the Delaunay-Belleville. This Parisian machine was, for some years, the height of chic. The Parisian coach-builders, quite undeterred by the fact that its bonnet was cylindrical and looked exactly like the boiler of the 6.15 to Brighton, laboured lovingly to produce landaulette bodies for it, of sumptuous hideosity, with buttoned upholstery and lace antimacassars, and silk rope-pulls, and trumpets to the chauffeur. They were monstrosities, and the Sheffield-Simplex which imitated them exactly, imitated them exactly.

It is true there were one or two early Vauxhalls, banging about on four cylinders. This car performed well in Flanders, and Sir Douglas Haig, who was constantly arresting my father for trying to report the war, used one whenever he had to leave behind the white charger, on which he looked so impossibly handsome, and so careless of two million lives. Only the Rolls and the Daimler and the dead Napier had in them the seed of the exquisite, fleet, lean, and lovely things for which the world had to wait until the thirties, and which in turn it will never see again.

When the war was over, things began to hum. It was the aeroplane that did it. The Rolls came out with an aluminium bonnet, which was immediately copied by Albert here, and Roamer and Moon in the United States. A friend of mine, who was rather rich, used to dash about the streets of Oxford in an all-aluminium A.C., and later in an all-aluminium Vauxhall Velox.

When my parents came to visit me, they did so in a Daimler of proportions so vast that I still dwell on the thing with affection and respect.

26

It began with the famous fluted radiator standing about five feet high. It then continued with about twelve feet of bonnet which sloped up at a rather ugly angle. Then came a tiny little man called Arthur, who controlled the machine. He was in constant movement, pumping up the petrol, moving giant levers, listening to my mother's voice in his ear, rattling controls on the steering column, pumping up more petrol (it did six miles to the gallon) and leaning this side and that as he swung the leviathan round corners like a man on a bicycle.

Behind him came an impressive sheet of glass, and after that rows and rows of softly sprung seats, stretching away, as it seems to me now, like the Albert Hall.

This astonishing conveyance, with its seven-litre engine, moved in complete silence. It would ascend the steepest hill without a sound, at seven miles an hour in top gear. Its maximum speed was fifty miles an hour—we only did it once. The people in the third row from the back all hit their heads on the roof and Arthur was in disgrace. I believe he had eleven children.

[4]

This leads me naturally to the naked body.

The most enchanted spot in Oxford was 'Parson's Pleasure'. You turned left in the Broad opposite the Bodleian, passed the big Trinity gates which were last opened to admit Charles II and will never be opened again till a Stuart is on the throne, turned right just after the wall-flowers and old stone walls of Wadham, and came to a convent called Cherwell Edge.

I used to know most of the girls there. Very occasionally they gave little dances, to which we turned up in white ties and white kid gloves, accepted a programme with a pencil dangling from a piece of silk before cavorting respectively to 'Avalon' and 'Swannee' and 'The Japanese Sand-man'. They were officially registered as Home Students, and were supposed to be taking the university courses with the active assistance of a devout body of nuns. At the end of the year in question all eighteen girls were sent down for not passing their Responsions (a species of university entrance examination), and also two of the nuns.

Anyhow, you skirted the place, plunged down an exciting and mysterious path, with midges that danced between the boles of old willows, and came to a small wooden hut and a creaking iron gate. There was an old gentleman of the boatman breed, with a cloth cap and a white moustache.

'Member of the university, Sir?'

'Yes, I am.'

You gave him sixpence and he gave you a ticket off a roll. You opened the gate, which creaked open and clanged shut with a high falsetto groan, and came into an open glade. The river ran quietly at the bottom of it, past a tall tree with a diving-board fastened about eight feet high up on its trunk.

There was a semi-circular piece of grass on which the sun fell in splendour, and on the grass eighteen or twenty young men, as naked as the day they were born, stood and talked, and sunbathed and dived, and read and smoked. There was always one don, a white-haired, lean and brown-limbed man, correcting papers in a corner.

I have always been fond of the water, but there is an enormous release to the body, and the spirit, about taking off *all* one's clothes. I loved this place, not only for the pleasure of my own sensations, of the feel of the sun on one's body, and the caress of the water, and the quiet unbroken surface if one swam into the shadows round the corner, but with an intense objective delight in the physical and unashamed beauty of these young men. It was like Praxiteles, and Michelangelo, and Donatello.

The river was highly populated a hundred yards away. You could hear the reedy rag-time of the portable gramophones, the splash of punt poles and the laughter of the girls.

28

But all this traffic was kept away. Arrived at a certain point you disembarked from your punt or canoe and sent it over a contraption called 'the Rollers' into another arm of the river. Thus was preserved the naked seclusion of the University Bathing Place.

But not always.

At least once in an afternoon a punt with two girls, scarlet-faced and staring straight before them, would meander by. They did it on purpose, of course. No one paid them the slightest attention. Absolute disdain was the code of behaviour. And if they saw a little of the beauty of young manhood and went back to their colleges and thought about it, who can blame them?

Two or three years later, in an episode which I shall relate more fully in due course, a rather handsome German woman called Leontine Sagan, who had made a very successful film called *Mädchen in Uniform*, asked me a queer question.

'Is there,' she asked, 'much homosexuality among the boys?'

I had the greatest difficulty in persuading her that, not only was there no homosexuality, but no sexuality either, and I have no doubt that I shall have equal difficulty, in 1969, of persuading you.

There was no such thing as sex. The word had no meaning, and was never used. It was possible to be in love, a totally different thing, but even this was considered eccentric and was never mentioned. I myself was romantically in love, and had been for two years before I left school. She could play Ravel and Debussy on the piano like an angel, and studied under a famous old teacher called Mathay. We wrote to each other about once a month, and I kept all her letters. They told me who had been to tea, and how she had been to a concert by Pachmann, and how he kept tossing asides into the audience while he played. Nothing more. I wrote back, in adoration, but never disclosing it, except that after several years, I took to ending my letters, greatly

29

daring, 'with love from Tony'. We gathered blackberries once, in the Isle of Wight, and I still have a photograph of her, sitting with her basket on the Monocar.

Even this case of worship from afar would have been considered pretty advanced. There were quite a lot of personable young females in Oxford, but they were hedged about, not only with an elaborate chaperon system, but with their own remoteness.

The chaperon business was extraordinary. You couldn't invite any young female from one of the women's colleges, either to your room, or to tea in Fuller's, or to come on the river, without a formidable female turning up, talking and knitting industriously the entire time. And, of course, you had to pay for all the blasted éclairs she ate. Not to mention the salmon mayonnaise and the strawberries, and the hock, if you were really putting on a show.

Some of the colleges, as I have hinted, arranged little dances which always ended, thank God, at ten minutes to midnight. The formality varied a bit. At Lady Margaret Hall, for instance, a white-haired woman of distinguished aspect, with intelligent eyes and a forest of freckles, would hand you one of those little programmes *with the names already filled in*. You had to go round bleating, 'I say, can anybody introduce me to Miss Eileen Roxborough? We're dancing number five.'

The conversation would go like this.

'Been to any good shows, lately?'

'Not really.'

'I say, I'm terribly sorry. Was that your foot?'

'No. No. Entirely my fault. I'm afraid my mind was on theatres.'

'Did you manage to get tickets for the Gilbert and Sullivan things?'

'Good lord, no. Did you?'

'No!'

'I suppose you have been to *The Co-optimists*?'

'Rather.'

'Terribly good.'

'Awfully.'

'I rather like Melville Gideon.'

'Oh? Which is he?'

'Chap at the piano.'

'Oh, yes. He's *awfully* good.'

'Phyllis Monkman must be a hundred.'

'More likely two.'

'I say, you are priceless'.

'Shall we er—shall we er—shall we go in search of some of that cup?'

'Oh, do let's. I'm parched!'

At Somerville, on the other hand, things were a bit more matey. There were some rather amusing people. Helen Simpson, who wore a monocle, had her own studio in the Clarendon Hotel garage and was an expert in witchcraft, and wrote a book called *Saraband for Dead Lovers*. I mean you don't *kiss* a girl like that. And Dilys Powell. And a girl called Doris Mull, who was fantastically pretty, and danced like a puff of wind.

That was it, of course. We went there for the dancing. Those were the dancing years.

The bands were so good. Jack Hylton, Clifford Essex, The Savoy Orpheans.

There was an enormous variety of exciting new rhythms. The blues. The slow fox-trot. The tango. All the nuances of rhythm, which later flourished and were eventually stamped out of existence by rock and roll, were just invented. The voice of the saxophone was heard in the land. It sidled and slid and clucked in ecstasies of the most complicated syncopation. The bowler-hatted trumpet with its wah-wah. The desk of drums, the rhythm section with its roll and its cymbals and its tuned tympana and its odd-noise department which could do anything from a galloping horse to church bells and a motor-horn.

There were no set steps. Mostly you just walked. Clemenceau once called it, 'A country walk somewhat impeded by a member of the opposite sex.' But you walked interpretatively. Each dance was an exercise in individual interpretation. You could walk, simply on the first and third beat of every bar, and when the music seemed to require it, make a little sort of run with a step on *every* beat. You could walk for whole patches by keeping to the *syncopated* beat, and that was really something. You could swing round with a sort of delayed hesitation, and pass from one to the other, or almost pass, but slip back at the last moment. If you had a girl in your arms like Doris Mull who seemed to know exactly what you were going to do on the instant you did it, this was pretty sophisticated stuff, I promise you.

Most sophisticated of all was the waltz. Here, once again, you walked, but you walked *two* paces to *three* beats in the bar. Debussy wrote some of his music with four beats in one hand to three in the other. I can assure you, if you are younger than I am, that the deliberate asynchronous effect of this, the purposeful departure from the indicated rhythm and the coming back to it was exquisite suffering. A year or so ago my wife and I went to a local 'do' (a sort of coming-out dance for my daughter) where they put on a waltz, and the entire room did the damned thing in three time! One-two-three, one-two-three, they went, all together, lurching over the one and skipping dutifully over the two-three. Like the Penge and Crystal Palace Barndancers' Association entry on television.

But I was on sex. As my friend George Mikes said in his famous Chapter Nine, 'The English do not have sex. They have hot-water bottles.'

We did not have hot-water bottles.

[5]

Please do not carry away the impression that life at Oxford was all beer and Skindles. I learned all about the Defenestration of Prague, and the principles of political economy as enunciated by John Stuart Mill. I also joined the Cavalry.

32

Frankly I was forced into this. One of those South Africans at my college, who objected to the way I was constantly rendering 'Whispering' on the piano, gave me a severe talking to one day. He said I ought to do something for the honour of the college. So I joined the Cavalry.

The Gibbs family tends to have bow legs, obviously due to generations of horsemanship. My Uncle Cosmo, who liked to look beautiful, developed a very characteristic way of standing to disguise this, with the heel of one foot tucked into the instep of the other. That and the Hooper trousers did the trick. Apart from this patrician disability, recent generations have not been equestrian. I believe that my father was once bolted with by a very small Bulgarian pony during the Balkan War. I myself had never been on a horse in my life. However, I turned up in somebody else's riding-breeches, an Ascot stock purchased for the occasion, and a yellow waistcoat, looking really rather like The Pragger Wagger.*

The place was a big structure which resembled a film studio, except that the floor was carpeted with dung, from wall to wall. A tiny, wiry little man, smelling strongly of Brown Windsor soap, advanced and said, 'Good afternoon, Sir. I'm the Sergeant-Major but most of the gentlemen call me Daisy Bell.'

This seemed encouraging, and I was persuaded to climb on to the back of an enormous horse to 'see what I could do!' 'Feet out of the stirrups, Sir!' ordered Daisy Bell. 'Charge!'

The horse is an intelligent animal which learns to understand human speech. It waited for no signal from me but put itself in immediate motion. By God's grace I managed to get a firm hold of the beast's mane. Then I saw a large wooden bar blocking our passage.

'Hup!' shouted Daisy.

The horse leaped in the air, sailed like the A.V. Monocar, and put its two front feet on the ground. At this point I left it. I continued my flight for a few unearthly seconds,

* An affectionate reference in the period to H.R.H. The Prince of Wales.

calculated that I would probably land on the back of my neck, did so, and departed this life for quite some time.

I must say Daisy Bell was awfully nice about it.

Two of my friends who were in the Cavalry with me, Jack Neely and Michael Trappes-Lomax, escorted me to the Randolph and fed me on goblets of brandy. (The last thing I should ever have expected to happen was that Jack should turn out to be the principal ophthalmic surgeon of the R.A.F. and that Michael would enjoy a Mahjong-like existence as 'Rouge Dragon' at the College of Heralds.)

There were no actual broken bones, and I did not, like Augustus John after a similar mishap, turn into the marry-ing type. It was a simple matter to go into hiding on Wed-nesday afternoons when riding-school was held, and to hell with the honour of the college.

Then, one evening, Daisy called to see me in my digs. I became distinctly apprehensive, and I knew my voice would tremble.

'May I ask a question, Sir?' he began diffidently.

'Of course, Daisy,' I said.

'How many times have you been on a 'orse?'

'Well er—once actually.'

'I don't see,' he said, 'how you're going to manage about camp.'

'C-amp?' I repeated.

'Yessir. Rise at six-thirty, groom your own 'orses, parade seven-thirty sharp, spend the day in the saddle, feed the 'orses 'ay, bed 'em down, carry out the muck. D'you *want* to go to camp?'

It was a terrible confession to have to make, and I did not have the courage to make it.

'Why?' I asked.

'Because if you don't, Sir, and I thought perhaps maybe you didn't, a young gentleman called Wesley-Wellesley is very anxious to go, and as long as you didn't tell a soul it would be quite easy to arrange for 'im to answer your name at roll calls and suchlike.'

34

It is always embarrassing when people see through you, and are kind.

I rushed round to Michael Trappes-Lomax at New College.

'For God's sake, Michael, have you heard about this camp thing?'

'Y-y-y-y-yes,' said Michael, who had an endearing stutter.

'Can you ride?'

'N-n-n-no,' said Michael. 'Not very well.'

'Well, what are you going to do?'

'I've n-n-n-n I've n-n-n-no idea. Go, I suppose.'

He went.

I heard about it afterwards. He turned up by train at Arundel. The Duke of Norfolk was a sort of c-c-cousin of his. There wasn't any cavalry stuff that evening. He was introduced to his horse, which had a white nose. They went into the town and everybody got rather tight so that in spite of Daisy Bell's horrid warnings about six-thirty in the morning they stole noisily to their tents and in no time at all were sunk in sleep.

At six-thirty people started blowing bugles. Michael was never really a rapid riser. He was methodical. He folded things neatly and put them away. From another tent he could hear pawings and stampings and shushing sounds, and the ring of buckets.

When he was ready, not more than five minutes or so after the tent was empty, he made his way out and came upon a busy scene. He collected a bucket which seemed to have been set out for him, complete with cold carbolicky water and a floating brush, recognized an unoccupied horse with a white patch and began systematically and cautiously to brush it all over.

Every so often more bugles blew but nobody paid any attention. When Michael had got the horse really wet so that it was shivering with cold, another bugle went, and people began moving their horses out into the open air.

Michael was not at all behind-hand, but he was definitely last. It was at this point that a genuinely grateful young man arrived rather hurriedly, wiping the sleep from his eyes, and said, 'I say, that's *terribly* good of you, thanks *awfully*!' and led the horse away. Looking round Michael found that he was alone with a completely ungroomed horse with a white patch on its nose.

He took the bucket and began to groom it.

Arundel Park is a place of sweeping vistas and grand dimensions. It has broad acres of undulating turf ringed by noble trees, and man becomes minuscule in the scale of it.

Dwarfed by so much majesty, ninety-nine of the hundred members of the Oxford Cavalry were drawn up in two rows in the very centre of the green arena. The Colonel was parading his troops.

'Wars are won,' he was telling them, 'by the Cavalry, and don't forget it! I know there *are* people who say that war is becoming a thing of machines. Don't you believe a word of it! It's fellers like you, chaps on horses, bloody good horses and bloody good chaps . . .'. And so on.

One of the troopers half closed his eyes to look into the distance, and nudged the man next to him with his knee.

Far, far away, almost a speck on the green horizon beneath the trunks of great trees, a tiny horse was approaching. It was approaching fast.

'What happens,' remarked the Colonel, 'when the machines destroy each other? When the tanks are knocked out by the guns? And the guns are smashed by the tanks? Eh? Answer me that!'

The horse grew rapidly. It had a white patch on its nose and it was tearing across the field at a pace which could only mean that it was completely out of control. It was also on a collision course with the troop. Its stirrups were flying. Foam flew from its lips. There was a thundering of hooves. Its rider lay flat on its back.

'I don't know what you fellers are all lookin' at,' said the Colonel, at the exact moment when the runaway steed bore

36

down on him, snorting terribly, sent him flying, ploughed through the startled troop, and was soon a speck on the other horizon.

[6]

While all this was going on I stayed on to deal with an exam. It was called 'History Previous' and I passed it brilliantly on five doses of hashish.

There is rather an amusing formality about an Oxford examination. You wear a black suit and a white bow-tie. Except for the tattered gown and the tasselled 'cap'—which, of course, you did not actually *wear*—you felt rather as if you were going to a reception at the Elysée Palace.

Opposite the place where you had to go was a chemist. You went in there and asked for a 'pink mixture'. It was an American who told me about it. He told me that he had passed some Latin paper, in a shower of honours, without knowing a single word of Latin.

I went in, rather furtively in view of my eccentric costume, bought a tube of tooth paste as a cover, and then asked about a pink mixture.

'Oh, yes, indeed, Sir. Taking an examination, are you, Sir? I can recommend it strongly. A grand tonic for the brain.'

'Well er—how much is it?'

'Seventeen-and-sixpence to you, Sir.'

'Good heavens.'

'Well, Sir, it contains some very expensive ingredients!'

I delivered, and received a brimming wineglass of frothy pink. The chemist watched me drink it sympathetically, accepted the wine glass and gave me half a crown.

'Thank *you*, Sir!'

I walked across the road without any appreciable change and began to mount the steps. An extraordinary sensation of competence began to pervade me. By the time I had found my desk I was feeling masterful and assured. I

37

glanced about me at the other undergraduates, nodded briefly to those I knew, and waited confidently for my paper.

When it came I glanced through it. I knew, of course, the answer to every question, precisely, analytically and in detail.

I took up my pen and began to write. The whole thing, naturally, was about the Thirty Years War. There was absolutely nothing I did not know about the Thirty Years War. I dashed off a sensational description of the Defenestration of Prague. In the event that the examiners were unaware of it I appended the date—1618. In no time at all I had the Elector of Hanover doing his stuff. I had Gustavus Adolphus bounding about Europe at the head of his armies. I discussed his campaign and criticized his strategy severely.

Only one little problem bothered me. I could not remember which side he was on. But the problem did not bother me for long. I soon realized that I could see through the problem. I could also see through the paper. I could see right through the desk. I could even see through the floor. There was an underground rivulet there, an unsuspected tributary of the Thames. A large brown trout was nibbling at a stone.

This seemed to be going rather far. It was Gustavus Adolphus I had paid my money for, and I did not want to be distracted by the stratifications and faults of the Oxford subsoil. However, I found myself completely in command of that situation too. I could see where I wanted.

I could cut off the brown trout with a conscious flick of the eyes. If I wanted I could see through the desk and not through the floor. Just to be quite certain of this I spent a short time examining the feet of the man in front of me, viewing them through my own desk and part of his chair. He was wearing grey suède shoes. I particularly remember this, because I myself was one of the pioneers of this type of footwear. It's nice to know that, *en passant*, one has left one's mark on the contemporary scene. I claim to have inaugurated, among other minor elegances, the suède shoe, the double-breasted waistcoat, and a habit of wearing a felt hat turned up at the back and down at the front. With the exception of this last, which became a bit common because it swept the world and is still part of the national costume of America, I still wear the suède footwear, the double-breasted waistcoat, looking now, rather *ancien régime*.

I had a bit of trouble with the suède shoes. They didn't like them in America when I went there, after Oxford and I had had enough. And when I went to war in them in 1939 an officer of the Household Brigade spoke to me very severely.

'You're letting the front down,' he said.

In these days all sorts of people wear them. Paperback publishers. Shirt-sleeved people in Ford Consuls. But I carry on. After all I did it first, I and the chap in front of me in that exam. I came back to my paper.

I still did not know which side Gustavus Adolphus was on, but I could see at once that it was quite unnecessary to be pedantically specific about this. Obviously Sir Charles Oman knew, and if he were correcting the paper, there would be no point in informing him. I increased my strictures of his use of the cavalry, and enunciated a completely new theory that this was not a religious war at all but was the first of the really modern wars in which Europe fell naturally into two camps.

At the end of an hour I found that I had answered two questions too many, so I capped my pen, stood up, to the horror of several people round me who were still scratching away at their first pages, and spent the rest of the morning at Parson's Pleasure.

That afternoon I repeated the dose, and went like a knife through the principles of political economy. I told the story of how John Stuart Mill's maid had burned the manuscript of Carlyle's *French Revolution*, a story I happened to have at my fingertips, because my grandfather was a friend of the Carlyles, and founded the little museum in Cheyne Row where Carlyle worked in a sound-proofed room, while Mrs

Carlyle had imitation wood-graining done on the Queen Anne shutters. I was also very good on Marx and his manifesto, a document which I read for the first time a year or two ago, and found depressingly impressive, with terrifying inevitability.

After doing five papers in this fashion I had only the 'viva', a personal confrontation with the examiners, in the morning. That night I invited Doris Mull to come to a Commemm. ball with me, because I knew it was going to be my last night at Oxford.

These Commemm. balls were pretty terrible affairs, but this one was a disaster.

In the first place their tickets cost five guineas. In the second they started at ten and went on far too long. I picked Doris up in the Monocar at about a quarter to ten. The passenger had to ride side-saddle on top of the thing, since there was only one seat, and I couldn't help thinking what a splendid picture of upper-class youth we made, with this very pretty girl streaming with fichus, and me in white tie and tails and my scarlet machine.

The band was Clifford Essex, of course. But something seemed to go wrong with the time schedule. We danced to 'Swannee', and then three-quarters of an hour of utter silence ensued. I suppose they were providing us with an opportunity to make proposals of marriage, but as I didn't want to do that we wandered about rather miserably.

Then the band broke into 'Margie', and we did that, and then, by golly, there was *another* three-quarters of an hour. By the time we had knocked off 'El Relicario' and 'Whispering' it was two o'clock in the morning and I was getting seriously worried.

I am afraid I have always taken the line that anybody who isn't in bed by midnight at the absolute latest is in a state of mental unbalance and should be destroyed. In particular I had to face those examiners. They were going to ask me if I had read John Stuart Mill's *Principles of Political Economy*. And I hadn't.

40

I had already made these points with Doris, and at two-thirty I said I was really desperately sorry but I thought I'd better be getting along.

She was awfully decent about it. Most girls who accept invitations to Commemm. balls expect to be kept on the hop till seven in the morning. God knows how they can stand the drudgery. My wife, who was at the other University at the same time, still boasts that she did five in a row. I find this terrifyingly abnormal, like Indians who pull their eyes out on forks and put them in again.

We got in the 'toothpick', as my mother always called it, and I took her back to Somerville. I think she had to climb in. When she was about twenty feet up I waved and in profound thankfulness drove back to my college. For some reason I was in college again, just for those few days.

The place was shut. I rattled the gates, I rattled the doors. The damned thing was bolted and barred like a prison.

I have never been able to climb more than three rungs of a ladder without feeling dizzy, so climbing was out of the question. I decided to try a hotel.

I tried every hotel in Oxford. They were all dark, bolted and festooned with iron shutters. It was like London in the days of the Great Plague.

The only thing seemed to be to go back to that dance. So back I went.

They were again playing 'Whispering' as I got in. There was a stink of champagne. The floor was littered with cigarette ends. The band played on with dead white faces. A half-dozen couples stood clasped, motionless with fatigue. It was about four in the morning.

I collected some champagne, lit a cigarette, and added to the detritus. The idea came to me that if I could find some sort of corner here, I might be able to doze off for *some* of the night. There was no corner. There were some gardens outside, with idiotic fairy lights, and a temperature of forty-five degrees. So I went back into the dance room. Actually it was a tent, and none too warm. A phrase, often quoted by my father, of de la Rochefoucauld's kept drumming in my brain. 'Life would be endurable but for its pleasures.'

At seven o'clock I succeeded in waking up the Clarendon Hotel. A very early porter, with an expression on his face which meant that it was rather right and proper that figures in full evening dress should approach him from the break of dawn demanding breakfast, that youth must have its fling, did produce some food and coffee. At eight o'clock I managed to get into my college, have a hot bath, shave, and put on some reasonable clothes. At nine o'clock I presented myself to the examiners. They were extremely polite. Almost respectful. At ten o'clock I flopped into the Mono-car to drive to London. It was a two-hour journey. I arrived at six.

Somewhere on the route, I have no idea where, I must have stopped and slept soundly for six hours.

That American was right. I passed the exam. And I told my parents I was wasting my time and their money at Oxford and that I wanted to earn my own living. So I wrote *Little Peter Vacuum*, and this, in a way, is where we came in.

III

[1]

In a light-hearted moment I had dedicated *Peter* 'To My Father, who does this sort of thing so much better than I shall ever do.'

This went down very well with the reviewers, who pointed out that Sir Philip Gibbs was *not* likely to do 'this sort of thing'. How true! Sir Philip Gibbs was operating a particularly successful racket.

He would go to a place where history was in the making, such as the great famine in Russia, and send back articles to his newspaper. Then he would write a serious book entitled, say, *The Tragedy of Kazan*. Then he would write a novel in which a young American girl, working for the League of Nations Famine Relief Association, went to Kiev and fell in love with a young Russian sent down from Moscow to put some order into a collective farm. And in January of the same year he would undertake a lecture under the title 'The Russian Famine' in the United States. Next year he would go somewhere else.

I mustn't make fun of my father. As I have indicated, he was only just twenty-five when I was born, and we were always quite extraordinarily close. For years people mistook us for brothers. He was a small man. When we arrived together at the White House once, President Harding exclaimed, 'Well what do you know! A block off the old chip!' He was small, but he was packed tight with determination, and overflowing with generosity of feeling to all fellow men. He found it difficult to believe ill of any human creature, but if his spirit were once roused he was unconquerable.

43

That spring I went with him to America. We travelled on the *Olympic*, the sister ship of the *Titanic*. If you could stand up to the famous 'Olympic Roll', which would start the ship tilting in one direction and go on and on and on until you were convinced it was going all the way round like one of those Eskimo canoes, it was luxuriously comfortable. All the 'staterooms' had proper beds, most of them had private baths, the food was terrific, and everybody dressed up to the nines every night and came down to dinner when a trumpeter made the rounds playing 'The Roast Beef of Old England'. Of course, I'm not speaking of those people whom one occasionally saw travelling second class, schoolmasters, and so on, with tweed jackets and grey flannel trousers and round tins of tobacco. Come to think of it, I suppose there must have been people who were actually travelling *third* class. Lithuanian refugees, no doubt. One never even saw them. Probably kept in chains.

The trouble was that a great many famous people were on board, according to the passenger lists, but one never saw them either. The really posh thing was to leave your place permanently empty at table where the food was actually included in the price of the fare, and lunch and dine expensively in the 'Ritz Carlton' where they had foreign waiters and smoked salmon and presented a bill. Posher still was to have a private suite with a sitting-room, and have your meals served there. This avoided having to appear in the 'Ritz Carlton'.

In this way I never even got a glimpse of Margaret Whigham. As for Lord Beaverbrook, I am seriously of the opinion that he was not on board at all, which must be the apotheosis of posh.

But I did win one of the childish competitions. You had to eat three cream crackers and whistle a tune which your partner could identify before any other pair could do the same. As my partner was Myra Hess she took one split second to recognize 'God Save the King', and we won. I won a Dunhill pipe and she won a leather tobacco pouch.

Neither of us was a pipe-smoker, so I still have them both. And there was New York, sticking up out of the sea.

I love America. There was a time, not so very long ago, when I went through the first processes of becoming a prospective citizen. But in 1921 America was a totally different country from the relaxed, intelligent and civilized place it became twenty years later.

The people wore angular clothes and enormously high stiff collars, with the tie at the bottom. Apart from one or two skyscrapers, a style of building which has now become the most beautiful and uplifting in the world, the place was hideous. Iron fire-escapes seemed to run up the fronts of all the buildings. The electric signs were appalling in daylight, and the street-cars at any time. The motor-cars were revolting, black hunks of shapeless tin with flapping side-curtains.

The great feature of American life was the spittoon, or cuspidor. Every hotel bedroom in America had one of those. Every seat in every American train had one, except in the smoking cars, where half a dozen men in sleeveless vests would sit around and shoot at the one in the middle. In half-an-hour the thing was a soggy mess of paper, chewing gum wrappers, and tickets, all bound together with yellow phlegm and brown spittle. Add to this the fact that they were in the throes of Prohibition. The whole place was a factory for bath-tub gin. It not only made them tight, it made them literally blind. The Dodge brothers went blind and were mown down by the traffic on Fifth Avenue the day we arrived. The gangster was king and the sawn-off shot-gun was his national emblem.

That night we dined at my uncle's, at 1000 Park Avenue. A very famous American actress was there, and as we sat after dinner I had the astonishing thought that I heard her say the words 'Check my bladder'. When I focused one flushed and startled ear in her direction I heard her go on:

'Your young English officers are *awfully* charming, but whenever I went to sing to the boys—and I covered pretty well most of the front—I had the same trouble. I had to

45

check my bladder. They *would not* give me the opportunity to visit the little girls' room. Shy, I guess. I'm not accustomed to check my bladder. When I check my bladder things are liable to happen.'

'Dashed embarrassing,' said my uncle. 'Would you like to do something about it now? I think we might go on.'

We went on. God knows where it was. They said it was a 'Persian Party'. As we barged in across a lot of people sitting or lying on the floor, rather a pretty girl in a tinsel brassière and transparent trousers was doing a belly dance, knotting her stomach muscles and unknotting them with intense concentration. Nobody else was in the least degree interested. A pleasant man presiding over a beautiful cut-glass punch bowl said 'Have some dynamite!'

It looked like a sort of fruit cup.

He ladled me some into a beautiful cut-glass goblet. There were some bits of orange floating, I remember. It is the last thing I do remember. I drank it, counted eight, and went flat out on the floor. It was while I was out that someone told my father about the Dodge brothers. When I came to we were on the train.

For three months we lived on those trains. America, in those dim days, was still a railroad civilization, and the trains were its only arteries. Distances were vast in the terms of train-time, and every town was a night's journey from the next. The trains had a great air of romance. Vast locomotives with stabbing headlights and colossal bells. The sound of them comes to me now, the thunder of steam and the smooth, rhythmless rails, and the 'woo-woo' of the whistle in the night, and the rattle of the curtain rings in the Pullman-car, and the hoicking of men into the cuspidors.

All night and every night we tossed in our curtained bunks in a temperature of eighty-five. Outside the double-windows was the waste of snow and bright lights. There is no mistiness in the American atmosphere. If you opened the windows the air temperature was seventy-two degrees of frost. You could take your choice.

At seven-thirty in the morning, at some incredible place called Oshkosh or Duluth or Kalamazoo we tottered to a platform in sub-zero temperatures, haggard, blear-eyed, and with our eyeballs freezing between blinks. There was a deputation: some reporters, the secretary of the local Den of Lions. My father made a little speech. We bundled into open cars and set off through the snow with a crunch and rattle of chains. We went over furniture factories, schools, hospitals, China-towns, the Dodge works, schools, hospitals, the White House, and at night my father lectured.

'Lehdies and gentlemen!' Across the length and breadth of the American continent, I can still hear my father's voice.

'Lehdies and gentlemen! Then I travelled to Kazan, a distance of seven hundred versts. In Kazan they had only four hundred poods of grain.'

Nobody knew what a pood was. The verst is not in the American scale. But at night when it was all over we tumbled into a train again, and there were the hot Negro porters and the curtain rings, and the rush of wheels, and the 'woo-woo' and my father's voice talking in his sleep. 'Six hundred versts and only *two* hundred poods of grain.'

[2]

We kept on the move. We went off to Constantinople to see the Russians, and we went to Berlin to see the Germans. The Russians were great fun. Somewhere in the Black Sea area and the Crimea the war was still going on under Lord Milne, whom I got to know very well later in the *next* war when I wrote his military comments for him in a Sunday newspaper, and a couple of White Russian types called Denikin and Wrangel.

I don't think they really expected to expel the Communists. They were keeping the escape routes open, and thousands and thousands of princes, princesses, grand dukes, grand duchesses, admirals, generals, artists, writers, in fact

47

a whole social class, poured down into Odessa and so across to Constantinople. They seemed a gay, civilized and pathologically inconsequential lot. They were a different race from the button-nosed brachycephalic mob we now associate with Soviet Russia. Romanovs, Galitzines, Machiabellis, Obolenskys, the entire social register had descended on this slightly comic Turkish capital, and flung itself into the local life with happy abandon. They had no country, no money, no hope; but their merriment was inexhaustible.

Some of them took jobs. The admiral of the Czar's yacht ran a restaurant where the 'Chicken à la Kiev' was like a kiss. A perfectly genuine princess was doing a modified strip-tease twice nightly at a dive called the 'Petit Champs', before an appreciative audience of American sailors. Most of them lived on their jewellery.

They had two resident jewellers actually in the dining-room at the Hotel Pera Palace. My father and I descended to dinner one night, and there, splendidly isolated and banked with flowers, was a long table set for fifty guests.

They came in, the ladies laughing, pretty, elaborately décolletées and the men in full uniform with medals and swords. They looked superb and utterly ridiculous. With perfect, indeed with princely decorum they arranged themselves. The ladies fluttered. The men clicked heels and bowed over their chairs. Winterhalter could have drawn it. Buckets of champagne went into orbit. The great chandelier overhead set everything winking, diamonds and decorations and bright eyes.

Half-way through the meal one of the men rose, one of the few civilians, walked across the polished floor to a piano, and began to play Chopin. I have no idea who he was but he was as good as Pouishnov. Is it possible that he was? He was greeted with a polite chatter of applause. Then he began to play the old Russian folk songs, the C-minor melodies which have to be sung with a catch in the throat: instantly the people at the table joined in, humming at first, and then breaking into full-throated harmony. They sang like

Negroes, with a great spread of chords from deepest bass to highest treble, and there wasn't a note wrong in any of it. The tears were streaming down their faces. And when they had done that the men sprang to attention with drawn swords and the whole company went solemnly through the splendid old Czarist national anthem. The entire room stood up, except the two resident jewellers.

Then the lady who had been at the head of the table, a beautiful, sparkling lady with a rope of priceless pearls round her bare neck, walked over to the jewellers, took the pearls over her head and dropped them in a little heap before the jewellers.

The jewellers went to work. They examined the pearls through monocular lenses. They conferred together. They weighed them on a small set of portable scales. The lady took no notice. She stood with her head turned away and held high. I can remember the fair hair—the pretty line of her chin and neck, and the dress of white brocade, which just covered her nipples, but only just. The jewellers opened a drawer and put the pearls inside. Then they took some pieces of paper money and held them out. The lady didn't even look at her change. She waved at the head waiter and, when he arrived bowing, put it on his salver with a little flick.

Some days later we took a boat to the island of Prinkipo which the British Army had taken over for the Russians when they had become penniless refugees and where they fed them on British Army rations—bully beef and plum-and-apple jam.

They were still gay, still pathologically irresponsible. The place had been a summer resort for wealthy Turks. There were donkeys on the sands and little roundabouts for the children. The Russians rode the donkeys and the roundabouts. The women wore silk scarves on their heads, not as the present Queen and her subjects wear them but tied in flamboyant bows.

As we left I heard, through an open window, the Chopin Polonaise.

49

Then we heard that there had been a massacre at a place called Smyrna. Venizelos's Greeks had garotted all the Turks and flung them into the sea. We turned up and stayed a night or two at the Grand Hotel Splendid Palace which had bugs in it. There was no sign of anything much, except that there seemed to be a great many Greeks about, and very few Turks. We left. A fortnight later Mustapha Kemal arrived with his merry men, garotted all the Greeks and flung them into the sea. This was a pity in a way, because the Smyrna Greeks, being uncontaminated with the usual Balkan miscegenation, were real Greeks. They were beautiful, with fair hair and straight noses. *Kalos Kai Agathos*. All the women looked like Hebe. We also went to Berlin, to see the inflation, and to Geneva, to see the new League of Nations. We saw Sir Austen Chamberlain, and we saw Briand and Stresemann, and we rowed on the lake, one hot summer's day, with two journalists, one of them a red-haired character from the *Daily Herald* and the other a quiet, bullet-headed man from the *Popolo d'Italia*. I have forgotten the name of the first man, but the name of the other was Mussolini. And every year, on Christmas Day, we invaded three compartments of the Blue Train, and sidled off to the Riviera.

[3]

I had better explain at this stage that we were both, my father and I, looking for something to write about. I imagine an author has to do that. I was never, personally, able to do much about the Russians in Constantinople, or the Greeks in Smyrna, or even the Russians and the Greeks on my first trip to America, but the Riviera I definitely cashed in on repeatedly.

I liked the place. The winter sun shone in a way which happens nowhere else in the world except in Hollywood, where it has the same smell of chlorine and wallflowers.

I liked the sea for being blue, and the mountain villages for being Saracenic, the yachts in the Condamine and at

Cannes for being expensive, and the people for being slightly absurd. I knew of no other place, for instance, where you could share a bench in front of the casino with Sir Basil Zaharoff, the mystery man of Europe. I knew who he was. He didn't care who I was.

We sat there for some time. There was a tinkle of Russian music from the Café de Paris. There were some curious red flowers growing that looked like the heads of birds, with beaks and combs. From down below came the sound of rifle-fire from the *Tir aux Pigeons*. The birds who escaped added themselves with a flutter of wings to the trees above our heads.

Presently a very splendid Minerva drove up. It was a *coupé de ville*, with a chauffeur in pale grey sitting in front in the open air, with a strap under his chin. The moment it stopped an elegant man with a pair of gloves in his hand and co-respondent shoes on his feet descended, closed the door, walked up to the chauffeur, and struck him across the face with a vicious swipe of the gloves.

I was startled and angry, and said, to the universe at large, 'That man *must* be a German!'

'No,' said Sir Basil Zaharoff mildly, 'that is my brother.'

This whole set of circumstances would be unlikely in, say, Bexhill.

The Baroness Orczy was an unlikely lady. She inhabited a rich, terraced, metropolitan villa, a thing of balustrades and pots and bougainvillea and great rooms on different levels. She was a tiny woman on tall heels, very corseted, and, of course, she knew what she was doing. She wrote books about the Scarlet Pimpernel for money. Naturally she knew all the other writers. If you went to one of her parties you would find, as she did not hesitate to point out, 'three reigning princes'. Two of them, I imagine, were their hereditary highnesses of Monaco, Rainier's father, and the old man. But who was the third?

I have no idea. But E. Phillips Oppenheim would be there, and Aldous Huxley, and Maugham, and sometimes

Wells, and W. J. Locke. Wells was by no means an inhabitant, but he retained a Provençal mistress. In one of those angelic pauses in the racket I heard him say, in fluting tones and an atrocious French accent, 'Tu est horrible, mais je t'aime.'

W. J. Locke had an extraordinarily beautiful adopted daughter. Isn't it strange how Locke's works have completedly dropped from the scene? Yet *The Beloved Vagabond* was beloved by all. He was a tall, shy man, who found the world a difficult place to live in without far too much brandy. This girl—was her name Tony?—was the belle of the ball. She never had fewer than thirteen men round her, three of them reigning princes. Her father was an Italian, but you would never have guessed it. She was the English rose. The Italian brought a court action against Locke for her return, and when he lost it killed himself. This added to her attractiveness, for a certain type of mind. The Baroness Orczy was really Mrs Montague Barstow.

Mr Barstow never appeared at the parties. He occupied a separate part of the villa. There was something the matter with him, and if you wanted to see him you had to ask specially. Like the sun-dried man. There would be a certain amount of *sotto voce*, and you had to go through the door. There was Mr Barstow in a wheel-chair, painting nudes.

He was always painting nudes. He had painted hundreds and hundreds of nudes. The walls of three or four rooms were covered with nudes. The moment he finished one he started painting another. They were quite good nudes, rather greenish perhaps; and he never used a model. He invented them all out of his head.

I must say that I had a certain sympathy with Mr Barstow. If you were the husband of a very famous woman and you had, for some reason, to live in a wheel-chair, and upstairs a party was going on with three reigning princes, damn it, you'd paint nudes.

The point I wish to labour *ad nauseam* is that there was an atmosphere of expensive improbability about the Riviera in those days which made it absolutely right as a background for short stories, novels, plays and films. The whole thing was ready to hand. The sunshine. The palm trees. The statue of Massenet. The Russian grand dukes. Sir Basil Zaharoff. The old ladies who were pensioned by the Casino. The people who were establishing residence for divorces. The American matron who took an aspirin at the tables and was promptly rushed through a secret door to have a stomach pump applied. The Living Dead. I must tell you about the Living Dead.

One of my aunts, a nun, had instructed me in an infallible system for playing roulette. She was a nun for forty years before she emerged, dyed her hair red and married a garage proprietor in Curzon Street. This system was called the 'Abbé Labouchère'. It was incredibly boring, but it worked. You had to sit down at one of the tables in full evening dress with a large piece of paper and a fountain pen. You then did very complicated sums, with a great deal of crossing out, which earned some extremely dirty looks from the croupiers. I suppose they were nervous that you would ruin the Société des Bains de Mer. Sinister men with expressionless faces would be discovered standing beside your chair. If you made no mistakes in the arithmetic and had enough paper you could get up from the table at half-past ten or so, when it was time to go to bed, with a clear profit of four-and-sixpence.

This was going on one night when a man introduced himself as Marion Crawford and asked if I was using the law of probabilities.

I asked him if he was the son of Marion Crawford.

He replied that all Marion Crawfords were the sons of Marion Crawfords.

After this inauspicious beginning we left the table and he tried to explain to me about the law of probabilities. Of course you know what it is. But that man actually bought a paper every morning which the Société des Bains de Mer actually published which contained every actual number which had come up in every table both in the Casino and the International Sporting Club on the day before. Millions of numbers. Marion Crawford, who said that he was really a mathematician, worked his law on the numbers, and could produce with reasonable exactitude the numbers which would turn up on any particular table. He had an interesting phrase to describe this. He said that 'the probability that they would not turn up approximated to zero'. His only trouble was that although he knew with some certainty what numbers would crop up in the course of an evening, he had no idea in what order they would occur. He then said he had an engagement to have a drink with Lady de Frece.

I looked blank.

'Vesta Tilley,' he said, with a curious expression in his eyes.

'Good God!' I exclaimed. 'I thought she'd been dead for years!'

He solemnly took out a small book, ran his thumb down the edge till he came to the 'T's', found Vesta Tilley and added a tick to her name.

'I keep a score,' he said, 'of all the people who get that remark when I mention their names. There are lots of them in Monte Carlo. Poor Vesta's leading by seventeen.'

He showed me the cover of the book. It was labelled, in neat mathematician's handwriting, THE LIVING DEAD.

[4]

All this was far too good to miss. When we returned to Shackleford (did I mention we had moved to a biggish house in the country?), I adopted my father's routine for the working day. This was simple but exhausting. Immediately after breakfast we collected a dog called Fitz (for Fitz Gibbs) and tore across the common at a furious pace for three-quarters of an hour. Then we returned home, trembling and pale, and locked ourselves in our respective studies.

54

We wrote until lunch. We were then waited upon by a butler who had been a mental-home attendant, and played about in the afternoon. After tea we shut ourselves up again and worked until dinner.

In this way my father poured out a stream of successful books. But I didn't do too badly myself. I wrote a book called *The Elder Brother*, which was my masterpiece, and will no doubt remain so. Quite a lot of it took place by the statue of Massenet to the sound of the *Tir aux Pigeons*. It was a serious and a moving book and I am still proud of it. Having hit the jackpot twice I suddenly became successful. The book was published in New York, where a man called Ross read it. Harold Ross had just started a magazine called *The New Yorker*. He made me its first London correspondent. I suddenly found the trick, too, of the short story. It *is* a trick. I sold my stories to that Ray Long who signed the death pact with Mildred Temple, and they all appeared here in *Nash's* magazine. Then I wrote a play. I called it *The Living Dead*.

It was a neatly balanced pattern of an idea. I took a man like my uncle (the one who married the most beautiful woman in England), put him in Monte Carlo, and arranged things so that he had an attractive son by a first marriage and an attractive daughter by a second. The two young people, knowing nothing of this, met at the Eden Roc and fell in love. Then the horrified parents had to confess the truth. They couldn't marry, of course, because that would be incest. So they agreed, on a high emotional note, to part, and 'my uncle' was wheeled away to get on with painting his nudes.

Old Mr Curtis Brown, a charming and courtly old American, looking just like Benjamin Franklin, who was a literary agent and father of Spencer who later ran theb usiness, showed this to Leon M. Lion. Does that name mean anything in the theatre today? It meant a lot to me, for Leon M. Lion ran the Playhouse, just by Charing Cross Station. Many people thought of him as one of the most sensitive and successful producers. I certainly did. Mr Lion didn't send for me to go and see him. He came to see me.

He climbed out of his car, looking remarkably leonine. The wind had given him a mane of hair. He was wearing striped trousers and carried a brief-case in his hand. I was deep in the entrails of my car and covered with oil. It was an Amilcar.

'Are you young Gibbs?' he asked.

I said I was.

'I'm Leon M. Lion,' he said.

I gulped five times. I knew they had sent him my play. He took me by the arm and walked me up and down.

'Are you the son of your father?'

I asked him what he meant.

'You *must* know,' he said, walking me with a conscious adaptation of his steps to mine. 'Son of a famous man. The incubus. Is that how it is with you?'

I said that in some ways it helped, and in some ways it didn't.

'Forget it,' he said. 'I've read your play and from this moment you needn't give the old man another thought. I solemnly assure you, with the full knowledge of what I'm saying, that yours is the pen which is going to save British drama.'

All the birds in the air began to sing.

They needn't have bothered. He gave me a cheque for £100 and I shot off to Paris for a weekend.

[5]

I never know what to do in Paris. If you ignore the oo-la-la, due to fastidiousness or other cause, there seems very little else. The Opera, like all opera, is frightful. If you go to a straight play you can't understand a word anybody says. There seems really nothing for it but to saunter about, admire the perspectives, drift back to the Café Berri, buy an *Evening Standard*, and take the first plane out.

One night, I did, greatly daring, look up in the local evening paper to see if there was anything reasonably Parisian that I could visit impersonally and without involvement.

An advertisement caught my eye *La Danseuse Nue, Cinema de Bastille*.

I didn't see what harm there could possibly be in that, so I got into a taxi driven by a Russian prince, and drove for about thirteen miles. The only time we stopped dead was to allow a pigeon to cross the road. The driver took off his cap to it. He was an amusing man. The *danseuse nue* was a bitter disappointment. She wasn't *nue*, at all. Only *nue*-ish. And suffering from obvious malnutrition. However, we did see a German film about sunbathers and I decided then and there that one of these days there ought to be a plot in that. When the *danseuse nue* came on again, this time with a large wooden hoop, I decided there was nothing for it but the next plane out.

The plane I took out was an Imperial Airways machine, a biplane with wings made of canvas, a naked engine between each wing, and a fuselage, also of canvas, with a row of seats down either side. I suppose it held about sixteen people, and everything was lashed together by piano wire.

The stewardess had not yet been invented, but, presumably, there was a pilot in front, and there was a child of eighteen wearing a boiler suit and a leather flying helmet. He was known as 'the observer'.

I always like to sit at the back of aeroplanes in case we hit anything, and I duly ensconced myself in the last seat.

We took off with a great deal of revving up and bouncing about over the grass—I'm almost sure it was *grass*—and in next to no time at all everybody was sick. Those early machines had too much wing. They heeled and jumped and plunged with every breath that blew. It began to rain. The water lashed the canvas. The only thing to look at was the engine just outside the window. You could see everything working. The valves were bouncing up and down, the magneto was going round and round, and the thought was

57

inescapable that one's life was hanging by a slender thread. If anything happened to that engine . . .

After about an hour the weather improved, and there, down below, was the coast of France. Quite far down below. And there also was the sea, with all its waves and elements frozen into sudden immobility. I turned again to my engine. 'Good old engine,' I thought. The magneto was going round, the valves were popping up and down, and quite a lot of flames were coming out of it.

It took me about three minutes to reason it out with myself that it couldn't really be normal for flames to be coming out of that engine. They were quite big flames, about five feet long I should say, and they were licking the canvas of the wings. The observer was standing with his back to the pilot's door, looking agreeably down the aisle. He was a nice boy. I beckoned him urgently. He caught my glance and came towards me. I pointed out of the window.

'Great Scott!' he said, and hurried back to the pilot's door, went through it and slammed it behind him. Immediately the plane gave a tremendous lurch. A lady suddenly noticed the flames and screamed. That made everybody else notice the flames.

The strange thing was that nobody said anything or did anything. They just looked at the flames. The plane lurched again and seemed to become fixed in an awkward side-slip.

At that moment the young observer came back through the door and leaned against it. His face was green. I have often seen that phrase in books. His face *was* green. Very slowly he raised his hands to the people in the cabin, and turned both of his thumbs down. We all reacted in the same way and did so together. Soundlessly, and as one man, we stood up. Stretching away from me, in two rows, were the ears and cheeks of the passengers. They all turned green. The plane was canted at an impossible angle. The flames were like jets. They made a whirring as the wind caught them. The sea was very close now, and we knew that we were going to die.

58

This is the only time in my life when I have *known* I was going to die. The sensation was quite different from the *fear* of death, which occasionally came to one in air-raids. Just as with drunkenness, I found there was a little cell in the brain which remained intact, logical, and functioning.

I noticed, for instance, that I had no fear whatsoever. In fact I was amazed to discover in myself what I could only describe as an unsuspected bravery. Of course I thought it was rather a pity. It was a pity that I would never marry, and have children, and so perpetuate myself. On the other hand I had made a worth-while start. I had written two fairly good novels and a play that was going to save British drama. If the purpose of life was the improvement of the species and the justification of the individual, then at least I had done something of the second. These were very strange thoughts. I have set them down exactly as they occurred. Then I noticed something different about the engine. It had stopped.

The flames were still coming out of it but they were smaller flames. The plane was still tilted. The sea was about four hundred feet below. I knew at once what the pilot was doing, as if I could see him doing it. He had turned off the petrol to the engine, and he was piloting the plane with his head turned back so that he could watch the flames and keep the thing at an angle, so that instead of licking those canvas wings they slipped out between the two of them. Our whole angle of tilt and direction were governed by that necessity. If the other engine failed to support us and we drove into the sea, that was the calculated risk. The fire must not be allowed to catch those wings. And with the recognition that our movements were still, if only partially, at the command of skill and intelligence, a small hole opened and hope crept out.

The other passengers still stood in their two rows, bracing themselves against the roof. You could almost see their minds at work, sizing up chances. Four minutes passed and the sea was not much nearer. The *waves* were in *motion* now. A small ship steamed below us, tipped to an angle of forty-five degrees. The coast line of England appeared at the same strange diagonal. I thought of Bleriot. The wing above the engine was toasted black now. You could see the weave of the canvas. But it was not on fire. There seemed a distinct possibility that we should live.

We lived. While we were still over shallow water the fire went out. With our one good engine we achieved level flight at last, and went sailing, scarely more than fifty feet above the ground, through Shoreham Gap. One hour later we landed awkwardly at Croydon. We clambered out and ran to shake the pilot by the hand and clap him on the back.

'Just a bit of a hole in the exhaust pipe,' he said, grinning.

Next day the Lord Chamberlain refused to grant a licence to *The Living Dead*. He was very gentle about it when I went to see him in St James's Palace.

'My dear Mr Gibbs, I have a duty to perform. The play is on the subject of incest.'

I pointed out that the play was about the absence of incest.

'The subject of the play is incest,' he repeated.

It was a very pleasant, white-painted room. There were pictures of debutantes wearing their feathers. My great-grandfather kept two rooms in St James's Palace. I wondered whether this were one of them. But he wouldn't pass my play, and the British Drama remained unsaved.

Sometimes life approximates to zero.

So I did the other thing. I got married.

[6]

It was old George Doran's fault.

George Doran was one of those tremendously stately American publishers. He had flowing white hair and a flowing white beard. and he was always beautifully dressed. I sometimes wonder, if I had got myself up to look like this, whether I should not have made a better publisher. But that's a later story.

60

The family had acquired the habit of coming to London after the Riviera to finish off the winter. We just took houses generally within a stone's throw of Sloane Square. 6 Sloane Gardens. 43 Cadogan Gardens. 33 Cliveden Place. 4 Lyall Street. That was a flat, where a frightfully noisy man played the banjo underneath at four in the morning, who turned out to be Charles Graves. It was that same flat we passed on to a very tall man indeed, with a dominating chin, a commanding presence and a tonsure. He told us the only thing he was really interested in was the height of the door. The doors were O.K. He said his name was Reith and that he had something to do with the British Broadcasting Company.

We were very interested in this and asked, since he said he was coming back on Tuesday, whether he could bring something to show us. He very kindly agreed, and in due course he turned up, trailing wires. He spent about an hour draping these around the place. Then he plugged something into the electric light, and spent nearly another hour with an intent expression and a pair of earphones over his head. Then he passed them, very quietly and carefully, to my mother.

She said she couldn't hear anything at all.

My father listened, said he thought the thing must have gone off the boil and passed it to me.

The moment I put it to my ear a voice said 'The orchestra will now play "Who tied the can on the old dog's tail?" ' A tinny stridulation filled the ear.

We were amazed and delighted. We said it was the most staggering thing since the invention of speech. We asked Mr Reith whether we could buy one. He said that he personally didn't sell them. The B.B.C., as he called it, was simply an association of manufacturers.

He thought that if we went along to Harrods. . . . He strongly recommended something called a valve set.

We bought a thing like the instrument board of a Comet. You sat in front of this battery of dials with a pair of headphones on your head, and began to operate the controls.

61

You had four valves, each with its own switch like the thing that turns on the new hydro-electric station at Novorosikirsk, and you brought them in one by one with a heady sense of power. Then you had a 'Potentiometer', and a 'Grid Bias, plus or minus', and a 'Coil Turret' and a 'Grid Leak' and a 'Rough Tuner' and a 'Fine Tuner' and many, many more that I cannot remember. High skill was called for, and great qualities of patience and endurance, because every time you altered one thing, all the others, to use my father's phrase, went off the boil. At last, when you had the music fairly humming in your ears you threw another gigantic switch and a vast cornucopia in the next room exploded into sound.

But about this marriage.

One of my uncles was a brilliant bacteriologist, and he died in the cause of science in the first war by catching cerebro-spinal meningitis, on which he was working. They buried him at Étaples. He was an amusing, violent, unpredictable man with a touch of genius, who wore extraordinary clothes like deerstalker hats and sheepskin jackets. His purse was the scrotum of a kangaroo. There is a bronze plaque with a portrait of him in the Library of the Lister Institute of Preventive Medicine, just at the corner of Chelsea Bridge.

That was where he worked, peering down microscopes trying to grow bacteria in test tubes, delving into the world of the microscopic and the ultra-microscopic. His greatest friend was 'The Boss', the Institute's Director-General.

'The Boss' it was who used to drive backward up Grosvenor Gardens into Hyde Park. He imitated my uncle Rowland in many ways. Isn't it clear now, how everything begins to clock into place? He, too, wore deerstalker hats. *His* purse was the scrotum of a kangaroo. But he was a much greater man. Where Rowland was volatile and imaginative and brilliant and more than a little wild, 'The Boss' was just as intelligent, but accurate, empirical, questioning, never tangential, and a born administrator. His name was Sir

Charles Martin, C.M.G., F.R.S., F.R.C.P., D.C.L., LL.D., D.Sc. He terrified me. I'm always uncomfortable in the presence of someone who has a better brain than I have. Yet when George Doran rang me up, invited me to dinner at the Savoy and told me to bring any pretty girl I liked, I asked the Boss's daughter. Her name was Ysobel Maisie Howard Astraea. Maisie was a long-legged girl. She swam like a fish. She could inject two c.c.'s of something or other into the heart of a living guinea-pig without hurting it. She could play Debussy's *Arabesque* like nobody's business. She was very nice, and after George Doran's champagne I took her back to the Lister. I didn't say a thing to her, but she said something very odd to me. Something like 'admiration'. Chelsea Bridge seemed to detach itself at the Battersea Park end and come curling over until it investigated us like a sea-serpent. Other very odd things happened of an internal nature. I mean, of all things, *admiration*!

Somehow I got back into the car, and burst into our home, rang up George Doran, said, 'My God what have you done? I want to get married. I believe you did that on purpose.'

'Well, I'm awfully glad,' said George. 'We'll have to do what we can to make it possible. Tell you what—I'll up your advance to two thousand dollars on the next three books.'

Then I rushed into the drawing-room, where my father and mother were sitting, and said, 'The most extraordinary thing has happened. I've fallen in love.'

They both looked rather pleased, if anything.

In the end we got married, and after a honeymoon in Nice, where my Uncle Cosmo kept an empty flat to establish French residence so that he could divorce his new wife, we took a little house in Cheltenham Terrace, and have been married ever since. I may as well put it in here, however absurd it looks: I love her very much indeed.

63

IV

I have no idea whether it was the effect of marriage, but I sat down and wrote a thoroughly bad book, about Oxford again, and immediately sold it to the movies.

It was called *Young Apollo*, a ghastly title taken from Frances Cornford's *Young Apollo*, 'golden-haired, stands dreaming on the verge of strife, magnificently unprepared for the long littleness of life'. The whole thing was almost as bad as being born in Bolton. But it did produce the Kordas.

There was a lady called Miss Buxton, from Curtis Brown, who performed the introduction. She looked exactly like the way she sounds.

Miss Buxton and I walked up Grosvenor Street. She was chatty, businesslike, and a little breathless. I stalked grimly above her, like a nephew.

Numbers twenty-two and twenty-three. London Film Productions Limited. We went in.

I looked about. A perfectly new table covered with magazines, their contents devoted exclusively to the portraiture of young women in an advanced condition of what the film people call 'cleavage'. Four new chairs, of the comfortable, vaguely modernistic cut. Four other chairs. Four beflowered maidens of breath-taking beauty, provocative to a degree, of that blonde expressionlessness which takes so kindly to the camera. All four were attired for Ascot. All four had remarkably slim legs. Their manners and their intonations were elaborately beyond reproach. Their finger nails were pink. Their odours conflicted slightly. One of them appeared to be filling up some kind of form. Miss

64

Buxton remained perched briskly on the edge of a chair. Their names, if it interests you, were Merle Oberon, Joan Gardner, Wendy Barrie and I've forgotten the fourth.

'Miss Buxton, pl-oeuil-se!' said a small boy in the doorway.

The four lovelies stirred, falling into new and lovelier poses of sex-conscious ennui. Miss Buxton and I rose, rather primly, and picked our way among their tapering, silk-stockinged legs.

We followed the small boy upstairs into an ante-room. It harboured a lady at a desk, a motherly-looking lady of pleasantly Scandinavian appearance, saying, 'O.K., Mr Laughton,' down a telephone, 'Fine.' There were, in addition, a half-dozen men waiting about on chairs, with an air of patient, hunched dejection, as if they had been waiting for days. Miss Buxton blithely ignored these people and led the way to a green baize door.

'That's all right,' said the motherly lady. 'Go right in.'

We did so. One or two of the waiting men allowed a fishlike gaze to alight on us for a moment as we went. There was a strong smell of cigar smoke and a thick carpet, and from the tall drawing-room windows the Grosvenor Street sun made layers of the smoke and drew filtered parallele-pipeds across the figure of a man who sat at a massive table of the Napoleonic period. He looked exactly like Abdul the Damned. He was in his shirt sleeves and wore a green eye-shade, and he was talking very gently into a telephone in Hungarian. 'Egen. Oyosh, Loyosh,' or words to that effect. Miss Buxton and I waited respectfully, with a strong sense of attending upon the pleasure of the great.

When he had done he turned round and stood up.

'Good afternoon, Mr Korda, this is the young author I told you about,' said Miss Buxton in her jolly way.

Alexander Korda grinned. He had an attractive grin, which broke across a fleshy face so that he became suddenly boyish. He was tall, exhausted, energetic, civilized, and European.

65

We shook hands, or, rather, I shook his.

It was Miss Buxton who broke the spell. She started determinedly on contracts and percentages and sums down in advance of royalties.

Mr Korda waved it all aside. 'I have Leontine Sagan,' he said, 'of *Mädchen in Uniform*. I wish to make a film about Oxford. I read your book. It is a very good book. You help me work on it?'

I gulped. 'I was going to suggest that——'

'Naturally,' agreed Mr Korda quietly, and immediately began to look rather strained as if he grew afraid his first estimate of us was wrong and we were stupid enough to want to go on discussing the matter indefinitely. 'Good-bye,' he said.

[2]

The studios were at Wembley, a ramshackle building with an exhibitionist front. A little man came out to meet me with a very red face, and the pointed ears and nose of a faun.

'My name is Zoltan Korda,' he said. 'I work on your film. *I* do.' He tapped his tie. 'If you are ready we go, without any further.' He smiled and his mouth as he did so formed a perfect V, so that he looked more like a faun than ever.

'But first you must excuse——Commissionaire, you go to the chemist chop and you buy me lactic acid ferment. It is fourpence.'

'Very good, Sir.'

He handed the commissionaire a five-pound note from a roll of several, and tapped his tie again.

'I have to take,' he explained. 'It is good for me. We go.'

He had a caressing voice, and the clean, altogether enchanting appearance of having been born five minutes previously, and he struck me, even then at the first meeting, as extraordinarily strokeable. I am not given to fondling my fellow men, but I always wanted to lift Zoli up and pet him.

66

His eyes were so trusting and unblinking. If you have ever stumbled on a baby satyr in the forest you will understand what I mean.

He led the way down tall corridors, saying, 'I like not the title. You see what I tink. I tink to myself, "Who is Apollo? Is he not a God?" I tink, "What the hell, Apollo? Is it a film about gods? But it is not. It is a film about Oxfor'!" So if you excuse me, we change the title without any further.'

Then he stopped, put a hand on my arm, and smiled into my face like a disillusioned child.

'I am sorry, Mr Gibbs. The movie world it is a lousy world. One must have tick skin. My skin,' he poked his tie, 'it is tick already. Please.'

As he went we seemed to penetrate always towards a deeper and more sensible silence. Now he put his finger to his pointed lips, opened a padded door, and led me a silent dance, more satyric than ever, on tiptoe among a fantastic undergrowth of electric cables as thick as a tree's roots, that twined all over the floor, serpentine and not a little sinister.

We were in a vast dim world and the shapes of queer two-dimensional rooms came and went as we picked our way, now through an unillumined bed-chamber, now through the ghostly suggestion of a pub-parlour, with all the bottles and its dart-boards and its election notices quietly complete to the dingiest detail, in the dark.

We got through in the end to a great brightness, and there was a pool with goldfish swimming in it and real trees, other trees not so real, and suddenly we were on the blinding steps of a country church with a great crowd of bridesmaids gathered there. On the topmost step was George Grossmith, elegant, skeletal, debonair. He was wearing a silk hat, a stock, and fawn waistcoat, sponge-bag trousers and a monocle on a string, and he had one arm round the neck of Wendy Barrie and another round the neck of Joan Gardner. Zoltan Korda whispered their names.

In the foreground were three cameras on little rubber-tyred carts. All around and above intense lights blazed, in

67

the most unexpected places, on the top of the church tower, in the trees, dotted about among the guests, so that it seemed impossible the camera should not photograph some of them. Each, or nearly each, had its acolyte standing, hands on hips; the cameras were served by a little hierarchy of dishevelled priests, in flannel trousers and pullovers and unusual shoes.

Alexander Korda was squinting through one of the cameras. He was wearing an eye-shade and smoking a big cigar.

'G.G.,' he said, 'I want you about six inches further right.'

Mr Grossmith obediently moved, and his 'daughters' with him.

'Come down one step, G.G.'

Mr Grossmith came down one step. 'How's that old boy?' he asked.

Mr Korda went and looked through the other camera.

'This all right, Alex?' called Mr Grossmith.

'O.K.,' said Mr Korda, 'we go.'

Suddenly the microphone spoke. It had been dangling quite inoffensively on a long rod just above George Grossmith's head; and it startled me by uttering almost human sounds in a tinny, disembodied voice.

'I'm awfully sorry, Mr Korda,' said the microphone, 'but he's blasting.' The Oxford accent was irreproachable.

Mr Korda waved. Men rushed at it and moved it further away.

'Try,' said Mr Korda, round the end of his cigar.

'My darling, I love you,' declared Mr Grossmith.

'And I love you too.'

'Still blasting,' complained the microphone.

Mr Korda waved again and the men removed it further.

'Am I blasting now, blast you?' called Mr Grossmith.

Everyone looked up at the microphone anxiously, with that slightly awed religiosity with which her devotees must once have approached the Delphic oracle.

'No, that's all right,' it said. 'Sorry, Mr Korda.'

A fireman crept up behind us and touched Zoltan Korda's

cigarette. He stamped on it wryly. His brother's cigar was going nicely.

'All right, try it,' Mr Korda said.

'Is this a take?' asked an elderly lady with a velvet strap round her neck, who subsequently proved to be Lady Tree.

'Yes, take. Quiet'.

'Quiet!' repeated a man.

'*Quiet!*' repeated another.

'Quiet!' repeated another and another and the echoes.

A bell rang.

'Qui-ERT!!' roared somebody in the remoter distance. The hush was terrible.

The cameras were alive, soundlessly, without motion. A man stepped before them with a blackboard, and gabbled something like: 'Track thirty-two, take four, take six,' while another jumped forward with a wooden instrument like the jaws of a crocodile which he snapped shut before leaping lightly aside. Instantaneously the grouped figures on the church steps broke into motion. Faces moved, registering expression. Skirts billowed. Gentlemen stroked moustaches. The two girls who had been nestling so pleasantly in Mr Grossmith's embrace now sobbed hysterically on his bosom. There was a commotion from somewhere behind the people on the steps, and a man cried, 'Let me pass! Let me pass!'

'Cut!' said Mr Korda.

'Cut!' said the cameraman.

'Cut!' shouted people here and people there.

'Cut!' cried the echoes.

Zoltan Korda plucked pathetically at my sleeve. 'I am hungry,' he said. 'It is good for me to eat. You will come with me?'

We groped through the undergrowth to a frightful canteen. A frightful waitress came.

I asked for China tea.

Zoltan Korda said: 'I have not eaten today. I have tree eggs. You have oranges?'

The waitress had.

'Six oranges, please, in a glass and milk. Half a litre of milk.'

The waitress looked blank and adenoidal.

'Milk,' said Zoltan, measuring about a foot high with his hands.

'Any bacon with the eggs?'

'Yes, bacon. It is good for me.'

'Half a pint of milk?'

'Now listen,' said Zoltan. 'I order milk. What the hell? You bring milk, if you please, without any further!' He turned his eyes on me with a deprecating smile. 'The next time,' he said, 'I speak Hungarian.'

The waitress departed, muttering.

Everybody was very friendly at this first tea-party with the members of London Films. There was Monsieur Pallos, whose name was pronounced Pollosh. His English was fluently non-existent, but he spoke French with tremendous gusto. He had all of us speaking French. He was a dapper little person with dark pomaded hair and something elaborately Latin about the check of his suit and the pricking in his shoes. He was magnificently polite and something of a wit. There was yet another Korda, Vincent, a taciturn chap with a prognathous lower lip and a strong resemblance to Maurice Chevalier. I recognized him as one of the men who had been waiting in the back room that day.

I asked him what he did.

He looked deeply suspicious.

'Qu'est-ce que vous faites ici?' I tried.

'Sets,' said Vincent.

'You mean the scenery?'

'Oui.'

'You did that one I saw in there?'

He looked more suspicious than ever. 'Vous avez fait l'église la?'

'Oui.'

'Et les goldfish?'

70

'Oui.'

'You despise the movies?'

'Oui.'

'He exhibits au salon,' explained M. Pallos. 'He is a great artist. Très grand artiste. Assez moderne. Très connu. 'Ungarian. Vous comprenez?'

'Oui,' I said.

The commissionaire approached with a small bottle. 'Excuse me, sir, four pounds nineteen and eightpence change.'

'I tink I keep,' said Zoltan, pocketing it.

'I also,' declared M. Pallos, 'am 'Ungarian. You have been to Budapest? No?'

'No,' I said.

'Yes?'

'No.'

'It is not much. Moi, je préfère Paris. London, yes—but Paris. Moi je suis tout à fait Parisien. We 'Ungarians we 'ave no 'ome. Nous sommes toujours des étrangers. Mais à Paris, voyez vous, personne n'est étranger. Je demeure à Paris. Enfin, je suis Parisien. Waitress, apportez moi de la salade, s'il vous plâit. Et du café. Café noir, s'il vous plâit, et bien chaud. Vous comprenez? 'Ot coffe, et de la salade.'

'No eggs?' said the waitress.

'If you like,' agreed M. Pallos vaguely. 'Eggs. And so, you make film about Oxford with us, n'est ce pas? I 'ave been. Ah, quelle vieille ville! You 'ave met Madame Sagan?'

'No, not yet,' I told him.

'Très intelligente.' He shrugged his shoulders and said something in Hungarian to Zoltan Korda. Zoltan said quite a lot in Hungarian. M. Pallos became deeply moved. Vincent Korda clucked his teeth. Zoltan said something else. M. Pallos became very excited. Vincent Korda rose and walked vaguely away. M. Pallos and Zoltan Korda remained glaring at one another with bulging eyes.

Fortunately at this moment Joan Gardner came along. Apart from the fact that her face was painted a jaundiced

71

shade of London-and-South-Western-Railway gamboge, she struck me, in her flowered wedding frock, as a pretty person, and perfectly simple.

'You sit with us?' Zoltan asked, looking perceptibly affectionate. 'Mr Gibbs, this is Joan Gardner. She play Jane.'

M. Pallos rose with exquisite politeness and kissed the tips of her fingers. Zoltan, more childlike, stroked her arm with his fingernail, becoming absorbed in the business. . . .

So this was my heroine. She had a nice forehead, blue eyes, a good laugh, an honest look, no sophistication. I liked her very much.

'She is our starlet,' said Zoltan. 'Our little star. She is very beautiful.' He prodded his tie. '*I* tink she is beautiful. I am director, and if I say she is beautiful she is beautiful, without any further.'

M. Pallos said something in Hungarian. It made Zoltan Korda blush.

'You excuse,' he smiled. 'We talk Chinese.'

M. Pallos became businesslike. 'Mis-ter Gibbs, what is a good hotel in Oxford, please?'

'Oh, the Mitre.'

'The how you say?'

'The Mitre.'

'You spell that please?'

I spelled it and explained its significance.

'Ah oui! La mitre. We stay there. Mister Zoltan Korda, Madame Sagan, some cameramen, myself, we stay all together in the Mitre.'

I had alarming visions.

'You stay with us in Oxford tomorrow, please?'

I'm afraid I blenched. Maisie was expecting a baby at any minute. 'For how long?'

'One day, two days, three days, four days,' replied M. Pallos, magnificently uncertain. 'You no desire to go to Oxford?'

It seemed that this was going to develop into a situation which required the nomadic outlook.

'I engage a room for you? We live together there? It is arranged—no?'

'Without any further,' said Zoltan Korda, dropping ten tablets into his half-litre of milk.

[3]

The effect on the waiters of the Mitre Hotel was precisely what I feared. It was three o'clock as I came over Magdalen Bridge and the turreted shadows already reached like fingers across the High.

The porter and the boots and such servants as had their stations in the lobby looked rather melancholy I thought. Some secret grief was troubling them. The sounds of revelry swelled, and when I enquired if there were any people called Mr Korda and someone opened the door of the dining-room, they crashed into a mighty diapason. There were cutlery and china and the murmur of waiters, and the perceptible constituent elements of French, Hungarian, American, English and German. London Film Productions Limited had arrived.

Leontine Sagan was a bit mannish. She wore one of those floppy felt hats affected by Garbo. She shook hands in that peculiar, East-European way, extending it back-uppermost with the fingers falling. The man is supposed to bang his heels, exclaim, 'Küss die hand.' I shook it.

'Take me,' she said, 'to a very high place. I must go where I can see all Oxford, to get the feel of it. Is there a place where we can go?'

So I took her to the roof of the Bodleian. There, with her black hair blowing in the little breeze and the sun screwing her eyes, this woman first came into my young life. She was attractive. Although she wore the alarming checks which the American flapper of the period derived from the fashion of Berlin where, no doubt, they are regarded as *Schottisch*, her figure was evidently boyish. At the same time she was, emotionally, what the Edwardian novelists described

73

as a developed woman. She sat on the parapet for a long time, smoking a Turkish cigarette, with her chiselled face half turned to look over Oxford and to be revered.

A sensitive creature, I thought. I searched in my mind for adjectives. Handsome. Fine. Prussian, perhaps. Clever. Imaginative. Emotional? Above all, emotional, and I couldn't help feeling that she was sensitive to the occasion. 'Leontine Sagan looks over Oxford.'

'This Oxford,' she said, 'is so—so *aristocratic*.'

She looked about her, shading the sun from her eyes with her hand. 'Aristocratic,' she repeated, 'and poetic. I should like to get something of that. I tell you of my idea. I see a garden, a beautiful garden, and the boys are doing *A Midsummer Night's Dream*. I should like to make that almost the main scene.

I had no recollection of anything about *A Midsummer Night's Dream* in *Young Apollo*, but I accepted it politely.

'I was here yesterday,' she continued. 'I have already arranged with the O.U.D.S. There is a Mr Hunt. A charming boy, and very poetic. And then my idea was to blend in some way the story of your young man, your Christopher Allan Shepherd and the two girls Jane and Ysobel, so that they repeat always the *leit-motif* of *A Midsummer Night's Dream*. So we switch from one to the other all the way through. Could you write me that scene, please?'

I said a bit doubtfully that I would do my best.

'And another scene I want is a kaffee-haus scene. Perhaps a brothel? There is a well-known house in Oxford?'

'Well,' I said, 'there's Fullers, and the Kardomah, and of course—'

'A scene, you know, where the boys are sitting with their women, and the camera passes from one table to the other, and you hear snatches of conversation, the sort of thing boys talk about you know, when they are with their women.'

I said I thought that was a very good idea.

'Tell me,' she said. 'Is there much homosexuality among the boys?'

74

[4]

I told Zoli about our baby. He was touched and pleased. Then I asked him about the Kordas.

'Who are vee?' he repeated. 'You vish to know who are vee?'

'Yes, please,' I said.

He put an arm on mine, and his faun's eyes twinkled with a most endearing apologetic merriment.

'O.K. I tell. Vee are tree sons of an estate keeper.'

'Estate keeper, Zoli?'

'In Hungary are very big estates. Are rich noblemen and are serfs, and two times in every year some serfs must work for the noblemen on his estates. Mein vater is estate keeper, and two times every year he must take in—take on two, tree tousand serfs to work. You understand?'

'Igen,' I said.

'Mein vater is dying, but meine mutter is very good woman, and she stay many years, to take on two, tree tousand serfs. Vee have little house in middle of estate. From it vee see twenty kilometres in all directions.'

'Is this the rich black earth?'

'So! You know?'

'Go on,' I said.

'So. Comes time when Alex is eighteen, and I am sixteen and Vincent he is fourteen, and meine mutter tink is time for him to go into big world to make some fortune. So she buy him nice blue suit, and—how you say—chapeau melon?'

'Bowler hat?'

'And she say to him, "Bless you, my son, into big world must you go. Come back in one year." And she kiss him and he kiss her, and Vincent he kiss and I. Not very British I tink?'

He was an enchanting little man.

'Get on with it!' I told him.

'He is starting to walk. For twenty kilometres vee see him walk. Tree hours. Vee can see him no more. And tings

75

grow in the ground and a year passes and is once again a day.'

'And did he come?'

'From twenty kilometres. Tree hours he is walking and he comes zum hause and nobody is saying anyting. It is breakfast time. So first he eat my breakfast. And in a little time he eat breakfast of Vincent. Comes mine mutter, and she say to him, "Alex, not even a little fortune?" So Alex cries, and vee all cry, and it is another year.'

'It sounds biblical.'

'Biblical?'

'Never mind, Zoli. Go on.'

'Makes clean the suit my mother and presses very carefully, and brush the chapeau melon and once again,' Zoli smiled deprecatingly, 'vee kiss and he go forth. Tree hours before he disappear.'

'And it is another year.'

'Igen. And vee are looking twenty kilometres, and suddenly a very big cloud of dust is rising, and soon a motor-car, and in six, seven minutes it is here, a ver big motor-car, a Mercedes, and is open zis motor-car, and in back seat two very fine gentlemen each wit big tick cigar. And one of them is Reinhardt, and the other is Alex.'

'He'd done it.'

'Is very clever man.'

'Mr Reinhardt, or Alexander?'

Zoli made a gesture, a baby satyr flapping something away with his hand.

'Mr Gibbs I tell you something, His name is not Alexander. It is Ladislas ven he go. But, now, now it is Alexander.'

'And no more worlds to conquer?'

'Vee go to U.F.A. in Berlin. Vee go to Hollywood. Now vee are very, very British. Vee are London Films. A Big Ben there is. It is like B.B.C. vee must all stand up. You are an English gentleman. I—I am English gentleman too, without any further?'

Zoli laughed and laughed, and broke into a paroxysm of coughing and brought blood into his handkerchief.

V

[1]

We had engaged a friendly, efficient monthly nurse, and after that a Truby King, a pretty girl with bare arms, and after that a Norland. With the exception of the 'monthly' I chose them myself, and the standard of beauty was pretty high.

My son, of course, knew nothing of this, and began to show a marked reluctance to be born. Nurse Bradley became anxious. She had another date in three weeks' time. I had a camp-bed made up in the drawing-room beside the piano. The hall and stairs and the upstairs rooms were stacked with bulky and unmentionable objects, so that every time one moved there was a slither of rubber objects and a clatter of enamelware. The doctor was on a moment's call. And absolutely nothing happened.

There was an awful mess in the road in Ebury Street, and Nurse Bradley began taking my wife for short trips to Victoria and back on a No. 11 bus, just to shake things up. In the middle of this Ross turned up from *The New Yorker*, took one look at the hall and stairs, decided I was obviously the domestic type, and gave my job as London correspondent to an infantile phenomenon called Mollie Panter-Downes who has held it ever since.

He put me on to 'Profiles'. Above all he wanted the Prince of Wales. The complete low-down. How much he paid for his shirts. What he did in the evenings. I wrote a polite letter to Sir Godfrey Thomas at St James's Palace, pointing out what a good thing it would be to improve Anglo-American relations.

Sir Godfrey wrote back on splendid scarlet-headed

notepaper, all embossed with the Prince of Wales's feathers, and agreed to see me. I trotted round in the yellow Renault, parked it under the nose of a sentry, and was ushered in.

Sir Godrey was extremely cautious. He seemed to have no idea how much the Prince paid for his shirts, and as for what he did in the evenings. . . . Several more letters passed with the magnificent scarlet heading, and it became clear that no one was getting anywhere. Then the clouds parted. A tailor in Cork Street who was concocting me a suit, very snug over the hips and with the slightest of concessions to 'Oxford Bags', let slip that there was a special golf club— the place, not the thing—for tailors, and that everybody there would certainly know all about the Prince's shirts.

Bribed with bags of bullion for his trouble he produced the works. The twelve pairs of plus-fours for the trip to the Argentine, all of which were returned as useless. And so on and so on. Wonderful, wonderful stuff and just what *The New Yorker* ordered.

That afternoon I received another letter from Sir Godfrey Thomas. This time the notepaper, otherwise identical, was printed in black. 'Dear Gibbs, Would you kindly refrain from pursuing your enquiries at the servants' entrance?'

That evening the No. 11 bus did the trick and Martin turned up in the night, and I slept through the whole blessed business, a thing for which my wife has never quite forgiven me.

[2]

It was about this time that I learned that the part of Ysobel, a Somerville undergraduette of vaguely mediaeval tendencies, had been given to a lady from Tasmania with something alluringly Polynesian about her almond-eyes and the de-moniac tilt of her eye-brows. There had been some talk of giving the part of 'Horners', a self-confessed comedian, so styled from the material of his spectacles, to Giles Playfair, the son of Sir Nigel (*Beggar's Opera*) Playfair.

78

Playfair had just done something extraordinarily news-worthy with a balloon and Tallulah Bankhead. I forget now the exact details of the exploit, but the Oxford University Ballooning Society came into being as a result of his inventiveness. A balloon was acquired, the Press was informed, and at the specified moment a large crowd of reporters, photographers, and random undergraduates assembled on the ballooning field. The balloon swayed gently in the breeze, restrained from immediate ascent into the stratosphere by willing hands. Speeches were made. The President of the O.U.B.S. stepped into the basket, followed by Miss Bankhead, further speeches were made, bouquets were handed up, Miss Bankhead kissed her hands to the mob, orders were rasped out, the President of the O.U.B.S. went slightly pale, Miss Bankhead blew more kisses, the cameras whirred, the willing hands let go altogether, and the balloon failed to rise. At this point Giles Playfair stepped out and Miss Bankhead ascended into heaven, only to be saved at the last instant from physical assumption by a concerted rush for the last two inches of the guy-rope. For this, or for some other reason, the job of playing 'Horners', a faintly comic part, was given to a completely aspiring young Welshman called Emlyn Williams who has since acquired fame and fortune. The young lady who finally married the hero was Joan Gardner. She finally married Zoli Korda. The undergraduette who took her clothes off at Parson's Pleasure was the alluring Estelle Thompson, who became Stella O'Brien, who became Merle Auberon, who became Merle Oberon, until Alex ended the confusion by making her Lady Korda. The young medical student was a Lancashire Hungarian with a beautiful voice called Robert Donat. Nobody really knew very much about any of them. For all of them this was their first job.

[3]

I soon discovered that there are two troubles about writing

79

for the movies. The first is that nobody pays the slightest attention to anything one writes.

The second is that one becomes, on the face of it, disgustingly rich. Both are demoralizing. I forget now how much London Films were paying me. Could it have been a hundred pounds a week? D'you know, I think it was. The only difficulty was that I never got the money. At all events a man whose name I forget for the moment wrote a most charming book called *Greenery Street*. Of course: Denis Mackail. I am sure *Greenery Street* was Cheltenham Terrace. It described how the young married couples came and set up house, and were very happy and idyllic. Then monthly nurses descended upon them, and doctors in the night, and perambulators stood chained to the railings, and in no time at all they found the doll's houses too tiny and moved away, and another young couple moved in.

This happened to us exactly.

There was a man with whom I had once been rather friendly at that Oxford college who rejoiced in the name of Alexander Cadwallader Spearman. He had a very slight and rather attractive limp, and I remember, when I was helping him to pack just after that awful ball and just before that brilliant viva voce, my surprise when the first thing he put into his suitcase was a spare leg. The moment he came down from Oxford, it seemed to me, he became a member of Parliament, and a member of Parliament he has been without interruption, ever since. I have always wondered how he managed this. I stood for Parliament myself in 1945 and, naturally, didn't get in. On the whole, taking it by and large, nobody does. He married an extremely attractive lady, and got his wife in too, so that the whole business was extraordinarily well arranged.

This man lived at 39 Tite Street and wanted to leave for the country, so we moved in.

Do you know Tite Street? Oscar Wilde once called it 'a street of not unpretentious houses'. It was haunted by the ghost of Oscar. Sargent lived there, and Whistler lived there.

It was in Tite Street that Oscar Wilde, saying good-night to Whistler on the doorstep, announced pontifically, 'Meredith is a sort of prose Browning.' He walked away, turned back, and rang the door-bell again.

'And so is Browning.'

No. 39 was the very end house, cleverly arranged in a sort of fan-shape, so that you could look out over the river from all the rooms, both front and back. Another peculiarity was that every room was on a separate floor. The kitchen was at the top. The idea was that the brussels sprouts would be free to send their aroma upwards. This worked very well, but there was a disadvantage. The only sex-life of which the servants were capable had to be conducted through a speaking tube and a lift. You have no idea what an astonishing effect this had upon them. They would turn blue and tremble. My wife had to grab a whole succession of cooks by the wrist when they became hysterical and threatened to throw themselves in the river.

The river was a constant joy, and if we had stayed in Tite Street I would certainly have kept a boat for nine shillings a week at the Cadogan Pier, and used it for getting about. As it was I acquired a Daimler. One of the old sleeve-valve Daimlers. What a good car that was, as silent as the tomb. I cannot understand why they stopped making them. It had two seats inside, and two more taxi seats behind, separated by a walnut cupboard containing a cut glass decanter for whisky.

It was while the confusion continued at London Films that I thought I might as well begin to earn something by writing that nudist book and that as a first step, perhaps, I had better pop down to one of the places and see what went. This whole thing of taking off one's clothes in company, of course, had started in Germany after the First War. I suspect it was an aspect of defeat. If your country is proud, and your country is beaten in war, and you retire from the world to some sequestered spot and fling off your clothes, you can at least achieve the sensation of getting right back to the beginning of everything and being born all over again.

If there is any guilt involved, it is flung away with the clothes.

The cult spread to England, and in the 1930s there was quite a number of dedicated institutions which advertised quite openly in those magazines. With infinite stealth I slipped one into my pocket at Victoria Station, leaving my shilling to be discovered in due course. I picked out an establishment which looked within reach. It was called 'Oak Tree Camp' or 'Oak Tree Ridge', and was near Croydon. I dropped a line to the secretary explaining that I wanted to write a book, and asking whether I could have a look round. He sent a very civil letter inviting me on any fine Sunday I liked.

At about this time my wife developed a disconcerting habit of going off to stay the occasional week-end at Cambridge. So, one fine Sunday when I found myself alone and the sun was shining like nobody's business and the maids were all turning blue upstairs, I threw away my cigarette, started up the Daimler, and set off in a cloud of smoke.

One had to get to Croydon, turn left at the Whitgift school, and after that there was a map. It was quite a good map. You took a side road to the south, turned down a bumpy lane, crossed a field, and there were twenty cars parked by a gate in a thick-looking hedge, beside an electric pylon. It really was the most marvellous day. 'Oak Tree Camp, Private' said the notice above an electric bell. I got rid of the Daimler and pushed the bell.

The gate was opened by a rather suspicious man—in shirt, trousers and braces.

'Oh, yes,' he said. 'Come along in.'

He led me to a wooden hut. 'You can chuck your things there.' He pointed to some hooks and left me.

It was a biggish place, with a long line of hooks all round it. On the hooks was an exciting assortment of bowler hats, brassières, old Etonian ties, cami-knickers, a bone corset or two, grey flannel trousers, rolled umbrellas, rupture appliances, and Lord knows what else besides.

While I was gazing with some anxiety at this disarray of

82

the trappings of civilization another door opened and a girl came in. She was quite naked. About fifteen I should say, plump—with two little breasts coming along nicely and her hair hanging down over her shoulders. I thought she was the prettiest thing I had ever seen.

'Hullo,' she said, and began rummaging in a corner. Whatever she was looking for she didn't find it. I began to whistle and removed my tie.

She still didn't go.

I took off my shoes.

'D'you want any help?' she asked.

'No thanks,' I said. 'I think I can manage.'

She grabbed a tennis-racket and rushed off with a toss of her hair, slamming the door behind her.

Oh, well. I took it all off and arranged it in a neat pile, double-breasted waistcoat, suède shoes. It was like saying good-bye to my mother. Then I rescued a box of cigaretes and a lighter, opened the door and went out.

I ran straight into a chap I used to be at school with. We were completely starkers.

'Good Lord,' I said. 'Hullo.'

'Oh, hullo there.'

We shook hands.

'Can I introduce you to my wife? Darling—'

A naked lady stepped from behind a tree. He performed the introduction with polish and punctilio.

'How d'you do?'

'How d'you do!'

'Isn't it a marvellous day?'

'Yes, isn't it lovely.'

'D'you come here often?'

'Whenever we can get away. We rather like it. Don't we, dear?'

'Yes, it *is* rather nice.'

'Would er—would anybody care for a cigarette?'

'That's terribly nice of you. Thank you!'

'Haven't seen you before.'

83

'Well, this is my first time, actually.'

'Oh, really? Oh, well, we'll take you round. Is there anybody special you'd care to meet?'

'That's frightfully kind of you.'

'Not at all. Darling, you lead the way.'

She led the way with an uninhibited saunter. There was a criss-cross of grass marks on her bottom. We went through a gap in the hedge. On the far side of it there was a steeply sloping lawn. A little farther off a lot of people were playing some kind of 'tig'. Children mostly, though there were one or two bounding bosoms. We moved along in the shadow of the hedge.

'There's going to be a swimming pool over there, but I doubt if it'll be ready before much later in the year.'

'Oh, yes?'

'It should be gorgeous. But it's so difficult to enjoy *anything* these days, isn't it? We're so worried about the Stock Exchange.'

'Oh, is your husband on the Stock Exchange?'

'Yes, poor darling.'

We stood together, looking out.

'Any tips?' I asked him.

He scratched his penis mournfully. 'Only gold shares,' he said. 'I don't trust this Government. About the pound. They can't possibly save it, you know. There's really only gold shares—and, of course, property. Have you got a decent broker?'

'Yes,' I said, 'Conor. Do you remember old Conor?'

'Of course! Oh, is he—'

'People called Read & Brigstock.'

'*Really!*'

'You ought to look him up some time, darling. Oh look, there's Julian and that frightfully pretty girl. Would you like to meet them?'

'Very much,' I said.

We advanced on a couple who lay side by side, propped on their elbows, on the sloping bank.

84

'Hullo, Julian.'

'Oh, hullo.' He jumped politely to his feet.

'Can I introduce—'

'*Oh*, how d'you do?'

'How d'you do.'

'How d'you do?'

'How d'you do!'

I don't know how it happened, but somehow or other the 'frightfully pretty girl' and I were quite alone. I had imagined, you know, that everything would be quite different. Cockney voices and varicose veins. But that girl was staggeringly beautiful. Beauty shouted from every line of her perfect body. She was a red-head, and her whole skin was alive with the same tint. Her hair was naturally curly and cascaded back from a charming, intelligent face. Her throat, as she lay with her head back, was wonderful, her breasts were exquisite, the whole line of her tummy and legs, her ankles and feet, was instinct with grace and movement in repose.

'What d'you do,' I asked, 'when you're not—'

'Not in a nudist park? Can I have one of your cigarettes?'

'Yes, of course.'

Our little fingers touched.

'I'm a racing motorist.'

'Good heavens!'

'What's so surprising?'

'I don't know.'

'Aren't you interested in cars?'

'Passionately.'

'Well then!'

'Bentleys?'

'Short chassis. Six-litre. Double O.H.C. with eccentrics. What's yours?'

'I've got a new Daimler as a matter of fact.'

'Too many reciprocating parts. All those sleeves and toggles and things.'

'What's the matter with them?'

'Inherently out of balance. D'you think I'm beautiful?'
She rolled over. No grass marks.
'You've got the most lovely back.'
'You're a bit round-shouldered.'
'What my tailor calls a classical stoop.'
'Come on, let's go and play that damned silly game.'
'I'd much rather talk about cars.'
A bell clanged.
'Oh, my God,' she said. 'Peepers.'

She rose on her arms and ran like Atalanta towards the hut. At the same moment my friend and his wife appeared. They were both fully dressed. He was wearing a grey Homburg and she had a cute little number with feathers and a veil. I rose to meet them.

'Horrid little boys. Always climbing up the pylon.'

The bell sounded again. The air was heavy with crisis. Later on, one got the same feeling in the air-raids. A shadow seemed to come over the scene. All movement stopped.

'What happens?'

'Chase them away with sticks. Hand 'em over to the police if necessary. I think we'd better be toddling. Why don't you walk with us to the gate?'

They made room for me between them. She walked with an umbrella, swinging it like a man. He shouldered his like a rifle. I still hadn't got anything on.

'Tell me,' he said. 'Are you still Catholic?'

I hesitated. Could one possibly talk about this?

'Don't mind my asking?'

'No,' I said. 'Not really. No I'm not.'

'We chucked it too,' he told me. 'I suppose quite a lot of the chaps do.'

'As a matter of fact I had a sort of formal thing about it with old D'Arcy. I took it frightfully seriously.'

'Martin D'Arcy. Awful good feller.'

The lovely lady came out of the hut again. She was wearing a pair of black lace panties which made her look like a French post-card.

86

'But you believe in God?'

'Yes, I do. I've got it all worked out in my own mind. I can't possibly tell you now.'

'Why not? It's interesting.'

'I say, I do feel absurd.'

'Don't be ridiculous,' said his wife, sharply. 'We've all been in absolutely the same state all afternoon.'

'Well, it's all based—one of these days I'll tell you.'

'Oh, go *on*.'

'Well, it's based on the idea that we know enough now to do without faith.'

'Know enough?'

The lovely lady took off her lace panties, flung them through the open door, came up and joined us. As I've said, she had the most beautiful red curly hair. And her breasts were pointed.

'Yes, about creation, and the way life developed. It seems to me that religion is always man searching for an explanation, and when you don't *know* the explanation, you need faith to get you over the twiddly bits.'

'You mean the bits we don't understand.'

'Yes, absolutely.'

'What *are* you people talking about?' the lady said, putting her arm round my neck.

'Faith,' I told her. 'Faith in God. Faith in mysteries. Faith in miracles. Faith in Trinities.'

'Blimey,' she said, and took away her arm.

'But you said you did believe in God.'

'I think you must come to an intelligence. I always say I recognize intelligence when I see it. There must be intelligence. Somebody or something thought the whole thing out. It's too good to be an accident.'

'But isn't that Faith?'

'No,' I said. 'It's a deduction.'

'I think I'll go and get a cup of tea,' said the lovely lady. She went away rather petulantly. I never saw her again. Pity.

87

The stockbroker prodded about in the ground with his umbrella.

'And what do we actually know?'

'Oh, about the lot. How the first hydrogen atom was formed. How all the elements were formed from that, in radio-active suns. Then the planets, the atmosphere, the rocks and stones and the sea and proteins and animo-acids, and so on, right down to me, standing here without a stitch on, and feeling utterly absurd.'

'I think it's *terribly* interesting,' said the wife politely. 'You ought to write a book about it.'

'I will,' I told her, 'one of these days.'

One of these days I will.

There was a pause.

'I say, I really think I ought to be pushing along. I've got some people to tea.'

'That's a good idea,' said my friend the broker, brightening. 'Come and have tea one day. We might talk further. About that and about gold shares.'

'Yes, do.'

'I'd love to.'

'Where are you? We're in Pelham Crescent.'

'We're in Tite Street.'

'Well, there you are then. Perfect. I'll give you a tinkle.'

'Thanks, most awfully.'

'Good-bye then.'

'Good-bye.'

'Good-bye.'

'Good-bye.'

I watched them go out through the gate in the hedge. I nipped into the hut, assumed my habiliments, and drove back to London in the Daimler.

The house was still horribly empty when I arrived.

VI

[1]

Somehow or other they finished that film, but not before Zoli
had locked Leontine Sagan for three days, solid, in the ladies'
lavatory, while he re-took all the homosexual bits. It was a
very bad film, and is now never mentioned when the early
Korda films are referred to. That catalogue generally begins
with 'Fire Over England' which contained a remarkable portrait of Queen Elizabeth by Flora Robson and 'The Private
Lives of Henry VIII,' with Charles Laughton as Henry and
Elsa Lanchester as the 'Flanders Mare', which I wrote.

Despite the fact that my weekly hundred was ticking up
like sixpences on a taxi, and that I never received a penny of
it, I have to report that the Gibbs family, in those happy
thirties, was embarked on a sea of limitless prosperity. I was
doing a weekly article for the Hearst Press, which was
being syndicated all over America on something oddly
referred to as 'The Hibrow Section!' They paid me ninety
dollars. I wrote a novel a year, which, with both English and
American publications, produced about a thousand pounds.
I wrote a bitter, but I hope humorous account of how the
Kordas made their films, and sold it to *Nash's* magazine for
seven hundred and fifty. One way and another I suppose I
was knocking up something in the region of two thousand
five hundred a year—not counting the Kordas—and on
this we were living in reasonably well-bred luxury in Tite
Street, driving about in that Daimler, with Martin learning to
walk in Burton Court with his Norland nurse, and Frances
on the way, and two full-time servants, and a chap to stoke
the central heating, and pleasant holidays in places like
Cap d'Antibes and St Jean-de-Luz.

My father, of course, was earning far more than that. He once told me that he had paid two hundred thousand pounds in Income Tax between the wars. He and my mother were living more or less around the corner, in Cliveden Place. We dined with them once a week, but my father, who still kept that capacity for treating children as adults, which had so much endeared us to each other in the early days, now transferred his affection to Martin, and could not be kept away. I am afraid that Maisie, who has always respected the expert, turned to bringing up her children by the book, and thought that the occasional twenty minutes of 'crying time' was very good exercise for the lungs. My father, grim-faced with sympathy, would snatch the child to him, and this infuriated Maisie. I remember times of feeling acutely unhappy that the two people I loved best in the world occasionally looked at each other with daggers in their eyes. But apart from this, there did not seem to be a cloud in the sky bigger than a man's hand.

Mr Ramsay MacDonald suddenly decided to form a Coalition government to save the pound. This was the first time since the days of Diocletian when the pound had needed saving, and it was pretty clear that if Ramsay took as serious a view as all that, he wouldn't be able to save it.

It happens that I knew a bit about Ramsay. I had met his son Malcolm quite a lot at Oxford, a man who has since spent the major part of his life being High Commissioner for South-East Asia. For all I know he may have made an extraordinarily good job of it. And a highly, not to say alarmingly, intelligent cousin of mine called Mary Agnes Hamilton actually fell in love with Ramsay, and wrote a doting biography of him. What I am hinting at is that what emerged from these scraps of knowledge was that Ramsay MacDonald was that rare specimen, an utterly dedicated and sincere Socialist. It follows, *ipso facto*, that he was not a clever man. You have only to compare him with some of the modern figures on television and measure the distance between their eyes to see what I mean.

1. The author, aged nine

2. (*a*) The author's wife, Maisie, and her father, Sir Charles Martin

(*b*) Maisie and the two children, Martin and Frances

So I remembered the naked man. 'Only gold shares.' Plus the fact that old Conor, who came with us to St Jean-de-Luz, was a stockbroker, and presumably knew how to do it.

In those days you could buy and sell shares on option. This meant that you could plonk down, say, two hundred pounds, at the beginning of a Stock Exchange account, and acquire the right to buy and sell two thousand shares as many times as you liked until the end of the account. If you came out on the wrong side you just refused to take up the option and lost your two hundred. If on the other hand, you had made a profit at the end of the term, you paid for the shares at the opening price, deducted the two hundred, and trousered the change.

This seemed like an extraordinarily good idea, and in close consultation with old Conor I plonked down my two hundred pounds.

For two weeks neither of us left the telephone, even to eat. We bought and sold those gold shares half a dozen times a day. Every time they went up sixpence we sold them. Every time they went down sixpence we bought them. Day after day the newspapers came out with dramatic headlines. 'Battle to Save the Pound'. Very soon the public became aware that something was happening, and gold shares began going up and down, not by sixpences, but by pounds. Every time they went up a pound we sold them, within seconds. Every time they went down a pound we bought them in; it was very exciting. It was hair raising. On the very last day of the account Ramsay did his stuff and devalued the pound. Gold shares stayed at the top, and we sold and pocketed a nice little profit of just under five thousand devalued pounds. This is the first time in my life I ever made any money dishonestly. We bought six acres in Surrey and built a house on them, an agreeable, Georgian replica, with an exact copy of the Tite Street drawing-room, designed by a cousin of my wife who later became president of the R.I.B.A.

This rather uncharacteristic story has a place in history for various reasons. It helps to explain why I failed to notice that, for the first out of six or seven times, Alexander Korda had run out of money. It also explains why, when I received a telegram which read, MR GIBBS PLEASE YOU WILL PROCEED TO PARIS IMMEDIATELY FOR SEVERAL MONTHS WE HAVE ROOM FOR YOU HOTEL NAPOLEON AVENUE FRIEDMANN PLEASE BRING MRS GIBBS KORDA. I didn't go. Instead I went to Germany with my father. It was a long time since we had made a trip together, and I hate being ordered about.

We had been to Berlin for a week or two immediately after the end of the war, and again five years later. It had been very drab, and the only recollection I have of it was of a pale girl pulling my head down by the ear in some perfectly reputable café and saying, 'You will pay money for entertainment?'

I didn't know what she meant and blurted out innocently to my father, 'She wants to know if we'll pay money for entertainment.' At this she burst into tears and started a long rigmarole about how she was a doctor's daughter and how defeat and starvation had brought her to this. We heaped worthless German money on her.

This worthless German money was worthless in a really big way. My dear old friend Dr Hjalmar Horace Greeley Schacht, whose book I published a bit later on, under the provocative title *My First Seventy-Six Years*, swears that he had nothing to do with it. Whoever it was, some public benefactor had so arranged things that you could stay at The Adlon—with banked flowers all over the place, a bust of the Kaiser in the bar, waiters in white coats and gold epaulettes on every hand, gold-plated taps in the bathroom and the ability to say for ever after, 'When I was at the Adlon'—for half-a-crown a day. Champagne was ninepence. Lunch for three, with sturgeon's roe, sucking pig, a wonderful hock all round and Goldwasser to follow might run to three and eight. I have in my pocket a 100,000-mark note of the period. Printed across it in that archaic Gothic script are the words, 'In three months add three zeros.' Don't tell me! If that isn't built-in depreciation I should be interested to meet it. And whoever did that thing sold large chunks of Germany to the international set. If you had a cousin in New York and could lay your hands on ten thousand dollars, you could buy a ruddy great factory, with tall chimneys, a railway siding, hooters, ventilators, and three thousand workpeople! I know, because it was offered me by an unpleasant gentleman in the Adlon Bar who kept showing me photographs and ordering fresh dry Martinis, and saying to the barman, 'Pay you tomorrow, George.' That meant he got them for one-tenth their present price. There is something terrible about the Germans in victory. There is something pretty terrible about them in defeat.

Two days later I went for a walk in Munich. In some rather pleasant tree-lined, tram-lined street, I came across an air of expectancy. Sober citizens had ranged themselves along the kerb on either side of the road. Some of the men had shaving brushes in their hats and there was something braided about the women. Of course you *do* get Bavarians in the capital of Bavaria, but these seemed a little self-conscious, and I wondered what was afoot.

A tram or two passed swaying up the line, and then a little knot of men appeared, marching in an untidy column. You could see from a short distance away that they were dressed in bare-knees, khaki jackets and 'fatigue caps'. They had the slightly absurd look of a flurry of Scoutmasters, and as they came nearer you could see that they were led by a fanatical chap with a blob on the end of his nose, and a cascade of hair across his forehead. Beside him was a great fat man, and just behind, a sallow character with lunatic's eyes. They swung past, keeping within the tramlines, panting slightly, their eyes fixed on some unattainable goal, and I am sorry to say that I let out a carefree cackle of amazement and delight.

The solid citizen next to me gave me a sharp nudge, and took the meerschaum out of his mouth.

'We do not laugh at those men,' he said.

93

Looking back on it that is precisely what they should have done.

I suppose our friend Hitler had already written *Mein Kampf*. Certainly no one had bothered to read it. At the same time, just to get the picture right, there were three million unemployed in this country. It seems an awful thing to say, but I honestly don't believe many people paid much serious attention to either.

Poor Ramsay certainly didn't. He got up in the House and made that very peculiar speech about everything going 'on and on and on and up and up and up' and was led gently away, and Sir Oswald Mosley went with him. But, in an odd sort of way, he was perfectly right.

My own recollection of this period was that we were absolutely on top of the world. Perhaps it was the business of the now worthless money. Whatever it was, there didn't seem to be any unemployment in and around Tite Street, or in Peaslake where a lot of chaps were building the house. On the contrary. The habitable parts of London were richer and gayer than they will ever be again.

The streets of the Metropolis were absolutely choked with Rolls-Royces of the largest possible sort. You wouldn't dream of going to the theatre unless you sported at least a dinner jacket and a tall hat. Most people stuck on a white tie just for the hell of it. I don't think it's the nostalgia of advancing years if I say that the shows still seem to me to have been pretty good. There was always Gertie Lawrence (with the Prince of Wales in the front row) and Jessie Matthews. There was the Russian Ballet. There was Jack Buchanan and Jack Hulbert and Cicely Courtneidge and Leslie Henson and Herbert Marshall and Edna Best and Gerald du Maurier. There was Robertson Hare taking off his trousers at the Aldwych. We knew where we were with these people. A 'Jack Buchanan Show' was a Jack Buchanan show. If you went to see Leslie Henson in 'A Night Out' you knew exactly what you were in for. A damn good dinner first and then two and a half happy hours of rolling in the aisles. And there was always Noël Coward.

The music was good too. Irving Berlin and Gershwin and Cole Porter. I met Irving Berlin. A modest little man to all appearances with an inner conviction of superiority. And why not? He told me that he preferred to play in only *one key* and that at home he had a special piano with a crank on one side to shift the keyboard along. He would sit down, bang away on the white notes (to excellent purpose), wind it up a couple of times, and out it came in F sharp Major.

[3]

I can't help it. I was doing terribly well, and the world seemed wonderfully civilized. John ('phone for the fish-knives) Betjeman calls it the period of 'ghastly good taste'. So it was. So it was.

God forbid that I should harp on this, but I suddenly discovered the trick of the short story. It happened when my wife and I touched off in the Daimler one day for another visit to St Jean-de-Luz.

There were two cafés set side by side. One was called the Bar Basque. The other was called Le Véritable Coucou. There was tremendous rivalry between these two establishments. The casino being what it was, there was really absolutely nothing to do in the evenings except go and drink at one or the other.

One night the Bar Basque engaged a species of perspiring pianist, and, of course, everybody gravitated towards the music. Two nights later, the Indubitable Cuckoo hired a girl to play the piano in spangles and the entire population shifted over, like porridge in a plate.

Suddenly, I beheld the light.

I whipped this up into a short story called *A Tale of Two Cafés* which duly appeared in *Nash's*. Naturally I elaborated a little. The girl in the spangles was only the beginning. The rival café came back with an all-girl orchestra in two-piece bathing suits. Naturally too, the son of the proprietor of one café fell in love with the daughter of the proprietor of the second. So they got married, the two cafés amalgamated, after which there was no music of any sort.

Six weeks after this story appeared, or as long as it used to take to get a letter from South America, I received a furious communication from a young lady of Argentina accusing me of plagiarism, piracy and unprofessional conduct in copying out her story which had just appeared in *La Prenza*. She sent me the copy of *La Prenza* and the story *was* exactly the same.

But the most astounding coincidence of all time had its origin in that nudist book I fancy I must have mentioned. I cannot imagine how it got mixed up with nudism, but in it I invented, as Zoli would say, the following ting.

I invented a chap in Slough, and described in considerable detail his bungalow workroom on the Slough Trading Estate, in which he had perfected a new and startling method of making petrol out of coal-tar. I then introduced the usual 'magnificent Daimler', which drew up one day before his modest doorway. This was rather a special Daimler. It had double doors in the side, and when these were opened some rails were fixed in position, an invalid chair was slid down, and one of the governors of the Bank of England was pushed into the workshop, where he bought the process.

One day, while everybody was struggling with *Men of Tomorrow*, I received a communication from my bank manager asking 'if I could make it convenient to call?' Thinking that something frightful had happened I hurried reluctantly round, and was given a letter from a fellow customer who said he had read my book, and wasn't it an extraordinary thing, but he had invented a process of making petrol out of tar. The address he gave was Slough Trading Estate.

I went down to see him in the old Daimler. There was a snow-storm and his place was difficult to find. However, I found a sort of bungalow which looked vaguely familiar, went up and rang the bell. The chap opened it, went as white as a sheet, and backed away with coal-black eyes.

'Have you got second sight?' he demanded.

I said I didn't think so. 'Why?'

He told me that yesterday a magnificent Daimler had driven up, a door had opened in the side, a wheel-chair had been manœuvred down, and a man had come in, introduced himself and bought the process. His name was Baron Schroder, one of the governors of the Bank of England.

Like everything else in this book, this story is guaranteed a hundred per cent true in every particular. I believe his process was added to the giant refinery at Immingham, which was already producing motor spirit from coal, with a residue of coal-tar. Incidentally the man who invented it gave me a couple of gallons of his distillate, and I drove back to Tite Street with the car going as well as ever.

But to come back to this business of the short story.

All you have to do is to look for a developing situation. Like the cafés. Or a man who lends another man a hundred pounds on which he becomes a millionaire, and forgets to repay him until he reads of his death in the paper, when he sends the money to his widow. D'you see what I mean?

Then all you needed was a bright opening line, such as 'In this life, if you wish to keep body and soul together, it is necessary to sell one or the other'. And you're home. In those pleasant days, with the *Strand* and *Nash's* and the *London Magazine*, you could get two hundred and fifty pounds for a story, if you knew the right people. I did. I knew Dick Mealand, an attractive American who edited *Nash's*. He thought I was the best short-story writer living. I did too, with the possible exception of Somerset Maugham, who was pretty good in his rather archaic way.

97

So we prospered. But not alone. So did a whole new generation of authors. Priestley, who was really only just beginning, wrote a book called *Adam in Moonshine*. He dined once or twice, stocky, very Yorkshire and not yet established as a national figure. I remember him as having a very pretty wife and a growing family and a pleasant house in Hampstead. Lady Martin, my mother-in-law, who had a passion for the peculiar and tended to live on banana-meat, adored his plays about Time. They *were* extremely amusing, and, of course, he'd read that book about Time by a man called Dunne, written about this time. Everybody had.

I'm afraid I act on the superior assumption that if I can't understand a thing after really giving it my attention, there must be something wrong with it. On this rough and ready basis, I am sorry to have to inform you that there is something wrong with the conceptions of 'infinite mass', 'saddle-shaped space', the 'expanding universe', and Dunne's regressional theory of Time.

But my mother-in-law simply loved all this sort of thing. She took me along one day to a remarkable place in Queen's Gate when she proposed to get in touch with her brother.

I knew that her brother had died some years ago while running for a bus in Victoria Street, so politely I went along. We were shown in by a respectfully hushed gentleman in glasses. A plump lady with bare, brawny arms was sitting at a table with a little circle of people round her. The walls and ceiling were painted black, the two windows at the end of the room were blacked over with cloth, and the only light came from a table-lamp which shone up from under the plump lady's many chins, throwing the rest of her face into sinister shadows.

When we were all assembled, the hushed gentleman, with a great deal of clanking, drew some more curtains over the door, removed his shoes, sat down beside me, and began cranking up a portable gramophone.

This struck me as distinctly fishy. I mean, why remove the shoes? Unless he was proposing to creep about? So I'm afraid I asked him.

I said, 'Why are you taking your shoes off?'

'So as not to disturb Madam Medium if I have to go to anybody's help,' he said.

Well, I hoped he wouldn't have to come to my help. I wasn't at all sure, because when the light was turned out the darkness became a physical sensation which you could feel all over your body. It was like being in space, and you had to remind yourself forcibly that you were sitting in a room, and that, outside, a lot of buses were charging about in broad daylight.

'We will take five minutes,' the man said in a whisper, 'for Madam Medium to go into a trance, so that our dear friends will know and have time to gather. At the end of that time, if we are successful, an astral larynx will appear so that our friends will speak to us in the direct voice.'

We sat. For a minute. For another minute. For three minutes. For four minutes. There was no sight and no sound. Nobody seemed to breathe. Somebody was sweating though. I could smell it. And then the chap next to me got quietly to his feet, leaned over the group and held up something phosphorescent. There was an indrawn hiss of breath.

'The larynx!'

God knows what came over me, but the undevout thought was inescapable that the chap was dangling his wrist-watch.

At that moment a tremendous gurgle came from Madam Medium. In the dark and the silence she began to thrash about and make the most horrible noises.

'The larynx!' she cried in a great voice.

I crept to my feet, crossed over and dangled my own wrist watch. It was extremely convincing.

'Two larynxes!' whispered the man, in an expression of puzzled awe.

'Two larynxes?' echoed the medium in a voice of thunder. 'Two larynxes,' shrilled a little girl's voice, that seemed to come from nowhere.

It was eerie. I sat down again rather suddenly. We waited, with every nerve twitching.

'This is going to be ever such a lovely sitting!' piped the little girl. 'I'm on a lovely hillside with lots of lovely daisies and there are ever so many dear friends here just behind me who are longing to talk to their loved ones. So I'll just say good-bye now, for myself. I passed over, you know, in 1743.'

I suppose I can't possibly convey the extraordinary effect of that childish voice.

Then the silence started again. I should think another minute of complete silence and utter darkness.

Then the medium made another sound. A very tiny sound. It sounded like 'Eh—eh'. Like somebody very far away. Saying 'Eh—eh.' Perhaps somebody on a lovely hillside with daisies.

'Nelly?' cried another voice from the audience. 'Is that you, my darling?'

'Eh—eh. Neh—ly. Neh—ly.'

'Nelly, my sweet! Is that really you?'

'This—is—Neh—ly,' repeated the astral larnyx rather hesitantly, as if uncertain what exact voice it should adopt and what the relationship would turn out to be. 'I—am—not—very—close. Who—are—you?'

'Nelly!' groaned the lady with terrible loudness. 'Don't you know me? It's your very own sister! Maudie!'

'Maudie!' exclaimed the voice, more certainly, but still feeling its way. 'My dear sister! Maudie, my sweet!'

'Oh Nelly, Nelly! How wonderful to hear your voice again! I've been miserable ever since you went four years ago! Are you happy? Tell me, are you happy?'

'Yes, Maudie. I'm very happy here, except when I have visited you and found you crying. You didn't know I was there, but I came, many times, in the four years. But now that you have found me you mustn't cry any more. Promise you won't cry any more, my sweet.'

'I promise, I promise!' sobbed the lady.

'And you'll visit me often, now that you know the way?'

'Of course, sweetie pie.'

'I must go now because there are many dear ones. But now that we have found each other we'll meet many times and be as close as we were on earth. Good-bye, sweetie-pie.'

'Oh! Oh!' bawled Maudie uncontrollably. 'She called me my pet name. We always called each other "Sweetie-pie". Oh! Oh! Oh!' And she fell to sobbing.

I found this horrible.

Then the voice spoke again, very faintly.

'Eh—eh!'

No response. One could feel the emotion building up in the electric silence.

'Eh—eh.'

'Walter?' said my mother-in-law.

The trouble was, I couldn't think of a single deceased relative with a disyllabic name. There was my uncle Frank, and my grandfather whose name was Henry, though I didn't call him that, and my Domville grandmother who ran away with the brother of the Chancellor of the Exchequer and became 'Mrs McKenna'. I should have liked to have had a go with her, but I didn't see how I could put the astral larynx into such an awkward predicament, though I was sorely tempted.

It seemed to my irreligious mind that it was pretty clear what was going on. It appeared to me that the astral larynx was being absolutely brilliant in following the lead. Like a good dancer. Like Doris in fact. If a woman asked for 'Nelly', identified her as a sister, and used expressions like 'sweet' and 'Sweetie-pie', it was—I won't say easy—but possible to shift into step.

'Eh—eh!' began the larynx all over again.

'Walter?' said Lady Martin.

'No. Oh—eh.'

'You're not asking for Tony?' I suggested.

'Eh—eh.'

'Is that my Uncle George?'

It wasn't. It was Billy.

I thought that astral larynx was quite remarkable. For two and a half hours more it kept up a flow of conversation with the departed, absolutely without falter. Some of the people were regulars. That must have been easy. And the emotion helped. At the end of that two and a half hours there was not a man or woman in the room who had not talked with the dead, and been reduced to tears. It was appalling, and a tour de force.

I kept on about my Uncle George. Once I thought the larynx hesitated. It almost said 'Tony'. But it veered away again. My mother-in-law got her brother Walter.

'Eh—eh!'

I think I must have been the only person left in the room.

'I'm here,' I said. 'Is that you, Uncle George?'

'Oh—eh!'

My heart leaped in my bosom.

'Uncle?'

'Oh—ny.'

By gosh, I'd got him!

'To—ny.'

'Yes!' I said. 'Yes, yes! I'm Tony.'

There was a long pause. Madam Medium gurgled. I thought she was going to wake up. Then a cheerful bass voice boomed through the room like a thunderclap. I shuddered.

'That you Tony, old boy?'

'Yes, Sir.'

'This is your Uncle George!'

'Good God, Sir! Is it really you?'

He roared with laughter. The room rocked with it.

'Of course it's me! Who the devil d'you think it is?'

102

'Good Lord,' I said again. 'Uncle! That's absolutely marvellous! How are you, Sir?'

'Marvellous! Marvellous, my dear feller! Never felt so well in my life! By Jove, made a joke, eh?' The laughter boomed again.

I laughed back politely.

'Well, how are you, eh? How are you getting along Tony, my lad? Eh?'

'Not too badly, Sir, thanks awfully, Sir.'

'I'm glad to hear it! Everything all right at home?'

'Yes, thanks.'

A pause developed. It was an extraordinary thing, but neither of us seemed quite to know what to say next.

'Well,' boomed my uncle, 'now that you've found me out, I hope I shall be able to be of some help to you. If there's any little thing—'

'Oh, could you, Sir?'

'Of course, my dear feller! What d'you suppose? Word in the right ear. Anything like that. You've only got to say. I mean, in your career? Or anything?'

'That's terribly good of you!'

'Not a bit. Not a bit. Not a bit. I'll be watching you. Taking a bit of interest in my young nephew now, eh?'

'Yes,' I said.

There was another pause.

'Well,' said Uncle George.

'Well,' I answered.

'Well, good-bye, my dear old chap!'

'Good-bye, Sir,' I said, utterly exhausted.

Silence.

Madam Medium snorted and thrashed. The hushed gentleman arose and switched on the little light. I found twenty gleaming pairs of eyes fixed on me. Madam Medium drank a glass of water. I thought that if I didn't have a cigarette I should probably pass out. So I lit one. Madam Medium rose to her feet, looking at me strangely. She held out both brawny arms. She came towards me, waddling on little steps. She seemed to want to hold my hands. Rather reluctantly I held them out. She took them in a tight, baby grasp.

'Are you a medium?' she asked.

'Good heavens, no!'

'You should be. You,' she said, 'are mediumistic!'

'Really?'

'You have powers!'

'I don't think I have, you know.'

'I know it. Never, never have I had such a wonderful, such a strong, such a powerful manifestation as your Uncle George!'

She beamed upon me possessively. 'He must have been a wonderful man in his earthly life!'

'He was,' I agreed wearily. 'He was.'

'You must have been very close!'

'Yes. We got on rather well together,' I admitted.

It was craven of me. Craven and spineless. How could I tell her that I never had an Uncle George?

I went to bed for twenty-four hours.

VII

It could have been my Uncle George at work among the daisies because I got another of those telegrams. PLEASE COME AT ONCE DEAR MR GIBBS WE HAVE CHARLES LAUGHTON.

Charles Laughton was not the chap I met at the nudist park, thank goodness. But we were at school together. So when I was well enough to totter round to Grosvenor Street and saw the famous figure through Alex's open door, I went in and said 'Oh, hullo, Laughton.'

He replied, 'Oh, hullo, Gibbs.'

I said, 'Have you ever been back to that frightful place?'

He said, 'No, never. Have you?'

In those days he had already been gifted with that Falstaffian outline which is now famous, though his face was more virgin clay, being unmarked with any of the pouting petulance that came with fame.

I remember him as rather a pasty, expressionless youth, for all his plumpness, condemned, like the rest of us, to kicking a football about in the playground for hours at a stretch. I cherish the recollection of him in the ill-fitting regalia of the O.T.C., rather a figure of comedy, if I may say so, full-bellied, full-bottomed, and eccentric in the set of his puttees. An inch or two of bare leg and the tabs of his boots, that sort of thing. With abrupt motion consequent upon abrupt words of command, his jowls were inclined to jell. I have a suspicion that towards the end he attained the dizzy rank of lance-corporal, but since I also scaled that pinnacle this cannot by any possible stretch of imagination be regarded as a mark of distinction. Never a thought among us that we entertained a genius in our midst.

We acted plays of course, very good plays. *Arsène Lupin*, *The Private Secretary*, that good old favourite *The Bells*. But Charles Laughton never acted in them, or if he did we were completely unaware of it. The outstanding figures of our dramatic entertainments were the Archduke of Austria, Francis L. Sullivan and Glenny Creig, whom the world came to know as Colin Clive. The very last thing we should have imagined about 'Fat' Laughton was that he could act.

We were mistaken about that. The first time I saw him on the stage was on that most rash and amusing occasion when he disguised himself exactly as Arnold Bennett in the performance of *Mr Prohack* at the theatre in Sloane Square, a performance produced with Arnold Bennett's money and with Dorothy Cheston Bennett in the cast. It was a magnificent piece of impudence, though I believe Bennett took it well.

Incidentally, I was touched to discover that I had achieved immortality in the letters of A.B., published in Dorothy Cheston Bennett's book *Arnold*, in the following terms: 'Lunched to-day at the Reform Club with Philip Gibbs and his son, Anthony, also an author. Left early.'

Charles Laughton in *Mr Prohack* was the living image of Arnold Bennett, down to the peculiar stutter and the jig of his leg, and considering that Laughton is a short fat man and that Arnold Bennett was a tallish thin one, this was pretty good acting.

'I wish to make a film with Laughton,' said Alexander Korda.

'What?' I asked.

'You will think of something,' said Korda, rising to end the interview.

I asked how long he could give me.

'Three days?' he suggested. 'Then I shall be back from Rome.'

I opened my mouth.

'Is there something very special you want to say?'

I mentioned a little matter of some hundreds of pounds.

He picked up the telephone and spoke.

'Mr Gibbs does not get his money.'

A voice talked reedily for a long time.

'Very well,' said Alex putting up the receiver. 'Could you make do with fifty for a day or two?'

I looked at Alex in a startled way, but he only grinned.

'Yes, of course!' I said.

'Good. We talk when I come back.'

I went out and slapped Zoli on the shoulder.

'How goes it?' I asked. 'How is London Films?'

His eyes met mine.

'Comment ça va?' I said to Vincent, who still could not speak one word of English.

He curled his lip. 'Comme çi, comme ça,' he growled.

It rather looked as if London Films had only fifty pounds.

[2]

I had noticed among the mourners in Miss Fischer's room a distinguished, narrow-templed man who sat, not miserably, but politely, with his hat on his knees.

I asked Miss Fischer the next day, and she said, 'I guess that was Mr Guy Bolton. Do you know him?'

'No,' I said, though in point of fact I knew that he was the father of my uncle's two stepchildren.

'Ja,' continued Miss Fischer. 'I reckon he wanted to sell us an idea or something. Some historical thing.'

When Alex returned from Rome in a few days' time, I learned that the historical thing was about Henry VIII.

'What do you think,' asked Alex, 'of Laughton as Henry VIII?'

It was, of course, one of those happy juxtapositions which snick into position with all the brilliance of revelation.

'Of course!' I shouted.

'I think so too,' said Alex. 'It will be necessary to work up some kind of story. I don't think it matters whether it is true. Just to get Laughton as Henry. One takes perhaps just two of the wives. . . .'

I ran all the way home, and opened my 1898 edition of *Chambers' Encyclopaedia* which belonged to my grandfather. It gave the whole story of Henry VIII in a hundred lines. There was no work to do.

That evening I received a cheque for fifty pounds.

[3]

Take two of the wives? I thought of taking all six.

Since Alex remained in Rome for the best part of a fortnight, I went to argue this point with a remarkable old Hungarian gentleman called Mr Biro, who acted as a sort of story editor for all the Korda films.

I asked Mr Biro point blank what was the matter with London Films.

He smiled at me for a long time inscrutably, and then his face humanized.

'It is simply,' he said, 'there is no money.'

'Charles Laughton,' I said, 'at two hundred a week. Why Rome?'

Mr Biro spread his hands, palm uppermost. 'There is a man,' he admitted, 'in the Banco Commerciale d'Italia, who is in touch with Mussolini. . . .' He gazed for a moment into the bowl of the Cona coffee machine, as if he could read the future there. Then he seemed to regret his indiscretion. 'Now, Mr Gibbs, now—now we have to talk about Henry. I have made some worthless notes.'

'It is so difficult,' he cried, 'when it is true. How to get a story? There is no incident. There is no story line!'

'No incident? No—? But he had six wives!'

'If he had had six hundred,' said Mr Biro, 'that does not make a story. Never have I been beaten like this before.'

I asked if I might see his 'worthless notes'.

'It is useless,' said Mr Biro. 'It is no *good*. We will have some strong coffee.'

I asked if, at any rate, I might see them.

'You may see,' said Mr Biro, hunched in dejection like a

benign vulture. 'I have made two little stories, each with two of the wives. I have begun with Anne Boleyn, with Henry's spies following her because she has produced no male heir, so that he may execute her for what they call in the country the High Treason which is another name for adultery. And they make a case against her and she is executed, because all the time Henry is in love with Jane Seymour. And she has the French executioner specially so that he shall be neat, because she says 'she has such a little neck'.

I saw that Mr Biro was making triangles, but my eyes gleamed, perhaps, at that episode of the 'little neck'. It seemed to me like the beginning of a film. I began to see the crowds converging upon the Tower of London across old London Bridge, with the eye of the camera to pick upon individual people of the crowds, and then to converge suddenly on the woman who was the cause, speaking to her French executioner of her 'little neck'.

'It is not good,' said Mr Biro. 'The other is perhaps better. It is to take Katherine Howard and Anne of Cleves. You know that Henry married Anne of Cleves for purposes of state, and that he sent Holbein first to paint her portrait. It is my idea that Holbein, who was a young man then, fell in love with her, because really she was not so bad a looking woman, and that he warned her of what happened to Henry's women, and that when she comes to England she must speak with a guttural German accent so as to make herself unattractive to Henry, because she is afraid for her head and also is in love with Holbein.'

I could have embraced Mr Biro on the spot. It seemed incredible to me that Mr Biro was unable to admit that, by taking the two stories and adding the deaths of Jane Seymour (whom he loved), and Katherine Howard and ending with the aged Henry being ordered about like any inexperienced husband by Catherine Parr, he had enough material for six films, or the richest that was ever made.

But Mr Biro only shook his head.

I said that it was history, that it was England, that there were marvellous parts both for Laughton and for Elsa Lanchester.

'I am sorry, Mr Gibbs,' said Mr Biro sadly. 'I am sorry to *damp* your youthful *ardour*, but I am afraid. There is no film.'

'Oh damn!' I said.

[4]

Despite the profound gloom, I began to write out my idea of the film, and as I handed her the sheets the lady who did my typing kept asking me, with illumined eyes, 'Is it true? Is it true?' I admitted that it was all true, with mental, Galilean reservations regarding the Holbein–Anne of Cleves affair, the credit for which piece of invention is due entirely to Mr Biro. I was encouraged by this. I became a theoretical expert in falconry, and knew all the technical terms for holding the falcon on the wrist, and letting it go and calling it back, and all that. An agreeable sport as I must confess, among tall trees in Bushey Park or Windsor Great Park, when clouds were white in a blue sky and the tethered horses whinnied at their posts, and the birds were sunlit specks in the spring infinity, so that one must shade the eyes to keep track of the head-long dive for the neck of the prey.

I could see old Henry as he sat astride his caparisoned horse, his belly drawn up in front of him as he craned towards the sky. His horse was restive under the weight, I knew, but he bestrode it laughing, with a bellow of excitement, and stood in his stirrups and waved his cap in the air and slapped young Culpeper on the shoulder with a roar of royal pleasure, because young Culpeper was not so good a falconer as Henry. It was then, I knew, that the messenger came riding hell for leather on a foaming horse, and reined up all standing, and fell on the ground with a ceremonial wave of his hat and a bow before the outraged monarch. 'A son!'

But, of course, you've seen the thing.

Mr Biro, when he had read it, shook his head. 'It is not possible,' he whispered. 'It is not *possible*!'

The telephone rang, and when he lifted it the voice of Miss Fischer said, 'Rome wants you, Mr Biro.'

Mr Biro moved the cigar to the corner of his mouth.

' 'Allo?' said Mr Biro in the French way. ' 'Allo? 'Allo? Lozzi?'

I heard him admit, in Hungarian, that he was 'Biro'. For some time then he listened, saying every now and then 'Igen'—which I remembered as the Hungarian for 'Yes'. While I marvelled at the airy way in which the telephone lines of Europe seemed slaves to the business of London Films, Mr Biro listened, and I thought that as he listened he became graver. Then he began to talk rapidly himself, gesticulating with his right hand in an admirably explanatory manner. 'Mr Gibbs,' said Mr Biro in the middle of torrential Hungarian, and then again 'Mr Gibbs.'

I could only guess at what was going on in Rome, but I tried to imagine it for myself.

I imagined Alex and the man from Mussolini sitting up there, side by side on a sofa, going over the figures of London Films, its achievements and its possibilities. *Men of To-morrow*, *Wedding Rehearsal*, so much costs, so much made. Contracts with Arthur Wimperis, with Laughton, with the four starlets, with the best cameraman in England, Mr Biro with an unrivalled knowledge of scenario. My brother Vincent, my brother Zoltan. The quota laws. The untapped market. Thirty million pounds a year going to the makers of American films. And behind the figures the publicity. The propaganda. A hundred and twenty million lire could alter history if their results were slanted in a certain direction, in the direction of a certain man, and the splendid notion of Fascism.

It must have been something like this.

Suddenly Alex came home again with one and a half millions in his pocket, tied to a promise to make a film about dictatorship and, as if a current had been turned on, the machine was galvanized into furious motion. The typewriters, which had been silent, sprang into sound. The telephone bells set up a clamour. The halls of fame emptied of their loungers and became filled with a great rushing. In widening circles the vibrations spread. The newspapers, with their antennae tuned towards activity, caught the rhythm. The film critics were suddenly 'reminded' of London Films. Interviews with Alexander Korda leapt off the machines. Henry VIII! Henry VIII! Suddenly the world knew about it. Charles Laughton began to grow a beard.

I saw 'Henry' recently on television. It was a good film still, largely as I had written it except for a few touches and one whole scene re-done by Arthur Wimperis. When Henry tried, reluctantly, to go to bed with Elsa Lanchester I had her tearing up the sheets. 'Wimp' had them playing cards. It was, perhaps, more civilized because both of them found it difficult to get into bed with the other. It was strange though, I thought, that one of the ladies of the bed-chamber spoke American. It was a pity too, I thought, that the list of 'credits' at the beginning still contained the words 'By Lajos Biro and Arthur Wimperis'. But, as Zoli would say, 'Vat the difference?' The film made a fortune, but not for me. And it didn't save London Films, or not for long. Three years later, after *The Scarlet Pimpernel* and *Fire over England* and *The Four Feathers*, there was no money once again.

This time it was the Prudential Insurance which came to the rescue with three million pounds. In 1940 Alex took the whole party to America, two hundred of them at the expense of United Artists. In 1943 he brought them all to No. 1 Belgrave Square. This time at the expense of Metro-Goldwyn-Mayer. Finally he raised four million pounds on the Stock Exchange. It is only a guess, but it is my guess that the young man who set forth in a blue suit and a chapeau melon raised not less than fifteen million pounds before, having no more worlds to conquer, he became old, with startling suddenness, and died.

112

VIII

[1]

No bigger than a man's hand, did I say?

Quite suddenly, we all knew, I think, that unless quite a lot of people did something quite clever rather soon, the thing was liable to happen. One day at dawn an old boating friend of mine from Geneva days invaded Abyssinia.

We then had, of course, the Spanish war; but that was a private worry of the 'left-wing intellectuals', to whom, of course, one did not belong. Naomi Mitchison who lived in the costume of a Ruritanian peasant in an enchanting Carolingian house in Chiswick, defaced its wall with the inscription ARMS FOR SPAIN. If she lived there today, she would almost certainly daub it BAN THE BOMB. Various souls like Jack Haldane went out to fight General Franco, and worried the Spanish to death, I'm told, by firing off revolvers after lunch, so that a full-scale battle had to be fought when all decent Spaniards on both sides of the barricades were desperately trying to enjoy their siesta.

Apart from the killing, which is always disgusting, and which no intellectual of *any* persuasion ought to take part in, the Spanish Civil War was outside the main stream of history, like the Irish rebellion. But the Abyssinian business was unpleasantly different, coming at a time when the whole world had grown accustomed for nearly twenty years to living a reasonably care-free existence, in the knowledge that the age of reason was established and that the League of Nations was, indeed, the Parliament of Man. My boating friend seemed to be acting successfully in open defiance of the League.

This was something which opened a pit at one's feet.

There were horrible things at the bottom of this pit. Things like conscription, and gas, and bombs, and the whole writhing insanity of organized massacre. Patriotic women and happy padres blessing flags. One suddenly remembered the last time, which we all thought was dead, and buried for ever. But it wasn't. It was alive and down there. And Anthony Eden was openly advocating war.

I had an invitation to meet Eden one night, and at the back of my mind I kept rehearsing the things I would like to say, if only I got the chance.

I walked down St James's Street in the direction of the Athenaeum, where Lord Inman had bidden me, and as I walked I looked at the roof-tops on either side, with a queer vision of the bombing of London.

A voice addressed me. It was Vincent Korda.

'What for you look at the roof-tops?' he demanded sharply.

'Hullo, Vincent. I was thinking of the bombs.'

'You tink?'

'I tink, perhaps.'

'I tink, perhaps, too. We shall be refugees.'

Refugees! He stared at me with big round eyes. For too long. I told him I had to meet a man.

'Well,' he said. 'Visantlatasra!'

'Abyssinia!' I replied. It was the joke of the moment. 'I'll be seeing you.' H'm. . . .

In the Athenaeum I found Eden sitting in a chair, with a species of bar behind him covered with a white cloth and a row of sherry bottles, and a small group of people gathered in a semi-circle before him.

I didn't quite know what it was all about, since Lord Inman was a Labour creation, but there sat Eden, with his good clothes, and his ready smile, and relaxed good manners, looking every inch the younger statesman. We were introduced, and he made a little set speech lasting three minutes. Saying in a pleasant, drawing-room manner that we had established the Covenant of the League, that Mussolini had defied it, and that we ought to stand by our signature and go to war with him. 'As a warning,' said Eden, 'to other dictators.'

His words fell on the preserved air of the Athenaeum with a kind of chill logicality which was so logical that it seemed irrational. I mean, it was perfectly true that we had established the Covenant, that Mussolini had defied it; and it was exactly two months and three days since that 'other dictator' had re-occupied the Rhineland. Add the three things together and you get the necessity of a preventive war. But are the canons of human behaviour really subject to such simple arithmetic?

I'm afraid I spoke up.

'I don't want to die for Abyssinia,' I said.

'No,' said Eden quickly. 'That's the trouble!' And he gave me a friendly and understanding look, born of the consciousness of superior convictions.

[2]

My father and I talked a lot about this, in the quiet of his study at Shamley Green, with the old clock that ticked away the moon's phases.

He did not leave his study much in winter, and particularly after dark, because a horrid thing had happened. I had gone over there, one December afternoon, pushed the front door inaudibly (it was always open) and found him fumbling and stumbling down the stairs, with a tight hold of the banister and his eyes shut. He was practising going blind.

This was the first news I had of any such calamity; and, so absurd is the traditional reserve of the English people and so fragile the relationship between father and son, that I said nothing then, and never mentioned what I had seen for the rest of his life. But the fact was that he was growing a cataract in both eyes, and though he could see perfectly to play billiards in strong daylight, or to cavort about the lawn with a croquet mallet on a fine summer's day, to go into a dim room, or out into the twilight, was to step into utter sightlessness.

Coming back from the Charing Cross Hospital of which he was vice-chairman one afternoon after a meeting, he did that very thing. He successfully navigated Trafalgar Square, and then entered the comparative dimness of the Tube station and bought himself a ticket for Waterloo. He followed the stream of people to the head of the escalator, managed by some miracle of sound and touch to keep in step on it with the right foot, arrived at the bottom, made his way uncertainly forward down a completely invisible corridor, and went slap off the end of the platform on to the line.

They stopped the trains. They turned off the electricity. He couldn't climb back because he had broken something called the Achilles tendon, and he was bemused with what had happened, and the pain. But a helpful sailor, who was also making for the Portsmouth train, got him up, helped him into the tube carriage, hobbled him one-footed at Waterloo and set him down on the platform at Guildford. There, other friendly people put him on a bus to Shamley Green, and there it was at last, prone before his own front door and unable to move another inch, that the gardener found him and carried him in.

[3]

It was very shortly after the annexation of Austria that my father and I thought we had better go and see for ourselves. So we got out the Delage and drove through Soissons to Germany, to a place called Trier. It surprised me by having been, once, the capital of the Roman Empire, before Constantine changed his mind and went to Constantinople, so that it was full of vast Roman constructions of a debased sort of brick, of about the architectural calibre of any railway terminus. It was also Hitler's birthday.

I must say, things had changed a bit since I laughed at

those men in Munich. The birthday parade had a carefully calculated air of menace. Columns of men marched eleven deep past the old Porto Nigra, all moving like automata, faceless under their steel helmets, with that balletomane kick of the jack-boot which looks so frightening because it's so absurd, a deliberate affront to reason. There were vast tanks rumbling along three-deep, and horse-drawn guns and every conceivable engine of destruction and more and more solid ranks of robots goose-stepping by.

The thing was quite horrible, but the faces of the crowds were not alight. On the contrary, behind a thin veneer of spectators who lined the kerb-stones, the ordinary life of the pavements carried on as if absolutely nothing was happening. Women went in and out of shops, boys wheeled bicycles delivering sausages and bread. People stopped to chat and sat at café tables quaffing beer.

And then something occurred, like a bright splash of sanity. An old gentleman wheeled a bicycle across the pavement, and pushed its front wheel on to the roadway. He was wearing a yachting cap and had a big curly pipe stuck in his mouth, so that he looked exactly like one of the old German toys. One knew instinctively what he was going to do. He mounted the bicycle by its step, wobbled with stern concentration, and then rode as hard as he could, straight at the procession, with an air of absent-minded abandon.

The result was impressive. The horses of gun-carriages reared in the air and the carriages locked sideways at impossible angles. For a moment one thought of the Egyptians in the Red Sea. And then, right underneath the pawing feet of horses, the old man got through, and pedalled away with a happy smile. The people on the opposite pavement clapped, laughed and ran to thump him on the back while the disorganized birthday procession of Herr Hitler gathered itself together and proceeded, rather less remorselessly, upon its way. And I shot the whole scene on a small movie camera, and keep the film to this day as a record of the fact that in the city of Trier, on Hitler's birthday in 1937, civilized men were on both sides of the barricades. Not forgetting the Germans who reined in their horses.

[4]

We thought we had better penetrate a little further into enemy territory so we drove on through smiling fields, my father and my mother and I, to Munich. There is something very odd about the Germans which I notice every time I go there. They are incredibly like the English. In fact, they are more English than the English. It may be this which has saved us and failed them. They are the pure stock, whereas we have neutralizing admixtures. We are French, and Irish, and British, and even Roman, as well as Anglo-Saxon.

I remember feeling this very strongly when we stopped *en route* at the Schloss Hotel in Heidelberg. In that pleasant provincial town there were people who were so like the Englanders of fifty years ago that you'd think we'd come in a time machine instead of a Delage. At tables dotted about in the restaurant and observing a reverential hush in the presence of food were English men and women of about the period of 1906. The men wore country clothes, Norfolk jackets, and breeches and tall stiff collars. They had an air of authority, and made a quiet fuss about the wines. If they were married and had families, the wife and children sat respectfully silent, with one eye on Papa. If not, they bowed politely to solitary ladies, who inclined the head graciously in return.

Those ladies—I swear it—had lace collars upright about their necks, kept in position by a whale-bone at either side, and in one case by a couple of S-wires that reminded me of the caduceus. They wore tailored coats and skirts, and the one with the caduceus had more than a suggestion of leg-of-mutton sleeves. Some of them had, obviously, paid companions, who kept a tight rein on little dogs under the table, pretended not to eat, waved their little fingers, and passed the salt.

To arrive, the necessary number of hours later, at that charming hotel with the charming name, the Vier Jahreszeiten (it means 'Four Seasons') was to use the time machine again. As we tried to drive up to the entrance sundry uniformed persons held up their hands, and we had to wait while a magnificent white Mercedes drew to a halt, and out clambered a huge, jolly man in a perfectly white uniform with masses of brass.

'By God,' my father said, 'it's old Goering.'

And so, by God, it was. He was immediately surrounded by a clamour of little girls, and stood in the centre of the group, jovial and avuncular and bare-headed, signing autographs. Behind the little girls, S.A. men had ranged themselves in petrified positions of extravagant attention. For two minutes or so time stood still, while Goering signed and joked and patted heads. Then he went in, and all the cars and trams and people suddenly moved again.

Every night that week the white Mercedes drove up at seven o'clock and Goering went in to the separate entrance of the Restaurant Walterspiel. My bedroom was immediately over that entrance, and I used to lean out and look. Sometimes he came alone. Sometimes there were bevies of beautiful girls. He pinched their bottoms and they squealed with laughter.

For hours the Mercedes waited, while the sounds of muted music floated up. At twelve-thirty or one a.m. the street would be filled with sudden revelry and the white Mercedes, backing to avoid the grey Delage, would purr powerfully away.

I've often wondered if the idea wasn't at the back of my father's mind that, if he stayed in that hotel long enough, he might contrive a word with Hitler for no other reason than that he was at heart a journalist.

In a way, he did.

But I had to go. Maisie was due in Paris the next evening, and we had promised ourselves what we both felt might be a last fling—a fortnight at the Eden Roc.

So I got out the old wagon, and made it to Paris in the

day, with an odd sense of returning to a civilized world where people were decently afraid. We met at the Napoleon, had a drink with Rex Harrison, and got my lighter filled with sexy violets. I remember that, consciously, one did things like this as if one would never be able to do them again. Then we beat it down the old Route Nationale No. 7, spent the night at Valence or somewhere, and were just jumping for the gates of the Hôtel du Cap about tea-time when I drove slap into a small Fiat which came out from the right.

I never could remember the rule of giving way to the right.

The Fiat remained motionless where I had hit it, with a strong look of grievance. Then, with dignified slowness, all four wheels heeled over and came off, and out climbed about fifteen nuns, with fishing rods.

I think the French are charming.

My father's adventures were much more interesting. He stayed on at the Vier Jahreszeiten but had his room changed after I had gone and found himself next to Himmler. Two enormous black-uniformed, black-visaged S.S. stood guard at the door. Every time my father went in to clean his teeth or anything these people put their hands caressingly on their holsters. Himmler had a piano inside, and the faint sound of little French *chansons* mingled with the water from the tap.

That afternoon my father went down to get a cup of tea in the main lounge. The whole shooting match was there in one corner. Hitler, Himmler, Goering, Hess, and little Goebbels, laughing loudly among themselves and guzzling éclairs. What a bunch. My father got his pot of tea with some cress sandwiches and an éclair all to himself; and the thought came to him that if he had a loaded revolver in his pocket it would be a wonderful opportunity, and not a bad thing to do. Being a civilized man, he had no revolver.

When they had gone an American lady in another corner began to make a tremendous fuss. She said she had lost a packet of postal cards, and she knew for a fact she had them when she came in because she had bought them right there at the stand, so she must have put them down some place, and she wasn't going to leave the hotel until her packet of postal cards had been located.

All the gold epauletted waiters in the place began searching, down the backs of chairs and sofas.

One of them came up with a loaded revolver, which the chief waiter hurried away with, between two fingers, as if it were over-ripe fish. Someone, my father thought, must have had the same idea....

[5]

There was a fine croquet lawn at Shamley Green, which became celebrated far and wide, for a devilish game called 'Madders'.

The essence of it was that if you hit the ball of any of your opponents, you took his score, so that it was possible to be within one hoop of the winning score of thirty, and lose the whole thing to some underhand and cunning fellow with no score at all, who crept upon you from the farthest edge. When that happened the quiet sunny scene was rent with the sound of lamentations. Croquet mallets were raised high into the air and thudded to the turf and murder was nearly done.

In some curious contradictory way, this peaceful scene became embedded in the history of what looked like the end of history. Quite deliberately, though without, I think, deliberate purpose, my father began to make friends with Germans. They came at first in driblets, for tea and croquet on the lawn. There was Wolf Dewahl, the London correspondent of that admirable paper the *Frankfurter Zeitung*, and his pretty little wife.

There was General Wenninger, of the Luftwaffe, a charming blue-eyed man with rabbity teeth, a shy manner, a nice wife, and an enchanting little daughter. He was Military Attaché at the German Embassy. The German Embassy, indeed, began to feature rather prominently at 'Madders' so that the inhabitants of the Green detected a new and guttural addition to the cries of rage and anguish.

The result was that it was possible to drive over on any

fine Sunday afternoon and discover my father swiping his way through large groups of inarticulately protesting foreigners, who had been reduced by the appeasing English to a condition of deepest anxiety or vociferous despair. The experience unnerved them and seemed to awaken their worst suspicions of the English character.

This was not true of the von Dirksens, the ambassador and his wife.

Ribbentrop had departed, with his champagne, after he had given the King a Nazi salute at Court, nearly knocking his nose off in the process. I didn't see him go, but on my way to the R.A.C. one day I saw the champagne go, case after case of it, while the famous Embassy chow looked on. Von Dirksen was not a Nazi, nor therefore an *arriviste*. He was a perfectly straightforward ambassador, but his wife, I thought, was a tiresome woman.

The Germans, I discovered, had the 'gentleman' idea even more strongly ingrained than the English. For them class transcended even patriotism, so that a German gentleman could say to an English gentleman, 'Hitler? But he is not a gentleman. Beck, yes. Ludendorf, naturally. Goering, perhaps, just. But Hitler?'

Frau von Dirksen gave herself the most tremendous airs, and was constantly using the term *'en poste'*! 'When my husband was *en poste* in Tokyo.' 'When my husband was *en poste* in Venezuela.' When the time came to leave she would rise imperiously to her feet and, looking for my mother, cry in ringing tones, 'Wo ist die Hausfrau?'

The only man I could make friends with in this galère was Wenninger. He struck me as a civilized man.

[6]

On a particularly sunny Sunday afternoon there was another game of croquet. There was a gravely good-looking man with white hair who argued in clipped German with a group of rather amorphous people who clustered round him and

3. Four generations of Gibbses: Sir Philip (*aet.* 80),
Anthony (*aet.* 56), Martin (*aet.* 29) and Philip
(*aet.* two months)

4. Charles Fry

endeavoured, with a more than English wealth of gesture, to clarify the game's situation at that moment. My father with his jaw thrust out, his pince-nez slightly askew, a look of devilish determination and cunning marring his rather fine features, was pursuing his remorseless way in a frenzy of concentration on another part of the lawn. With his mallet he jabbed and prodded and hooked sharply to the left. The holocaust was in full swing. Balls were lying dead in every direction. Loud teutonic shouts rent the air. An American journalist went suddenly pale. A professor of geology from London University flung up his hands in torment. My small son shouted, 'Go it, Gruffer!' having been brought up to treat his elders in this manner. My father re-doubled his efforts. He went viciously through two hoops, demolished Dwye Evans, the publisher of *The Bible as Literature*, whanged against the stick, and evoked cries of anguish and surrender from the tall German with the very blue eye and the jolly rabbit teeth, from the very furthest corner by the house. With fiendish accuracy my father aimed, sent his ball on its unerring flight and routed the Military Attaché at the German Embassy at a distance of forty-three yards.

General Wenninger hopped down on to the concrete path which borders the lawn at this point, and rescued both the balls with perfect affability.

'I'm extremely sorry, General,' said my father, with mild apology written faint upon his look of triumph.

The General smiled and clicked his heels. He had the eyes of an airman.

'I would have you notice that the Germans did not start *this* war,' he said.

War, actually to break out in six days, seemed very far away. . . .

[7]

There was Dewahl the newspaper man. He sat in the drawing-room after tea, occupying the exact centre of the sofa in his rather heavy, stiff way, and fixing me with his penetrating, heavy-lidded eye, while his wife perched on the back and smiled down adoringly on the top of his head. The top of his head was spanned by the spring of his ear-phone. The orifice of the metal box on his waist-coat seemed to fix me with the same unwinking attention as Dewahl himself. Outside the big bay window the rest of the party were submitting themselves with exhausted good grace to a further manifestation of my father's berserk abandon.

I argued rather hotly with Dewahl. The storm was very close now, and I suppose all our nerves were a little frayed. The thing seemed serious, and I remembered a sort of exasperated frustration at coming up against a stone wall in his mind. I remember saying, rather stupidly perhaps, that we had already had a war which had settled nothing, and that it was still so close that I doubted if it was humanly possible for human nerves to stick the same thing all over again twice in twenty-five years!

I'm sorry I said that now. I saw the statement register in those pale eyes and the amplifying machine, to be filed for future reference. It was an indiscretion perhaps. But I went on angrily. I tried to put the English point of view, the obvious point of view about how England always sympathized with the under-dog, how we had almost championed the Germans once we had beaten them, how we had protected them against the avowed *amorcellement* of the French, how we had been shocked at the business of the black troops in the Ruhr, how we had held back the French time and time again from exercising their undoubted rights of retaliatory invasion. I said there were limits to which we thought the Germans should be allowed to go, but that those limits were exceeded by the invasion of Austria, the martyrizing of the Jews, the seizure of Czechoslovakia in unholy violation of Hitler's signed word and the irritating reiteration of his racial principles.

Such arguments made no impression on the man whatsoever. He defended 'Austria'. He sat there and remarked expressionlessly that the Austrians *wanted* to be united with the Reich, and that they had asked the League of Nations no less than twelve times for permission to 'Anschluss' without result.

'The Führer,' said Dewahl—and he is the only German I ever met who called Hitler by that name without knowing that to the English ear it sounded faintly ridiculous—'the Führer thought he had been betrayed by Schuschnigg and told him so. He offered to hold a plebiscite. And what did Schuschnigg do? He went back to Austria and armed the Communists! Made violently anti-German speeches! The situation became rapidly untenable. The Führer had never limited himself by supposing that altered circumstances do not alter the ethics of a situation.'

I stared hard at Dewahl's inscrutable visage. Altered circumstances altering ethics? Did I detect a hint of sarcasm, veiled by that mask-like muscular control?

'So the Führer gave the order to march in order to prevent bloodshed.'

I stared again. 'Go on,' I said at length. 'Czechoslovakia.'

'Czechoslovakia? The Führer is from Moravia himself. He is one of these Sudetens.'

I stared again.

'But not one of these Czechs.'

'It was a military measure.'

'All right,' I said. 'Poland.'

'Have you looked at the map?'

'Yes.'

He shrugged as though that settled the matter.

'There *need* not be war.'

'Are you going in?'

For the first time Dewahl looked sideways. Then he looked me in the eyes again. 'I have a very nice flat here in London. We are all packed up ready to go. I have sold the furniture—our furniture—to a little Jew. It may not be worth much, but we are fond of it. We are fond of London. We are fond of the English. The English do not like us, but at least we have made one friend. Our housekeeper has cried all this week because we have to go. We are very fond of her. We are waiting word from the German Embassy. *There need not be a war.* Perhaps we shall be back after a long week-end.' He rose suddenly, and held out his hand, showing the top of his head, which his wife liked so much, in a stiff little bow which struck me as being incredibly 1914.

His wife shook hands, in a friendly, romping sort of way.

Then Dewahl said an oddly significant thing. 'It is time,' he said, 'that Europe was organized.'

It was only after they had gone that I realized he meant 'organized', of course, 'by Germany'.

[8]

I only saw Wenninger once again, before I saw him in the war.

They were distributing gas masks in Peaslake, at the War and Spottiswoode Memorial Hall. It always reminded me of Sinclair Lewis's hotel, the Deux Hémisphères et Dijon. My wife was in the village distributing blankets to 'evacuees'. My father's new novel was called *This Nettle Danger*.

The rooks cawed over Shamley Green. Two armoured cars came, their bare-throated young drivers gazed at the signpost, dropped their jaws and with great difficulty turned round and went back the way they came.

There were to be three more days of peace. The sands were running very low.

I walked through London savouring those last few moments. The pulse of the city seemed to beat more slowly.

London was ominously quiet. Already the streets and the houses and the windows had broken into an inadequate rash of sand-bags and criss-crossed paper which were of no more use against bombs than so much paper and sand. I walked the old haunts of my beloved Chelsea. The King's Road was filled with fire pumps and special constables and girls in khaki. In Burton Court, where my children used to play in the sun and watch the officers of the Guards at cricket, a few, a very few, Chelsea children still played listlessly among the trenches. The smooth turf of the Guards' cricket ground was scarred with the tracks of lorries, and in the centre an ugly barrage balloon wallowed with its belly on the earth.

I went down Tite Street. The house was a hive of little Wrens with black stockings and pert eyes and naughty bottoms. In Cheyne Walk they had painted bands of white about the bases of the immemorial elms. The smoke above the immense brick funnels of Battersea Power Station was absolutely motionless. There was no traffic in the road. A solitary tram was stationary on Battersea Bridge, and for a moment I was guilty of some foretaste of the future, of terrified forebodings, in which some invisible cataclysm seemed to have struck London into the abrupt immobility of death.

[9]

That afternoon I took tea with the Prime Minister at No. 10 Downing Street, in company with five hundred other people.

In view of the menace of the international situation and with my mind filled with the thought of universal death, I fear I made a serious misjudgement of the English character. I went just as I was.

As the door was opened to me by a black-clad menial and I passed up the iron staircase, I knew that I was treading on what had once been hallowed ground. I was impressed by the situation of finding myself in that historic place where so much haphazard history has been made by high-minded men after tremendous thought, and where the last decision in that present chapter of human affairs had in all probability been already taken. I climbed the stairs rather regretfully, rather reverently, for I knew in my heart that death was the verdict

127

and that these chaste walls belonged now to a finished phase.

The door at the top of the stairs was flung open, and the sudden reminder of what the English character can do in an emergency smote me between the eyes with all the impact of a blow. There was abrupt diapason of tea-party sounds. The tail coat was universal, the striped trouserings, the neat hair cut and the white carnation had been chosen to a man. The ladies wore gloves and gracious smiles, and were in excellent chatter.

In the middle of the room was Mr Chamberlain himself, ruddy of countenance, bright of eye and completely carefree of manner. I met the publisher of *The Bible as Literature*. I ate two coffee cakes, supplied, I fancy, by the survivors of the late Joseph Lyons. I observed that Sir John Reith was present and that his Eminence the Archbishop of Westminster, seated on a chair in an oil-cloth floored passage was holding an unofficial reception on his own.

I spent some time covertly observing Mr Chamberlain at a little distance from behind a tea cup, and I thought to myself that either the English were not blessed with imagination, or were devoid of brain, or that we were the very salt of the earth. My father led me to him. And Mr Chamberlain lifted the sides of his moustache in a very friendly smile, wrung my hand and said, 'You're exactly like your father!'

I shall carry with me till I die the confused impression of the rattle of tea-cups, the murmur of diplomatic conversations, the well calculated frivolities of the polite feminine voice—and outside as I left, the long row of anxious watchers with open mouths and white faces wondering what all the coming and going was about, and whether it was peace or war. Once again the lamps were going out all over Europe.

[10]

The Wenningers had a charming house on Chelsea Embankment, and they had suggested that I go along there when I got away from No. 10.

I must have arrived too early, for only Prince Friedrich was there, a young man who looked so like his cousin the Duke of Kent that it was impossible to tell them apart. He had a job, curiously enough, in the Ford works at Dagenham.

I remember the autumn sunshine coming in at the windows across the river and Battersea Park, and this young man with the parted hair telling me he liked England better than Germany 'under that fellow', and would stay here if there was a war.

If there was a war. It seemed incredible. Wenninger's little girl, awed perhaps by the presence of royalty, handed round those nice little nut wafers which are filled with chocolate paste, tripped in her confusion, and sent the whole lot of them rolling across the floor. She wept, and Prince Friedrich von Hohenzollern and General Wenninger of the Luftwaffe and I went on all fours like pussycats to catch them under the chairs. If there was a war. . . .

I asked about 'that fellow'.

Wenninger explained about the curiously vertical divisions of German power.

'I am of the Luftwaffe,' he said. 'Herman Goering is my personal friend. Goering with the Air Force behind him, has great power. Perhaps the greatest power in Germany, because Hitler has only the Storm Troopers, and, if there is a war all the Storm Troopers will be in the Army, and the Army is loyal to its generals.'

'And aren't the generals loyal?'

'Of necessity,' he said, 'they are.'

'Only of necessity,' said Prince Friedrich, smiling, like one Englishman to another.

I thought this a very strange conversation.

General Wenninger smiled, showing his wet rabbity teeth.

'You see we can talk here,' he grinned.

'Can't you—can't you talk anywhere else?'

'Not anywhere.'

'Not in the Embassy?'

'Least of all in the Embassy,' Wenninger automatically looked over his shoulder.

'You mean, not even in your own room?'

'Least of all in my own room.'

I said I was damned.

'Do you mean there is a spy there?'

'On behalf of Himmler.'

'Good God,' I said. 'Fitz Randolph?'

The Prince and the General smiled with faraway eyes, neither confirming or denying.

'Our good friend Himmler is *very* powerful. His men are *everywhere*. There are reports on *everybody*.'

'Even the Ambassador?'

'Natürlich!'

'On you?'

'Natürlich! But I am very careful.'

'On—on Goering?'

'I am sure.'

I left the last but obvious question unspoken, looking from one to the other.

There was a little silence.

'This conversation is getting a bit treasonable,' said Prince Friedrich.

'Even from here,' Wenninger added.

I apologized.

'Listen,' said Wenninger. 'What would you do if you were going along and you suddenly saw a madman in the street?'

'Cross to the other side,' I said.

Suddenly, the people poured in.

There was an extraordinarily beautiful lady with blue eyes and a blue turban. She was not only extremely beautiful but extremely intelligent. There was a dark and rather sinister man with an electrically shaven chin whose name I did not catch and whose politely one-handed conversation referred constantly to something which he called 'The Crissis'.

There was that rather elegant individual we had just mentioned with the English name Fitz Randolph, whose letters to *The Times*, elaborately reasonable, never quite reconciled the readers of that paper to the more dramatic utterances of the Nazi regime. There was a handsome, Britannia-like lady who was something to do with champagne, just like Herr Ribbentrop. There was Maisie, wondering what on earth had happened to me.

I do not move much in exalted diplomatic circles and the sudden and deeply respectful punctilio which heralded the arrival of the German Ambassador and his wife was a surprise to me. Frau von Dirksen entered first. Dr von Dirksen followed, a big man with a shaven head and an expression of fleshy discretion. Frau von Dirksen carefully made the tour of the room, bowing distantly to each of the guests who was presented. My wife, Maisie, who is rather tall, seemed to attract her attention.

She regarded her fixedly for some moments with an air of strong disapprobation and then said suddenly, 'Hum! Your legs are too long.'

My wife said that she was extremely sorry and ventured to ask why the lady held that opinion.

'Unhealthy!' snapped Frau von Dirksen. 'There is much too far for the heart to pump the blood. You should have big body, so, and little legs, like this, so! Who think you has the healthiest race today?'

'The Germans,' said Maisie with ready diplomacy.

'Nein!' exclaimed Frau von Dirksen with the utmost seriousness. 'In Germany there is many very long legs who have. So! This is not good. But the Japanese! Ah! They are healthy! Very big bodies. Very little legs. For heart there is very good pumping. It is so near. I admire very much the Japanese. I think very much of their health. I believe much in the spirit, but for the body there is homeopathy.'

The Dirksens passed among the guests, and when they had condescended to the last of them, like royalty, they departed.

When we left, Wenninger came out with us. He stood with the sunlight shining on his face. I got the impression there was something he wanted to say. 'Not much hate there,' I remarked.

He shrugged with an oddly Gallic gesture. 'The English can hate,' said he. 'In the war I was in command of a Zeppelin. The English captured me.' He shrugged again. 'It was the fortune of war. They took me to a prison camp in the North of England. On the way it was necessary to change trains and to wait two hours at Crewe. They put us—there was another man—in a glass bookstall of W. H. Smith & Son. They locked us in, and for two hours—'

'What happened?'

'The English crowd discovered us. It was not very nice being there. It was the women who were the worst. They spat—'

'I can't believe it.'

He shrugged again. 'They spat on the glass.' Then he smiled in that disarming way of his. 'After all,' he said, 'we were the Zeppelin menace. We had been bombing women and babies without warning.'

We were silent for a while.

'What's going to happen?' I asked.

He looked very grave.

'Is it really true,' I asked, 'that you are Goering's friend?'

He nodded, once.

'What about those six thousand aeroplanes?'

He licked his lips nervously. 'They will not come,' he assured me.

I looked at him in amazement.

'Listen,' he said. 'We shall go into Poland. We hope that you will not do anything. But if you do—we shall go into Poland anyway. In four weeks we shall have conquered Poland. Perhaps England will declare war. They will send men to France. The people of London will come out into the streets and gaze into the sky, but no aeroplanes will come. For month after month they will gaze into the sky.

Not one German plane will fly over London. I tell you we shall absolutely refuse to fight this war!'

'Supposing we attack?'

He shrugged again. 'With only a million men? For the Siegfried Line? We shall defend ourselves. *We will not attack*. We do not *want* a war with England. If you insist on it, we cannot prevent you, but *we shall not fight*!'

'How do you know all this?' I asked.

'It is the German plan,' he said. . . .

Two miles along the Embankment the rattle of tea-cups, I imagined, was becoming stilled.

'As for me . . .' said Wenninger, and sucked his teeth to a stop.

'Yes?' I prompted.

'I shall not be in Germany. I shall not be found in Germany if there is war with England.'

I was startled by what he seemed about to say.

'I shall be found in some neutral capital.'

'Found?' I repeated. 'Why "found"?'

'If you want me,' he said, 'you can find me. I am a friend of Goering.'

At the time that struck me as a very peculiar thing to say.

When we drove home that night the roads out of London had been closed to incoming traffic and were filled with motor-cars travelling very fast. and sometimes four abreast, with ungainly luggage on their roofs and perambulators strapped behind. Vincent Korda had been right. For the first time in over eight hundred and fifty years there were English refugees from a foreign invader on the roads of England.

IX

[1]

So we went to war, and I went off to report it, because my mother died.

I will not dwell on that because I am not fond of death, and because it is so intimate a thing. But my father was heart-broken. As the doyen of war correspondents, it was natural that he should be invited by Lord Kemsley to report another war. But he could not face it, and, after dark, he could not see. Since I had been working for the Kemsley papers for the last year or two, it seemed obvious that I should volunteer to take his place. And, if the world was to go to war, it seemed to me that the only way in which I could fit into such a scheme was to observe it, and put into writing what I saw.

Somebody at the War Office had designed us a very pretty uniform consisting of an officer's tunic with the words 'War Correspondent' embroidered on the shoulder in a tasteful shade of green, a cap with the letters W.C. in gold upon the front, two extremely shy-making arm-bands of black and white alternate stripes (as on the Belisha Beacon) and the one frightful word 'Press' emblazoned in inch high letters of a fiery red. The genial major at the War Office who seemed to be in charge of our sartorial arrangements told us that complete latitude would be allowed us below the waist, but suggested trousers without turn-ups and Wellington boots.

[2]

I had my own ideas about the correct equipment for a gentleman going off to report on war, and since Lord Kemsley, who owned both the *Sunday Chronicle* and the

Daily Sketch, which I was supposed to be representing, was paying, I gave them—I admit it—rather free rein.

I took one look at the queue in Moss Bros, hurried round to my own tailor, and asked him if we could possibly cook up and have ready to wear something rather tasteful in the way of uniforms by Friday. His natural desire to do what he could to help the war effort spurred him to declare he would sit up day and night if necessary, and we evolved a few distinctly natty variations on the official theme.

We had leather buttons everywhere instead of brass ones —I was determined to avoid that W.C. business—and a belt made of self-material so that there should be no nonsense about Sam Brownes. Permanent turn-ups, naturally. I asked him to fit the jacket on the long side as I had noticed that Wilkinson's in Pall Mall were selling bullet-proof waistcoats, and this seemed an awfully good idea.

I bought one of these, and then went along to the Burlington Arcade to collect a couple of pairs of rust-coloured suède shoes, and as I was leaving I spotted another shop which sold rolled umbrellas which fitted inside a telescopic walking-stick. So I bought one.

I hugged this to myself as a very typical gesture. I am not fond of war. In my opinion it is not ennobling. As a civilized man I wished to dissociate myself from mankind's insanity, and the inevitable collapse of civilization.

With my mind, if I must admit it, writhing with these simple clichés, I cherished the thought that whatever happened, in whatever circumstances of spilt guts and decaying flesh I might find myself, at least I should always go— even to my own death—clutching this secret totem of my own personal disdain of the whole bestial business.

And so it was that, clanking musically with the waistcoat, swinging my gas-mask in one hand and my rolled umbrella in the other, I presented myself at the door of a first-class carriage of the train in Waterloo Station, which was to carry no fewer than thirty-nine accredited war correspondents into the jaws of death.

There was only one other person in the carriage, a sensitive-looking man who had made his own gesture of non-compliance. Tied neatly round his throat and bellying from the front of his British warm was a charming silk scarf in a Paisley pattern, not yet fashionable in Army circles. He was reading *The Times*.

'Can I introduce myself?' I started. 'My name's Anthony Gibbs.'

He lowered the paper with a tiny show of distaste.

'Oh yes?' he answered. 'Mine's Kim Philby.'

I have described this part of the war in another place, so I will not weary you with it now.

Its main and most provocative feature was that there was no war. Exactly as Wenninger had prophesied, not one shot was fired. For week after week and month after month the Germans built up an increasingly terrifying preponderance of forces on the Dutch and Belgian frontiers, which the poor little British Expeditionary Force was quite unable to match.

The British Expeditionary Force was led by frightfully nice chaps. They couldn't have been nicer. They had food parcels sent out from Fortnum and Mason, and swore that their men were bloody good chaps. There was a difference. When I left there were four divisions of bloody good chaps in France. On the other side of the border the Germans had two hundred divisions; and not nearly so nice.

They did not attack.

The High Command seemed to accept this situation with unquenchable gaiety and good humour, but some of the correspondents, including Philby and myself, became haunted by a conviction of doom. Philby could only stand up to it with drink. It was painfully obvious to anyone who had not received his education at Sandhurst that if ever the Germans *did* attack, a lot of awfully nice and bloody good chaps could look forward to massacre.

Then my father finally emerged, a small, stooping figure

in khaki, fumbling his way down windy steps from the doorway of a Dragon Rapide, so that it was time for me to go. Philby and—was it?—Philip Jordan begged me to try to get published the story of almost certain disaster for the B.E.F. which I could then so clearly foresee.

Well, I did try. Lord Kemsley, over whom I spilled the facts and figures in a passion of anxiety, reminded me of the existence of one Admiral Thompson, the chief Press censor, and told me it was as much as his newspapers were worth.

Through Ian Hay, who, as Major-General Ian Hay Beith, was now in charge of correspondents at the War Office, I managed an interview with Hore-Belisha, who had passed on from pedestrian crossings to become Secretary of State for War.

He believed me. I begged him to go over to France and see for himself. He went, and was sacked for his pains.

It was then that Lord Kemsley hit, as he thought, on the solution. There was no censorship of books.

I sat down and wrote it all in a book. When I had finished, I took it round to Hutchinson's, who had always published my father's novels and my own.

I am not certain of what happened. Perhaps some craven patriot sent it, after all, to Admiral Thompson.

All I know is that I received the manuscript back, heavily blue-pencilled, and a letter from the Foreign Office with the signature 'Anthony Eden' where ordinary mortals stick their stamps.

It said: 'Dear Gibbs, I must ask you as a patriotic English gentleman, not to publish this book.'

So I remembered Wenninger.

[3]

The winter was turning into spring, which is the danger period in war, and I ran into a friend of my father's called Ourmousios. He was Secretary to the King of Greece, and as a Greek was neutral in the phoney war. He told me he had heard from General Wenninger who was established as German Military Attaché at The Hague. (He also told me he had an innate distrust of people like Peter Scott, and that the only English bird he could distinguish readily on sight was the hen.)

So Wenninger was at The Hague, was he? And Goering was his personal friend. . . .

Two things happened which stirred those thoughts round in my mind.

A man called Best and a man called Stevens were kidnapped across the German frontier at the little Dutch village of Venlo. The newspapers made a breath-taking but insoluble mystery of this. Nobody seemed to know who Best and Stevens were, what they were doing in Holland, why they went to Venlo, or why a gang of Nazis headed by a German General with a monocle and a shaven head, should have violated Dutch neutrality to seize two perfectly respectable British citizens, one a retired Army officer and the other connected only in the vaguest way with the Foreign Office. There were dark hints of 'the papers' being thrust down a lavatory while the Germans waited outside the small frontier café in their cars. The plain fact was that nobody knew.

The other thing was that the Germans invaded Norway, and held it in the face of a British expedition which returned abashed and wholly unsuccessful. The Germans had won their first victory. I was afraid they might shortly win their second.

I made up my mind. I got in touch with somebody at the Foreign Office and asked if I might look in some time and make a suggestion.

I was most civilly received in an agreeably Etonian atmosphere. There was a largish room which one gained through the usual series of outer chambers containing quietly attractive girls. One half of the room was hidden by a series of green screens. The obvious half contained two nice men wearing the proper tie. There were handshakes and cigarettes. Before sitting down I moved one of the screens slightly to see what lay behind it, and was greeted with flashing smiles by two stenographers with their notebooks on their knees. I explained about General Wenninger. I said I had met him several times at my father's house, and that I had been to his flat, and I thought he was a civilized man and a friend of this country. I remembered now—and told them this—that he had assured me on that day just before the war came that if it did he would refuse to be in Germany, and would try to get himself appointed to a neutral country. I explained about his friendship with Goering and argued that, since I knew from Ourmousios that he actually was at The Hague, the friendship obviously worked.

They admitted all this.

'But what, exactly, do you propose to do?'

I said they would probably think I was absolutely crazy, but my feeling was that the phoney war was telling on everybody's nerves, because nobody seemed to have the faintest idea of what really was in Hitler's mind. Was this whole thing a game of chess with all the pieces swept off the board and the game continuing on the floor? Did Hitler want to get out of the war? Or was he really going to attack? I said I was offering my services to go and find out.

Their heads were nodding like the Teddy Bears in toy-shop windows.

'Go on,' they said.

'If I could go and see Wenninger—I should have to have some definite proposal. A phoney peace proposal. You move all your men ten miles back from the Dutch and Belgian frontiers and we'll do the same.'

'Well?'

'Well, if I could swing that one on Wenninger there's just a chance he might pass me to Goering. I have a feeling that if I went out as a correspondent or something, doing the neutral capitals, and then produced this idea to Wenninger,

I might get to Berlin. What's more, I believe I could get back. Can I do that for you?'

They looked at each other with expressionless faces. Then both of their heads began to swing the other way.

'Not for us, you won't,' they said.

'Why not?'

'We'd never send a chap out with our blessing on a thing like that. It's too bloody dangerous.'

I wasn't quite certain whether he meant too bloody dangerous for me, or too bloody dangerous for the Foreign Office.

'Can I do it without your blessing?'

They shrugged. 'Anything you like in a neutral country, until the balloon goes up, but don't expect us to get you out of trouble.'

'Thanks,' I said.

We all rose and moved towards the door. One of them opened it.

The other said, 'Don't do it, old boy! Don't do it!'

He startled me. 'Why not?'

'Look what happened to Best and Stevens.'

'Good Lord! Was *that* what. . . .'

'Same thing, old boy. Exactly.'

'Not original!'

He smiled.

'Oh, hold on, don't go. You need a pass. Anybody can get into this place. It's getting out that presents the difficulties. Like Berlin!'

He scribbled something on a piece of paper.

[4]

Lord Kemsley fixed me up. A 'tour of the neutral capitals'. My visas arrived without a hitch. I wasn't quite sure how the Secret Police would be viewing my antics, and decided to spend a few days in Brussels first, with some amateurish idea of putting people off the scent. My father was now at home again, having decided he was far too old to be a war correspondent. Maisie and the two children had moved in to look after him, and my own house had been taken over as a convent of evacuated nuns.

A good friend of my father's, and of mine, Harold Callander, the London Editor of the *New York Times*, put me in touch with a man in Brussels who rejoiced in the name of Capitaine du Vaisseau Gade, who invited me to stay for a week.

This Captain-of-the-vessel was one of those intelligent Americans, tall, gangling and grizzled. He occupied an elegant flat in the most expensive part of Brussels, in that Square just round the corner from the Royal Palace, and immediately accepted without any question that I was an obvious spy.

'I assoom,' he said, 'you're Military Intelligence?'

It was the first time this happened to me and I didn't like it. It happened with increasing frequency later on, and I never became used to it.

'Martinis?'

'Thanks,' I said.

'After all,' Gade went on, stirring away, 'I'm the local representative of American Naval Intelligence. I think I'm pretty good at my job. In fact, I'm the only man who ever obtained a complete copy of the Stalin—Ribbentrop pact, with all the secret clauses.'

I looked at him in disbelief.

'With all the secret clauses,' he repeated. 'And believe you me, some of 'em are pretty secret. Have the British Government got them? No sir. Cheers!'

'Ch-cheers,' I said.

'So if there's anybody you'd like to meet?'

'What did you do with it?'

'The Ribbentrop pact? Right here in this apartment.'

My eyes must have been like saucers.

'Doesn't that make you frightfully nervous?'

'Nervous? Hell, no! Why should it make me nervous?'

'I should have thought—you know—being followed about, and people climbing in and searching the place and all that.'

He gave me a sudden sharp stare, and then roared with laughter. It was suddenly borne in upon me, that he thought I was putting on a damned good act.

'Let me do that again for you, Mr Gibbs.' He took up my glass. 'If you must know, it's pretty well protected.'

'Protected?'

'Sure! Little bits of black cotton all over the place. First of all you have to find it. Then you'd have to avoid all the little bits of black cotton. Break one of those bits, and I'd know, see? Cheers!'

'Cheers!'

A most absurd situation was developing. The drink, after a day of travel, was giving me migraine. It's a partly cyclical and partly incapacitating disease to which there is no cure.

'So I thought—I'm supposed to be dining with Browne tonight. He's Military Attaché at our Embassy here. Kind of rivals. I don't want awfully to have to leave you alone here on your first night in town. So would you—care to come along?'

Recklessly I swallowed the second half of the second Martini. I knew exactly what it would do to me. It did. The first sledge-hammer blow on my left temple.

I apologized profusely.

'I'm most terribly sorry, but I've got one of those cursed migraines coming on. Could you possibly leave me out of it?'

He nodded very, very sagely.

'Surely,' he said.

'I really am very sorry. I get them you know.'

'That's perfectly all right. I'll be back'—he looked at his watch—'at about eleven-fifteen. Eleven-fifteen. Can you remember that?'

'Yes, of course.'

'Oh, there's some cold chicken in the dining-room.'

'No little black wires?'

'No little black wires in the dining-room.'

He gave me a solemn and amused salute, and went away. The front door clicked behind him. Presently I heard the gates of the lift, and its Doppler whine. I was left alone with the only copy of the Stalin–Ribbentrop pact, with all the secret clauses. . . .

[5]

I remember going into the dining-room and turning on the light. It was right at the end of the passage, with its door open, the only open door among, perhaps, four on either side. There on the table was a plate of cold chicken, a bowl of salad, a potato salad, a Cona coffee machine, with a box of matches.

Only one thing was quite clear in this whole mystifying affair. I wasn't expected to dine with Colonel Browne. What *was* I expected to do? Was I being offered the Stalin–Ribbentrop treaty on a plate? As between spies? As between friendly Governments?

Or was I genuinely being warned not to snoop?

Or was the whole Stalin–Ribbentrop story a myth and was this some sort of test? 'Break any one of those little bits, and I'll know, see?'

I munched a bit of chicken and drank a little red wine out of a decanter, wincing at the pain in my temple which had now grown into the full fury of its rhythm. It was very quiet in the flat.

If the treaty really *was* there, and I really *was* being offered it on a plate, was it my duty to pinch the thing and take it to London—before eleven-fifteen?

I drank quite a lot of that wine. Once you start the thing you may as well drown it. There was a copy of *The New Yorker* on the table. I began to read it in desperation while I ate. I found a London letter signed Mollie Panter-Downes. It said that everybody in London was walking about with gas-masks in cardboard boxes. So they were. So they were.

I put it quietly away, got up from the table, tiptoed into the hall and stood listening to the silence. Which of the doors? I went into the dining-room, and lit the Cona. It is a mistake to drink coffee, too. My watch showed two minutes to nine already. There was a radio in the room where we had drunk the Martinis. I went in there and switched it on. Big Ben boomed out automatically. A friend of England then. 'Here is the news, and this is Alvar Liddell reading it: On the Western Front today there was the usual activity. In the House of Commons, the Prime Minister . . .'

I went back to my coffee, bubbling balefully and picked up *The New Yorker*.

At eleven-fifteen, when Gade came in, I was discovered reading it.

'Well?' he asked. 'Did you find it?'

X

[1]

I am pretty positive that no one followed me to The Hague. It was a short journey by train and I had the feeling I was on my own. I had booked a room at the Hotel des Indes, and this turned out to be a very sumptuous hotel indeed, set across one end of a small square where the young trees were already in bud.

I expand greatly in the caress of luxury. There were soft carpets, and quiet respectful voices, and shaded lights and the subdued click of well-run elevators. From the window in my bedroom I looked out on beautifully weathered Georgian bricks alight in the setting sun, and a most exquisite little building all in white and gold, which turned out to be a royal residence.

I picked up the telephone book, and, almost unconsciously, looked among the W's. It was about five o'clock. The name sprang out at me.

'Wenninger, General von. 99 Badhuisweg, Scheveningen.' And the number.

I began to tremble. My left hand lifted the telephone without volition. A girl's voice answered. A pretty voice.

'Do you speak English?'

'Of course! Everybody in Holland speaks English.' There was just the right amount of laughter in it.

'Oh, good.' I gave her the number.

I could hear the telephone ringing, and then Wenninger's voice.

'Hier von Wenninger.'

'Hullo, Wenninger,' I said.

There was a very long silence indeed. I sensed—don't ask

me how—that he was frightened. He knew my voice all right, and he was afraid of something.

'Can I come to see you?'

'To see me?' His breathing seemed almost out of control. 'Why?'

'Is there any chance of peace?'

Another long silence, then a click in the telephone, and the peculiar certainty that a third person had added his presence on the line.

'Very well.' He made it sound like a desperate decision. 'Don't take a taxi from the hotel.'

He hung up quickly. In a rather more leisurely fashion so did I. I went down to the entrance hall. It seemed full of uniformed porters. I made my way towards the swing door. Two of the porters advanced on me.

'Where to, Sir?'

'Can I help you, Sir?'

'It's all right. I'll pick up a taxi.'

'I am sorry, Sir. For a taxi it is necessary to ask at the desk.'

'D'you mean to tell me I can't walk out into the street and take a taxi?'

'I am sorry, Sir. You must ask at the desk.'

This struck me as very unusual. I had the odd sensation of being the centre of attention.

'Very well,' I agreed, and approached an elegant in striped trousers.

'Can you get me a taxi?'

'Certainly, Sir! Where to, Sir?'

Why did everybody want to know where I was going?

'The British Embassy,' I said.

'The British Embassy, Sir, of course.' He spoke into a telephone.

I went out through the swing doors. Leaning against one of the young trees was a man. He was wearing a bowler hat. That struck me as unexpected too. Did the Dutch wear bowlers? I gave him a second glance and met his eyes. There was a most odd expression in them. Then the largest sort of Chrysler drew up. One of the porters ushered me in and we surged away.

The British Embassy seemed remarkably close. We went round six corners and the Chrysler wallowed to a stop.

I tapped the driver on the shoulder and showed him a piece of paper on which I had taken the precaution of writing '99 Badhuisweg'.

He produced a string of unpronounceable gutturals, and presently we were in a Victorian suburban area, absurdly reminiscent of St Leonards-on-Sea. At the end of it was a barn-like structure with a fussy roof-line, and beyond that nothing. The sea. Then Yarmouth or somewhere. We stopped.

'Negende negende,' the driver announced, making the 'n's' sound like the noise some people emit when they have just trod in a dog's mess. A lace curtain moved. Wenninger half opened the door. He didn't shake hands or say anything. I slipped quickly in.

The room was crowded and fussy. Knick-knacks, wall paper, a cuckoo clock, toughly cushioned armchairs with a pattern of baldness, an india-rubber plant, the whole gim-crack fretwork of Victorian suburbia.

'Sherry?' asked Wenninger. He poured out two glasses. It was Bristol Cream.

'Cigarette?' He held out a packet of Craven A.

'This is very dangerous,' said Wenninger, at last.

'Is it?'

'For me just as much as for you.'

He *was* frightened. I thought he was.

'I think you don't understand the German system. I hope this is the only time you come to see me.'

I stared at him. I hadn't thought he was going to be awkward.

'D'you mind if I sit down?'

'Please.' The rabbit teeth showed apologetically, without smiling.

'All right,' I said. 'I'll be quick.' I told him, speaking rapidly, that the British people had never really meant to go to war, that Mr Chamberlain had only given the Polish guarantee because he thought it would call Hitler's bluff. I said it looked from our side as if Hitler had judged that same guarantee to be a piece of bluff on the part of Chamberlain. In other words, we had each bluffed the other into a position from which we would both like to withdraw if only the formula could be found. Was that right? I asked him.

He seemed to evade the question by looking at his knees.

'What is it you want me to do?' he said.

'Could you get me a safe conduct to Berlin to see Field Marshal Goering?'

'Impossible.'

'Why?'

'*Impossible!* You don't understand.'

There was a long silence. He was extremely excited.

'No,' I said. 'I don't.'

'Listen, my friend. I try to make this clear. In Germany there are five men, each with his private organization. Almost his private army. There is Hitler, with his S.S. Stormtroopers. There is Goebbels, with his army of Press and radio. There is Ribbentrop, with his men in the Foreign Office and every Embassy. There is Goering, with the Luftwaffe and some respect from the Army. And there is Himmler, with his Gestapo. There is a sort of balance of power, but of these Himmler is infinitely the most dangerous, because he operates in secret and can upset the balance. If Himmler learns that Goering is entertaining an Englishman—call it holding conversations with the enemy—and goes to Hitler with his story, then that could be the end of Goering. You do not know what you ask. It is *impossible*.'

He poured himself another glass of sherry with a trembling hand, and knocked it back in a single gulp.

'Would Goering,' I asked him, 'be interested in peace if he could be presented with a formula?'

'I don't understand.'

148

'If Goering could be presented with a way out, to which the English were committed, could he go to Hitler and tell him?'

'It is possible,' admitted Wenninger, 'but I don't see . . .'

'Can you get in touch with Goering?'

'I telephone to him. This line is safe.'

'Very well then, my dear laddie,' said I, 'you and I are going to find the formula. I'm going to come here every day for the next fortnight if necessary, and we're going to knock out a provisional peace treaty, and if you'll see that it gets to Goering, I'll see that it gets to Chamberlain.'

'You are empowered to do this?'

'Yes,' I lied.

'I do not think we have a fortnight.'

It was my turn for something cold to turn over in my stomach.

'You mean . . .?'

'Germany has a plan. It will be very unpleasant.'

I could have used some of that sherry.

'Very unpleasant,' he repeated. 'We can win the war in fifteen days.'

'My God, you believe that?'

'I'm afraid that it is possible.'

'And starting . . .?'

'I cannot tell you.'

'All right. Have we got three days?'

'A few more perhaps.'

'Then we've got more than three days to save the world it seems to me. Will you do it?'

He gave me a sharp glance and became silent. Something like a minute passed. There was a horrible clock in the corner, with nasty little weights and a pendulum that ticked away. The silence became oppressive. There was a great struggle going on inside the man. He really was afraid. But he had a conscience. Two minutes. The clock ticked away. You pulled a gilt chain to make the weights go up. Two and a half minutes.

'Well?' I prompted gently.

He put his hands on his knees and stood up.

'Very well,' he said.

I wrung his hand.

'But not tonight. You go back now to your hotel. You must be very careful. Did anyone see you come?'

'I don't think so.' I told him about the British Embassy business.

'That is very good. Every country has a porter in that hotel. Always say "the British Embassy". Best not to take a taxi from the hotel. It is not so bad going from here. I'll send you back in the car. It can drop you a short distance and you can walk, but in the morning be careful. I'll see you at half past ten.'

I thanked him. He went out to telephone for his car. In a minute it was there. A giant Mercedes convertible with a man in uniform and an enormous swastika dangling from the top of the bonnet.

I got in the concealed back seat and the thing slid away on rollers. The swastika fluttered bravely. And I had a terrible secret. In perhaps five days the German Army was going to attack, and across an area that I knew all too well. It seemed to me I had the whole ruddy future of humanity in my pocket. What the devil was I to do? Was there anyone I could get in touch with? Could I telephone somebody in England? My father, perhaps? How did spies manage about this sort of thing?

The Mercedes swooped silently through the traffic and stopped. Its driver leaped out and opened the door, standing smartly to attention. I got out and gave him a couple of guilders. He stamped his foot and his right arm shot out.

'Danke schön! Heil Hitler!'

'Not a bit,' I said.

The man with the bowler hat was leaning against his tree when I came round the corner. This time he raised it with an air of sarcasm. I found the action chilling.

The swing doors swung. One porter employed by each

nation, Wenninger said. They bowed as I passed among them. I went up to the man at the desk, and asked him if it was too late to ring Imperial Airways. I wanted to book a seat on a plane the next morning.

'I ring Schipol,' he said. 'It is not too late.'

I stood about while he did so, fussing and smoking cigarettes.

There was a lot of jiggling the hook, and cranking the bell, and then a lot of Dutch, not one word of which could I understand. Then he addressed me, holding one hand over the receiver.

'I am sorry, mynher, there are unexpected bookings. The first available seat is in seven days.'

I flapped a speechless hand at him. He booked it. I could see a bar round the corner. Somehow, I made it, just in time to stop the death rattle.

'Could you make me,' I said brokenly, 'one very large Manhattan?'

It looked as though I was caught.

I drank the Manhattan. I ordered another.

A pleasant English voice addressed me.

'Manhattans? What a splendid idea! I'll have one of those.'

I looked into a smiling face. 'I'm *The Times*.'

Relief flooded over me. 'Thank God,' I said. 'Have one on me.'

'Marvellous! Then you can have one on me!'

'Cheer ho, then!'

'Cheer ho!'

'I er—I thought you were looking pretty grim. What's up?'

I moved away from the barman's hearing. 'Can we sit down somewhere?'

'Anywhere except that table over there.'

'What's the matter with that one?'

'Permanently wired. Want to hear some secrets? Have a word with the manager, get the people shown to that table, and listen in the office. This is a very first class hotel.'

151

We fell into two chairs.

'This war,' I said under my breath, 'is just about to start.'

'I know.'

'You know? D'you know when?'

Two ladies drifted by.

'Of course, everybody knows that Heinrich Himmler is a homosexual. And he masturbates. If the Führer had had any sense, he'd have had the man done in with Roehm, on the Night of the Long Knives.'

I looked at him in amazement. The two ladies sidled coyly crabwise, past the table.

'What on earth——?'

He waited with a smile, till the ladies were out of earshot. 'Don't you know who those females are?'

'No?'

'They're the resident members of the Gestapo. The wife and the daughter of the former German Consul in Prague. They have to report on everybody in the hotel. Very dull for them, mostly. I like to give them a little something to pass on, just to brighten their lives.'

One of them was grey-haired with a knotted neck, the other was fluffy and about thirty-five. They clanked a bit, with necklaces and bangles and handbags.

'I can't think how you stand this place. I only got in this afternoon. I can't get a seat on a plane for a week.'

'You should be just about right.'

'So you know.'

'Everybody *here* knows. Whether anybody in London believes what anybody here tells them is another matter. Why, were you hugging the awful secret?'

'I was, rather.'

'No wonder you look grim. Waiter, two more large Manhattans.'

I suppose I ate dinner. I have no recollection of it. Nor do I remember the name of that friendly man. If he survived all that followed, the escape from Dunkirk, or the Nazi concentration camps, or whatever happened to him, and should chance to read this, I hope he will accept this salute across the years. He saved my life.

All I do remember is that some time that evening I pushed past a bearded man and entered one of two telephone boxes in the hall. As I did so the bearded man entered the other. I told my friend the telephone girl that I wanted to dictate a telegram, and she took it down for me.

'SIR PHILIP GIBBS SHAMLEY GREEN SURREY ENGLAND ARRANGE APPOINTMENT P.M. WEDNESDAY'.

She asked what 'P.M.' meant. I told her 'in the afternoon'. As I left one box the man with the beard left the other.

At ten o'clock the next morning I was in the hall.

'Taxi, Sir?'

'Where to, Sir?'

'Can I get you a taxi, Sir?'

I waved the whole gang of them away.

'I'm just going round to the Embassy. It's very close. I think I'll walk.'

They seemed disappointed. As I came out of the swing doors into the bright spring sunshine, the little man with the bowler hat immediately left his tree.

'British Embassy, Sir? This way, Sir?'

'Thanks, I know the way.'

'Do you, Sir? Are you *sure*?'

'Quite sure.'

'Oh, well,' he said, 'in that case——'

When I had walked furiously for about thirty-five yards, I knew, through the eye in the back of my head, that he had put himself in motion. So had at least two other men in nondescript macintoshes. I joined the happy, sauntering shoppers, coughing and hoicking at each other in that extraordinary language. Presently I came to an arcade.

I nipped rapidly into it, and dodged into the second shop on the right. It sold chocolates. I bought a pound box. They would be nice for Frau Wenninger. Had he seen me? He had. He went smilingly by, looking straight ahead. Did he know I was in the shop? I think he did. There was something about that smile. And what about the men in macintoshes? Everybody was in macintoshes.

The lady in the chocolate shop wondered why I didn't go. There was an electrical shop across the way. When the coast seemed clear I bought an electric fire. This took time. My friend in the bowler had not come back. That meant he was waiting for me, or had I given him enough time to double-cross me by leaving the arcade and dodging smartly round to the entrance again?

It was impossible to tell.

In the end I emerged, bearing my chocolates and my fire, and turned further into the arcade. In about twenty yards it splayed out in four different directions. The place was God's gift to hunted men. Down one of the passages two men in macintoshes stood stolidly gazing into a window. I took one of the other directions. No sign of bowler hat. No sign of anybody. I came out into a pleasant residential street with a good church and some trees, and *there was a taxi*! It might almost have been waiting for me.

I got in and slammed the door, and started to feel in my pockets for my piece of paper.

'Negende negende Badhuisweg?' asked the driver stolidly.

I gave up. It was entirely hopeless.

'Ja,' I told him, 'or whatever you say in your unpronounceable language.'

'It is fortunate,' he said, 'that so many of us speak English.

[2]

General Wenninger was waiting for me. I produced the box of chocolates for his lady, and showed him my electric fire. I didn't tell him about the taxi. It was obvious that something had happened to him as well. The moment the door had closed he announced his news.

'I have telephoned Field Marshal Goering. We are to go ahead.'

154

I swallowed. 'That's marvellous,' I said.

'We may do some good.'

'Please God.'

'Please God,' he agreed. 'Some plans have been made. We have three days. If we can get a document on paper, in two copies, I will show my copy to Goering. You will go back and show your copy to Mr Chamberlain. It is just possible we might——'

'Stop the war?'

'It is just possible.'

'It's difficult to believe.'

'To stop *this* war, that is. We need a free hand in the East.'

'My dear fellow, it's yours. Take it.' I said magnanimously. His eyes lit up. 'You mean that?'

'After the Stalin—Ribbentrop pact, nobody cares a damn what you do in the East.'

'That is very satisfactory,' said General Wenninger. 'Shall we begin?'

He dealt out two wads of paper. I took out my fountain pen and wrote the words THE HIGH CONTRACTING PARTIES in capital letters.

'What is that?'

'All treaties begin this way. You are one contracting party. We are the other. Both very high.'

'That's very good,' Wenninger declared.

I wrote some more.

'*THE HIGH CONTRACTING PARTIES,* by this signed instrument, do solemnly pledge each of their respective governments to faithfully adhere [this seemed one of those rare moments when split infinitives were *de rigueur*] to all the conditions and clauses comprised below to which they have set their hands.'

'But that's remarkable! Have you ever seen a treaty before?'

'Never,' I said. '*AND WHEREAS* the High Contracting Parties do hereby avow their desire to revoke the formal declarations of war entered into in September of last year and to live in peace each with the other, then the following conditions shall be binding upon both parties to this instrument.

'One.'

'What's one?'

'That's where we start arguing.'

'The free hand in the East?'

'I'm not sure we can actually put that in. Couldn't we put it by implication.'

'What sort of implication?'

'Something like "The two governments realize that, as a first step, the neutralization of the Western Front must take immediate precedence over all other matters, and to this end, et cetera, et cetera, et cetera"?'

'Et cetera?'

'That's right.'

'What sort of cetera?'

'Some sort of troop movement, I suppose. Back from the frontiers.'

'Would the British pull out their forces from France?'

'Good God, no!'

'No?'

'No! No! No! Not until ratification of a peace treaty. This is only a sort of armistice.'

Wenninger suddenly showed his rabbit teeth in an apologetic smile. 'The British are such gentlemen. They won't cause us much trouble.'

I was furious.

'That's all very well,' I said angrily. 'Here are your blasted German armies threatening every frontier in Europe, talking about winning the war in fifteen days, and you expect me to pull out the B.E.F.! God damn it, man! Have a sense of proportion!'

He stared at me with his pale blue eyes. 'You must not forget that this document is expected to find its way to Hitler.'

'I don't care a damn. If that bloody man Hitler thinks I'm going to—'

He leapt to his feet. I thought he was going to pulverize me with a blow. But he went to the curtains. He opened the door.

'*Please!*' he whispered. '*Please! Not even here!*'

'I'm sorry.'

He sat down again, wagging his head, and mopping his brow.

'I really *am* sorry!'

After some minutes he put his handkerchief away.

'Now! Let us talk business.'

'I thought we *were* talking business.'

'Serious business. You forget one thing.'

'Oh?'

'The blockade of the British Fleet.'

I hope I didn't show that I was absolutely staggered. The blockade of the Fleet, eh? Was this a really effective thing? Were the Germans really worried by it? Were they hemmed in? I must confess that, coming from Flanders, thinking in military terms, I had actually forgotten the British Fleet.

'Ah!' I said, with an attempt at a stall. 'So you don't like that.'

'It is very effective,' Wenninger confessed. 'As you know, we have many submarines. We have even pocket battleships. We have Narvik, it is true, and this is very important for any Eastern operation. But of what use is that if we cannot get there? It is vital for us that we can put to sea.'

I was really learning things!

It was my turn to go into a five-minute think. The horrid little clock began to tick, occasionally tripping over itself. Wenninger waited patiently. This really was a most extraordinary situation.

'O.K.,' I announced at last, with tremendous, not to say awesome emphasis. 'This is the whole basis of the thing.' I spoke at dictation speed. '*If you'll take your men ten kilometres back from the French and Dutch frontiers, I'll call off the blockade of the British Fleet.*'

We stared at each other for minutes more, unblinking. He got to his feet.

'Excuse me,' he said. 'I'll make a telephone call,' and he went out of the room.

He was away for twenty minutes. Was it possible that he was talking to Goering? I didn't know what on earth I thought I was doing, but whatever it was we seemed to be getting somewhere.

He came back smiling.

'Agreed,' he said.

'Have you—have you been talking to Berlin?'

'He agreed.'

You could have knocked me down with a feather.

[3]

That evening, when I climbed into the Mercedes, I had in my pocket a rough draft of what I can only describe as a peace treaty.

Even now, twenty-nine years after the event, though I am still word perfect, I am not at all inclined to accuracy about my own psychology in this bizarre affair. I think I have to confess that, from the very beginning, I had the wild notion that there was indeed the faint possibility that by some fantastic fluke I might be able to get back with something or other that might start a chain of circumstances that could conceivably make it possible for somebody else to stop the fighting. Put it no higher than that. I had no idea how this would happen. It might be through a newspaper article on the lines of the 'Lansdowne Letter' of 1916. It might be that my father could take it to the Prime Minister, or that the Foreign Office could make official unofficial contact through somebody in Stockholm.

But with that piece of paper burning a hole in my pocket it really did look as if the million-to-one chance had come off, and I allowed myself to dream dreams. Eight million men had died on the Western Front in the first war. If only I could get back to London intact with that piece of paper intact, I could perhaps save the second eight million.

The driver and I went through the same silly rigmarole. When I made my way round to the front of the hotel, there were the little men propping up trees. There seemed to be more of them. I went straight to my room and closed and locked the door.

There was a strange sense about the place that puzzled me at once. A greater tidiness. I opened my suitcase. Without any photographic memory one knows, I fancy, how a suitcase looked when one last closed the lid. The open sponge-bag here. The three dirty handkerchiefs and the five ties there. There was no doubt about it. Someone had searched my room.

I went to the bathroom. The same touch of difference. The clothes cupboard. The writing-table drawer. Even the bed with my pyjamas too neatly folded.

I sat down and read my notes. It wasn't difficult for me to memorize them since I had helped to write them. It was obviously unwise to continue carrying them around in my breast pocket because if anybody wanted to get hold of them they would first have to get hold of me, which would be uncomfortable. Remembering Best and Stevens I tore my notes into very little pieces and flushed them down the loo. I suffered from a bad attack of nerves. I remember stumbling, and staring at my white face in the mirror above the wash-basin. I had a little flask of brandy in my rifled suitcase. I took a swig and felt not much better. I examined the lock on the door. There were two. A wavy, horizontal handle was opened by the equivalent of a Yale key from the outside. Beneath it a smaller, matching handle worked a bolt. Short of a jemmy or a battering ram it looked pretty good. The windows, behind their thick damask pale green curtains, were lockable. I locked them.

I rang down to my lady friend, if she was a friend, and asked if I could have dinner in my room. She said it was perfectly feasible. I asked for ham sandwiches and lager beer. She wanted to know if I was ill. I said I had a headache. She was most sympathetic.

A waiter tried the handle and knocked with his keys. I

159

undid the bolt for him. He was quite alone with a trolley. I thanked him and bolted the door behind him.

When I had eaten the sandwiches I kept the beer, put the trolley out in the passage and bolted the door again. I didn't leave that room until the following morning. When I did, I left little traps. My brush and comb just so. The corner of a cigarette packet exactly there.

At ten I ran the usual gauntlet. At first I had found it amusing. Now it was not amusing at all. The bearded man by the telephone box, the half-dozen porters, various—I now realized—apparent guests of the Hotel. The wife and daughter of the former German Consul in Prague. They lowered their heads in a typical hotel greeting. Two or three single men, reading newspapers, turned pages at my approach.

I had discovered a Cook's office quite close and started off there on foot, tracked, this time by no fewer than five vague men in macintoshes, and, of course, my bowlered friend. Spying must be a nerve-racking occupation. I had had precisely two days of what some men must put up with for years. Imagine doing that in the enemy's country. It was more than enough for me as a neutral among the neutrals. And it was not as if I was on anybody's side. I was simply saving civilization from itself—or if that failed, carting about in my head a whole pattern of German thinking, behaviour and plans which seemed to me to make sense and might be extremely valuable to Ian Hay at the War Office—if only I could get to the War Office in time.

[4]

I drew completely blank at Cook's. There was not a single seat on a single aeroplane going anywhere out of Holland. I made the man ring up every airline I could think of. Paris? No. Sweden? No. Switzerland, Denmark, Brussels—not a hope. The trains, of course, were running. But they did not cross the Channel. I told the man I had a seat at nine o'clock on Wednesday.

'Better let me check with Schipol,' he said, 'in case any-body steals your ticket.'

He checked. It was all right. My name and my passport would do the trick. My passport! I had something else to guard . . . and I had five more days. I wasn't sure I could stand the strain.

Since everybody seemed to know, I took a reckless taxi to Wenninger. My bodyguard faded away once I was inside.

Wenninger's face was white when he let me in.

'There has been somebody on the telephone,' he said.

'Who? What? What did he say?'

'A warning to be careful. You do not come here after this morning, I think.'

'I quite agree. The devil of it is I seem to be caught here.'

'Caught?'

'I can't get a seat on a plane before Wednesday.'

'If it is too late we'll fly you in a Luftwaffe plane.'

'Oh, for God's sake! Can you see me arriving at Croydon in a Luftwaffe plane.'

He shrugged. 'To Sweden, perhaps.'

'How do I know you're not going to invade Sweden?'

'We have no plans to invade Sweden.'

'I think I'll stick to good old Imperial Airways.' I made a mental note. Not Sweden.

He shrugged again. 'There should be time. Now. We will make today two copies.' His voice and his grammar were becoming more Germanic. 'You will take one to Mr Chamberlain. I will take the other to Goering. It is understood?'

'Yes,' I said.

'When you get to London, I will send you a message.'

'What sort of message?'

'When you get back you will read every day *The Times*.'

'Oh?'

'If all goes well I will send no message. It is out of our hands. If all goes badly, you read in *The Times* that the German Embassy in The Hague is burning documents. Our document will be one of those which is burnt.'

161

'Good Lord, how can you do that?'

'Just read *The Times*.'

'I never read *The Times*. Couldn't it be *The Telegraph*?'

'It must be *The Times*.'

'Oh very well,' I said. 'Come on, then.'

So we started again. 'THE HIGH CONTRACTING PARTIES. . . .' He picked it out on the typewriter. It took a great many hours:

THE HIGH CONTRACTING PARTIES, by this signed instrument, do solemnly pledge each of their respective governments to all the conditions and clauses comprised below to which they have set their hands.

AND WHEREAS The High Contracting Parties do hereby avow their desire to revoke the formal declarations of war entered into in September of last year and to live in peace each with the other, then the following conditions shall be binding upon both parties to this instrument.

AND WHEREAS the two Governments realize that, as a first step to a peace treaty between the Sovereign states of Germany, Great Britain and France, the neutralization of the Western Front and the Freedom of the Seas must take precedence over all other disputed matters, the Governments of Germany and Great Britain do now agree that within five days of the signature of this agreement the following decisions shall be put into absolute effect.

I. The German Government will order all forces of men and military material to withdraw not less than ten miles from the frontiers of France, Switzerland, Holland and Belgium.

II. The German Air Force will be ordered not to fly over a corridor ten miles in width within German territory outlining the frontiers of the Sovereign states mentioned in Clause I.

III. The British Government will order all forces of

162

men and military material to withdraw not less than ten miles from the frontier between France and Belgium, and will use their best offices with the French Government to require that their military forces remain passive within the fortifications of the so-called 'Maginot Line'.

IV. The Government of Great Britain undertake to allow free passage of the ships of all nations into and out of all German ports, and will not molest on the open sea any ship, under whatever flag, which is proceeding to or from those ports upon its lawful occasions.

V. Immediately upon the implementation of these clauses, the British and German Governments will confer together to agree speedy arrangements for the negotiation of a full Treaty of Peace which shall be honourable to both parties, and will undertake to do everything which in their power lies to include the Sovereign Government of France into the deliberations and signature of such a treaty.

Given under our hands this .... day of ....
in the year one thousand nine hundred and forty:

For the German Government ....
For His Majesty's Government of Great Britain
....

When we had finished Wenninger and I sat looking at each other, pale and unblinking, for what seemed to be a very long time indeed. Then he disentangled the papers from his typewriter, took one of the documents, pinned it with a pin from under his lapel, and gave me the other.

I folded it neatly and put it in my pocket.

'Well,' said Wenninger. 'You like some tea?'

'I wish to God,' I told him, 'I could get out of this country tomorrow.'

He nodded and went to the door.

'Liebchen!' he shouted. 'Some tea?'

Presently Frau Wenninger came in.

163

'Lyons',' said Wenninger.

It was the first occasion I had seen Frau Wenninger since my mother's death. She came in with an odd gravity. It was clear that she was frightened too.

When I took my leave of them she held both of my hands in hers.

'You are very good men,' she said. 'I do not approve, but you are good and brave. You may both be killed. You are doing what you think is right. That is the thing.'

I felt slightly absurd, and very frightened.

[5]

That evening Wenninger sent me to the door of the hotel in the Mercedes. 'We must not seem to be afraid now,' he had said. I knew what he meant. Showing the flag. It was such an embarrassing flag. We went through our rigmarole of the Nazi salute. As I shouldn't be seeing the driver again I didn't see why I should give him any more guilders. The car sidled away. I stood for a moment or two, watching it go.

The little man with the bowler advanced upon me. He had a copy of the *Evening Standard*.

'I thought you might like to have a look at this, sir.' He held it out and I took it gratefully.

I could have sworn the man was not English.

'That's very good of you. Thanks.'

'Horrible job.' he said. 'You've no idea.'

'What job?'

'Watching people. Out here in all weathers. All day long and half the night. Just watching people. It gets me down, and no mistake.'

I couldn't think of anything to say at all.

'It's not too bad now. But in the winter I get very bad bronchitis. I tell you, it's a horrible job.'

He had a way of looking at me as if his eyes were not thinking the same thing that his lips were saying. He saw the expression on my face.

164

'I hope you don't mind me speaking to you. It's a pleasure to speak to an English gentleman.'

'Not at all,' I said.

'It isn't as if I am well paid for it. The pay's very bad. Got left behind at the end of the last war. Been here ever since. Dutch wife and a couple of kids. Sometimes I hardly know how to make ends meet.'

There was no doubt of it. The man was begging. There was something just not absolutely perfect about his pronunciation.

'I'm very sorry to hear that.'

'You're all right,' he said. 'Nobody on our side's going to make any fuss.'

I put my hand in my pocket. His face was dejected but his eyes gleamed.

'Is it all right if I—'

'Oh *thank* you, sir!'

Bribing? Begging? Extortion?

I gave him a couple of one pound notes. He saluted like a veteran of the First World War. I went upstairs to my room. Everything was not quite as I had left it.

Once again the lavatory bowl resounded through the Hotel. I had to pull the thing twice to get rid of all the pieces. The last lot to go flipped once as it went. I read the words, 'THE HIGH CONTRACTING PARTIES. . . .'

Somehow the next four days went by. For the life of me I can't remember what I did. I waited for the days and the hours and the minutes to pass, counting backwards, until I could get on that plane. The simile did not then exist, but it was exactly like the countdown for a rocket-launching.

At about six o'clock on my last night I began to toy with the distinct impression that I was going to make it. My bag was packed. A car was laid on at 7.30 the next morning to take me to the airport, on the edge of Amsterdam. Nobody had invaded anybody. Nobody had molested me. The spring sun was setting. Everything was reassuringly normal. I decided to go brazenly downstairs. Only thirteen hours and I should be on my way to London. I hoped my father would meet me and that we could go together to No. 10.

The bar was quietly busy. No sign of *The Times* man. But the two resident members of the Gestapo were at their table. One of them was knitting. The other toyed with a pinkish drink. Both had woollen spencers draped over their shoulders with the sleeves hanging down, as in Bognor or Bexhill. They inclined their heads graciously. I was minutely gracious in return.

'One very large Manhattan please.'

'One very large Manhattan coming up.'

What a fool I was to have been cowering in my room while down here were lights, Manhattans and ladies of the Gestapo.

I had never actually *met* anybody in the Gestapo, if you excepted that chap with the English name at the German Embassy in London. I began to wonder about this Gestapo business. How serious was it? I remembered my Father's stories of Himmler playing the piano in the next room of the Vier Jahreszeiten in Munich. But those people were *women*. And this was neutral Holland. They could hardly haul me away to the Lubianka or whatever their place was called. Damn it, I was supposed to be a journalist in search of a story. And damn it, this was my last night in Holland.

I approached their table.

They looked delighted. Almost as if they had been expecting the move.

'I understand,' I said ingratiatingly, 'that you're the resident members of the Gestapo.'

'Oh, no!' they cried. 'Where did you get such a silly idea?' They really looked awfully happy to see me.

'Won't you sit down,' said the young one, turning on a kind of grotesque sex-appeal.

'Well *actually*,' I said, 'I was wondering whether I could invite you ladies to dinner.'

They cooed like doves.

'That is *most* kind of you.'

'We should be *delighted*.'

'I say, how perfectly splendid.'

'Do sit down, Mr—er, Mr—er.'

'Fox Strangways,' I said at random.

'It is early yet,' said Mama. 'You must have a drink first.'
After all, it came from the bar.

'Well—perhaps just a very small Manhattan.'

The younger one laughed girlishly. 'Just a teeny-weeny
one, Mr Strangeways?'

'Strangways.'

'I am sorry. Your English names are difficult.'

The waiter brought it. No prussic acid, unless that also
was part of the service of this very superior hotel.

'Now you must tell me yours,' I said. 'I believe you're the
wife and daughter of the German Consul in Prague.'

'Not the Consul,' said Mama. 'The First Secretary of the
Embassy. It is not the same thing.'

'No, no, it's vastly superior. I do apologize.'

'We are not Germans. We are Czechs,' said Mabel.

'Really!'

'We are allies. Those terrible Germans!'

'Quite, quite,' I said. 'I say, would you mind frightfully if
we had dinner a bit early? I've got to catch a dawn plane in
the morning.'

'And you must *sleep*!' trilled Mabel. She seemed to think
she had uttered a *bon mot* of the most elaborately amusing
nature. Her mother reproved her with her eyebrows.

Both ladies rose. It was a difficult and dangerous manœu-
vre. There were reticules to be opened and bags inserted
and reticules to be closed again, and Mamma's glasses to be
popped in their case, and the knitting to be collected, and
the reticule to be opened again to receive both the glasses
and the knitting, and the flying sleeves of the spencers swept
within millimetres of a row of glasses on the next table. As
we entered the restaurant we sounded like the gun carriages
at the Royal Tournament.

'For three, please.'

'This way, Sir!'

We disposed ourselves. We ordered. 'Just something very light.'

A bottle of Liebfraumilch.

'We are great admirers,' Mama said, 'of your national poet Shakespeare.'

'Really! Do tell me—have you any idea of what is going to happen?'

Mabel froze defensively. 'Happen?'

'About the war, I mean?'

'We know nothing.'

'We know nothing,' Mama said, 'except what we read in the newspapers.'

'But not so great,' Mama continued, 'as our national poet Goethe.'

'Ah, Goethe!' Mabel exclaimed, rapt.

'Do you read Goethe, Mr Gibbs?'

'Er—Fox Strangways,' I said. It was on the tip of my tongue to tell them the story of my father and Lord North-cliffe. But, of course, his name wasn't Fox Strangways. So I changed it to, 'No, I'm afraid not.'

'Oh you should,' they cried. 'You should.'

'I don't believe he was as good as Shakespeare. Wasn't he the chap who wrote *Faust*?'

'Ah, *Faust*!' Mabel trilled ecstatically.

We toyed with a lot of soup and a little fish. I was beginning to think that this was an extraordinarily boring conversation to hold with the Gestapo. They thought so too. I intercepted a glance between them. It seemed to me they were waiting for something. Almost as if Mabel had asked 'Now?' and her mother had answered 'Not yet.'

Mama tried again. 'Have you been to Prague, Mr—er, Mr—er?'

'Yes, I have,' I told them. 'There's an exact copy of Chelsea Bridge across the river. I suppose you were there when the Germans came in?'

'We were in Italy,' said Mabel, severely. 'On holiday.'

'My husband was so fond of Italy.'

'We read about it in the newspapers.'

'The Italian newspapers?'

'Naturally.'

We had finished the fish. There was a hiatus. I began to long for a cigarette.

'Do you speak Italian?' I ploughed on.

'We speak all languages,' Mabel announced proudly.

'I suppose you have to in your job.'

They were very pained. Evidently I had violated the first canon of inter-espionage behaviour, not accepting a denial.

'I beg your pardon. Would you mind very much if I smoked a cigarette?'

Once again the odd glance between them.

'Please!' said Mama.

I pulled out my case. It was empty. I waved at a waiter.

'Could you bring me some English cigarettes?'

Mabel began to fuss girlishly with her reticule, poking delicately in its interior.

'We have English cigarettes,' she announced, and produced a packet of du Maurier.

I was never very fond of a tipped cigarette and I hesitated.

'He'll bring some more. I don't want to smoke all yours.'

'We have plenty.' She opened the lid. The box was quite full.

'Until he brings the others,' Mama urged.

I didn't want to be churlish. I took one. Mabel whipped out a lighter. Both their eyes were upon me, semi-triumphant, unashamed. I took a deep inhalation. They gazed at me with the most extraordinary expression.

'Oh well,' I said. 'Let's have some more of that wine.'

They went all gay as I poured it out. I held up my glass.

'Goethe!'

'Shakespeare!'

Their laughter tinkled like little bells. Like little bells. Tinkled like little bells. Tinkled. Just like little. . . .

169

The restaurant gave a sudden lurch. I grabbed the table. I could see them watching me. What the devil? In order to steady myself I took another drag of the du Maurier, filling my lungs. A cold serpent crawled into my head.

'Don't you feel well, Mr Gibbs?'

I certainly did not. I felt like immediate death. In the distance the waiter began approaching with more food. How he kept his balance in that lurching, plunging room was more than I could imagine. I got unsteadily to my feet.

'I'm awfully sorry. I'm terribly sorry. I'm afraid I— excuse me.'

The place was turning upside down. With a supreme effort of will I plunged out of the room and into the lift. It rose sideways. I have dreamt about this ever since. Somehow I staggered out into a heaving, undulating corridor. I got my door open, slammed it shut, and flung myself across the bed, with my arms hanging on one side and my feet on the other. I was only just in time.

Within half a second I was insensible.

[6]

My watch said twenty-five minutes past two when life returned. I had no idea what had happened to me. All I knew was that I felt like a man lying across his grave. My head was expanding and contracting like an oxygen bladder. My heart was flapping around. I was streaming with sweat. Perhaps I ought to be sick? I went to the bathroom, but didn't know how to begin. A small bottle of aspirin was on the shelf. I swallowed a couple and drank a lot of tap water. I felt sure it was the wrong treatment. It was. Brandy then? I went back into the bedroom, and as I did so I saw the tiniest movement in that horizontal handle of the door. With infinite stealth it was trying to descend.

I flung myself towards it, quite silently on the thick carpet, and watched it turn. And with the same stealth I began turning the lower handle which would lock the door.

There was no sound from the passage. But the handle went on turning. I was on my knees, turning too. We both reached forty-five degrees together. That took about three minutes. It was impossible, turning so quietly like this, to tell whether or not the bolt was going home. It might be that only in the last few seconds of travel . . .

We went on turning. The big handle was down now. A little pressure was applied to the door. More pressure. The bolt held. I stuffed my fingers into my mouth. The handle stayed vertical, and once again the woodwork of the door creaked—the bolt held. Very slowly the handle resumed the horizontal and then began to turn again.

'Oh, go away,' I shouted. 'I want to get some sleep.'

I heard faint whispers. Were they female whispers? It was impossible to tell. Then quiet footsteps. Mabel's footsteps? Or two giant S.S. men, with black gaiters and silencers in their guns?

It was about three o'clock. The room was blazing with light, as I must have left it. I had only three hours to go before my early morning call to catch that plane. It occurred to me that it would be extremely foolish to go to sleep. I began to think in terms of the trajectory of bullets, fired either through the door or through the windows. As these were opposite each other, no part of the room was really safe.

I spent the rest of the night locked in the bathroom, without a single cigarette, reading and re-reading that copy of the *Evening Standard*.

In the morning at last my breakfast came. I couldn't touch it. Very shakily indeed I made my way down to the hall. I paid my bill, spilling guilders all over the floor. I still have an impression of understanding glances. The taxi was standing at the door. I didn't see the Gestapo ladies. I didn't see my friend of the bowler. I didn't see anything. I crawled into the back of that vast machine and closed my eyes. I think I slept.

At Schipol I recovered very slightly, enough to notice

that the place seemed to be crawling with impossibly hand-some Lufthansa pilots, and air-hostesses with the face and figure of Marlene Dietrich. I cursed them mentally and found my little English plane. There was nothing to indicate that it was the last one to get out of Holland.

My father met me.

'That was a damn silly telegram of yours, old man,' he said. 'What's the good of saying, "arrange appointment afternoon"?'

'Didn't you arrange it?'

'You didn't say who with, my dear fellow.'

'Oh, for God's sake!'

We went to the R.A.C. And there, on the writing paper provided, I wrote, word for word, the entire text of 'THE HIGH CONTRACTING PARTIES' right to the bitter end. I wish I had a copy. It would have been a piece of literary curiosa. Perhaps, in the archives of Downing Street? . . .

I took it round there, unannounced. I was received, very pleasantly, by a skeletal young man who smiled uproariously at the corners of his mouth on either side of a motionless upper lip. His eyes twinkled too. He really seemed extremely amused. Mr Chamberlain's Principal Private Secretary in those days was called Lord Dunglass. He is now Sir Alec Douglas-Home.

In Whitehall the 'evening' posters were flapping.

'GERMANY INVADES HOLLAND.'
'ROTTERDAM ATTACKED.'

In the R.A.C. I looked at a copy of *The Times*. There was a short piece saying that smoke was rising from the chimneys of the German Embassy at The Hague. It was understood that they were burning documents.

The rest of the story is melodramatic.

The German Luftwaffe bombed Rotterdam into systematic dust with a ruthlessness which added a new word to the English language until they did the same to Coventry.

Wenninger did not like this. He was a good man and he had done his best. War was war, but he did not like the thought that his own Luftwaffe, in which he was a general, of which he was proud, should have done this brutal and unnecessary thing to a sprawling, undefended city of neutral, harmless Dutchmen.

Already the Germans were attacking now with their armies against a resistance which was heroic but lilliputian. They were across the Yser. The Panzer Divisions were pouring down the road to Lille. Wenninger was telephoned from Berlin, and told that, from that moment, he was to appear in public in the full uniform of a Luftwaffe general. It was an order.

Wenninger did not like this either. I can see him, in my mind's eye, in the ugly little villa on the road to Scheveningen, putting on those clothes with rabbity reluctance, and pinning on his medals.

He emerged into bright sunlight and got into that Mercedes. He was driven towards the centre of town. When they were outside the modern broadcasting studio Wenninger stopped the car and told the man to turn off the engine. He could hear something, a noise which, later, we grew to know so well, the faint asynchronous sound of many planes, still far away, but homing on their target. He knew, with certainty, they were on their way to 'Rotterdam' The Hague.

He left the car, rushed across the pavement to the great glass doors of the broadcasting station, flung through, thrust aside officials, tore up the stairs, hesitated, heard voices, pushed open the door of a studio, and burst inside.

An announcer was on the air with a hand microphone. He was reading an impassioned Dutch translation of the last speech of M. Baudouin, ringing with Churchillian phrases: 'We will fight them in the fields, we will fight them in the streets, we will fight them in the—'

Wenninger tore the microphone from his grasp and began to shout.

'Hier General von Wenninger! Hier Wenninger den

173

Haag! General von Wenninger to the General Commanding the squadron of Luftwaffe now approaching The Hague. Turn back! These are my orders! The Luftwaffe will not bomb The Hague. The Luftwaffe is to return to base immediately. Hier General—'

There was a scuffle as the Dutch announcer yanked the cord out of his hands. A great many people tried to seize Wenninger but he shook them off, ran out into the street, and shaded his hands to look into the sky.

A Dutchman with a revolver in his pocket saw a man in the full uniform of a General of the Luftwaffe and thought, 'God damn those bloody Germans,' and shot him dead.

As he lay on the pavement, surrounded by an excited crowd, the menacing thrum of the aeroplanes altered its note, and they went away.

As I have said he was a good man.

And at least we tried.

[7]

I saw the men come home from Dunkirk, and knew that I had been right. Train after train after train at some level crossing, jammed to the windows with sleeping men. I was convinced, and am still convinced, that Hitler had spared them the massacre, deliberately, partly because, being not altogether rational, he thought the English were Nordic gentlemen, and partly because he wanted a separate peace. The massacre could so easily have been arranged.

There was another thing I knew, and the knowledge made me arrange for Maisie and the two children to flee to the United States. If the German armies had cared to arrive anywhere in England in the next six weeks, with their dive bombers and their motorized columns, they could have over-run the country in six days flat, for there was nothing and nobody to stop them except a few strands of barbed wire at Littlehampton, and a posse or two of Local Defence Volunteers.

174

I went down to a place called Biggin Hill to watch the young Spitfire pilots scream their defiance at Goering's Luftwaffe. There was a large, chintzy room, with a bar at one end, and thirty or forty young men spreadeagled in easy chairs, reading old copies of *The Tatler* and *The Illustrated London News*.

Suddenly a loud-speaker would cough and crackle into life: 'Bandits six thousand angels vector one-five. Number eight squadron, SCRAMBLE!'

A dozen young men would fling down their papers and rush for the door, and the place would shake with the roar of engines.

Twenty minutes later eight young men would come back, pick up their papers where they had fallen, and resume their study of the beautiful Maharanee of Cooch-Behar.

So I went again to Lord Kemsley. I said I thought this country could possibly have 'had it', unless somebody went to get help. That meant the Americans. Kemsley agreed and sent me with a chit to the Ministry of Information. The director-general, Sir Kenneth Lee, an extremely intelligent and successful manufacturer of fabrics under the name of Tootal, took precisely one second to decide. He told me to report to the British Information Services in New York.

After sixteen days, having survived an extraordinary relic of the First World War called an Atlantic convoy, I was in the express elevator at Rockefeller Center. There was a nice chap wearing an O.E. tie. He assigned me to the 'schools and colleges division'.

The Americans were marvellously friendly, and this made it easy to be successful. Indeed, if the right thing is to make a contribution to the winning of a war, and I would agree that it might be provided that one does not take any personal part in the dishing out of death, this was my contribution.

I parked Maisie, Martin and Frances with that uncle who had married the acres in Massachusetts, and went round places like Harvard, and Boston College, and the

Massachusetts Institute of Technology, and Milton Academy and Yale, 'shooting off my mouth'. I treasure some marvellous letters of thanks from these people. I used to take them through a night of the blitz, and wring their withers with the howl of air-raid sirens, and the lapse into silence, and the distant irregular throb of German planes, and the crash of bombs, and cheerful Cockney voices in the shelters, and the riot of the ack-ack and the cries of children. . . . I used to have them sobbing in the aisles, and in a silly, ignoble sort of way, I am proud of what I did.

In the end, of course, the Japanese rounded off my job for me. Pearl Harbor was followed within hours by the American declaration of war against Germany, and I knew that, however long it took and however many people died in the process, in the end we would not lose.

The difficulty was to get home. The Ministry of Information, who had been able to arrange for me to take a few hundred dollars of my own money to America, now, rather ungratefully I thought, under the new aegis of Brendan Bracken, decided to abandon me to my fate. There was also something known as 'Exchange Control'. To put it crudely, I was stuck in the United States with a wife and two children, and I hadn't a sausage.

I had read in the papers that Alexander Korda had turned up in Hollywood with his entire organization. That must mean, thought I, that little Zoli was in residence. I sent a telegram into the blue:

ZOLIKAM STOP STUCK IN MASSACHUSETTS
MAISIE MARTIN AND FRANCES WITHOUT A
SAUSAGE STOP SOS.

Zoli was the best friend I ever had. He wired me the plane fare to Hollywood, put me in a hotel, found me a job writing a scenario for Twentieth Century-Fox, and, after I had sent for Maisie and the children, said: 'Now you can pay me back.'

176

When I had paid him back, received three thousand dollars and also a nasty little buff card calling me up, and spent an air raid—yes, a genuine air-raid on Los Angeles—locked up with Marlene Dietrich, I bought four tickets home on the good ship *Serpa Pinto*.

XI

I went down to a place in Ealing and danced, naked, in front of some young doctors. I also did an intelligence test. I never can do those things. They were the usual syllogisms and I spent much time looking for the secret trap when the obvious answer was the right one. If my naked body had impressed them I fancy they would have decided I was not officer material. However, fortunately, as I was reassuming a gentleman's habiliments they gave me the impression that the choice was mine.

'Are you dead keen to get into the Army, Sir?'

'No, not awfully,' I replied.

So I became a publisher.

In a roundabout way this was due to Princess Marie Louise.

Princess Marie Louise was so like her first cousin the Kaiser that if you scrawled that rectangular moustache on her photograph it would have been impossible to tell them apart.

Two or three times a week, at about six o'clock in the evening, an ancient sleeve-valve Daimler set out from Kensington Palace and, in a cloud of blue smoke, made the journey to Durrant's Hotel, a most respectable establishment just behind Manchester Square. Out stepped the Princess, military parasol in hand, and asked the porter if she could go up to Mrs Savory.

'Certainly, your Royal Highness,' said the porter, whose name was Arthur.

Now I knew Mrs Savory. When I was writing what seemed to me the entire weekly issue of the *Sunday Chronicle* (because I was the only man who had not been called up), including the leaders, the diplomatic correspondence, the film notes and the war commentary of Field Marshal Lord Milne, I lived at Durrant's Hotel, where I soon got to know everybody on account of the air raids.

These would generally occur at about one o'clock in the morning. The place would be peacefully asleep. Then, exactly as described in my American lectures, the sirens would start. First the mad Wagnerian chorus, then the growl down through the chromatic scale, then the long silence with one's ears pricked for the noise of the planes.

In Durrant's there were special noises. Doors opened quietly. The floor of the corridor creaked and exploded to the tiptoeing of ancient feet. Arthritic knuckles knocked with delicate insistence on rattly doors.

'Are you awake, dear?'

'Do you think we had better go down, dear?'

'I think I heard the alert, dear.'

'Oh, did you, dear?'

'Yes, dear. I think I shall go on down.'

'I suppose we'd better, dear.'

And all the old ladies, left over from the days when ladies were ladies, with blue veins in their hands and caps on their hair, and fluff at the wrists of their dressing-gowns, and grubby pom-poms on their slippers, would troop decorously down.

In the main hall, with its revolving door and its cane chairs and its two palms, Arthur would receive them. Somehow he had always found time to put on his uniform with the gold braid on the trousers and the first-war medals on his chest, but his feet were bare. There was an ageing notice propped on his desk. It bore the words ALL CLEAR. Now he would turn it round the other way. On the back it said ALERT. Then he served tea, while nasty things rained down from the skies, and the hundred-and-thirty-year-old bricks of Durrant's Hotel stirred on their foundations, and the palms rattled with faint irritation, and the staircase shifted its boards.

Mrs Savory was a bright little American lady. She was as bright as a bee, and as unafraid as the rest of them. About four feet high, she had the game touch of American aristocracy which I like so much. Her husband, she told me, had been Admiral Savory, who had moved up all the rungs of the Navy in the same places and at the same times as Lord Mountbatten, so that she took royalty in her tiny stride. She also seemed to have an unlimited stock of gin.

The combination of the two produced some fascinating evenings, after a short trial run to test my suitability for Princesses.

There wasn't a drop, said Marie Louise, in the whole of Kensington Palace. So we used to sit on Mrs Savory's bed while she sat on the upright chair, and drink the stuff out of tooth glasses.

It really was a most peculiar experience, raising an opaque glass to a female version of the Kaiser who really was—I think one must admit—responsible for the first war, at the fag end of the second. I used to cross-question her about her cousin, calling her 'Ma'am', just to be on the right side.

'What sort of man was he, ma'am?'

'Oh, a very charming man. Such a nice man. And so clever.'

'Oh, really? In what way, ma'am?'

'So clever at tennis! To see him hold the racket and two balls in the same hand and toss one of the balls up and hit it with the racket was really quite remarkable. Dear Mrs Savory! Well, perhaps a very little.'

I sometimes wonder about royalty. The point of this tangential vignette is that Mrs Savory had a son called Archie, who had just been engaged to do production by a publishing firm called Allan Wingate, which had been founded in 1944 by a brilliant young Hungarian called André Deutsch.

It was after standing for Parliament in the Liberal interest, fruitlessly, that I took the step. André Deutsch had quite remarkable projects in hand when I joined him. One was a book called *The Naked and the Dead*, by a man called Norman Mailer, which had been turned down by no fewer than seven publishers because it contained a great many four-letter words.

When I read the book I thought it was an earthy masterpiece, written by a sensitive young Jew who had suddenly found himself transplanted from Harvard to a Pacific atoll, where he had set a mental tape-recorder going in his brain and faithfully recorded everything which everybody said and did for the next two years.

Its great power, I thought, lay in its absolutely faithful accuracy, with no attempt at philosophizing, and if four-letter words were a part of that accuracy, they needed no excuse.

It was decided to go ahead, and on two Sundays before publication *The Sunday Times* appeared with an article 'boxed' in the middle of its front page, saying A BOOK WHICH SHOULD BE BANNED.

This had an extraordinarily good effect upon sales, and a very bad effect indeed upon the nerves, because there was a gentleman called the Director of Public Prosecutions just lying in wait for this sort of thing, and the last position in which I, personally, wished to find myself, after so recent an attempt to save the world, was in the dock at the Old Bailey facing a charge of obscenity—even if I had been at Oxford with Toby Matthew.

André called a board meeting. There were really only two alternatives. One was to withdraw the book hastily and admit defeat. The other was to order an immense number of fresh copies to the tune of five thousand pounds, which we did as soon as the book was cleared in the House of Commons on 21 or 22 May 1949.

[2]

When I became a publisher I had told myself it was a gentlemanly, not to say a scholarly, occupation. Yet within

181

the first six months here I was a prey to sleepless nights, with all kinds of horror staring me in the face. It has been like that ever since.

Of course, we took the courageous course. We ordered the copies to meet the orders, and got in touch with everybody we knew and pretended we knew, and begged them to write letters to the papers, protesting against this attempt to suppress a masterpiece. A flood of alarmingly eulogistic reviews spread like a rash across the pages, headed by Desmond MacCarthy. A question had been asked in the House; the copies were delivered and sold within minutes. We ordered more.

Fortunately, there was in the House of Commons at that time a gentleman called Colonel Wigg on the Government benches. Just as Toby Matthew lurked in the purlieus of the Old Bailey waiting to pounce on publishers, so Colonel Wigg lurked in the darker corridors of the Palace of Westminster, his tremendous ear to the ground for anything which might become embarrassing to the Opposition.

Colonel Wigg was absolutely marvellous. We met, if I remember correctly, at the Wig and Pen Club. We told him our story. He promised to espouse our cause and we ordered a lot more copies.

Later on Archie Savory who, if you remember, was half American, produced an American advertising man with magnificent offices in Berkeley Square, who gave it as his opinion that publishers had no idea of the uses of advertising.

'You advertise like drunken sailors,' he said.

'You don't really mean that?'

'Four inches there. Four inches here. "The book is an undoubted masterpiece . . . Desmond MacCarthy." What the heck's the good of that? What's the paper with the biggest circulation in this island?'

The *News of the World*, we told him.

'Fine! Take the whole back page of the *News of the*

World and turn it into one big coupon. I AM OVER 21. PLEASE SEND ME A COPY OF THE NAKED AND THE DEAD.

We stuffed our fingers into our mouths.

We couldn't do it. We couldn't possibly do it. But later, at least a year after we had been given a definite undertaking not to prosecute, and we had already sold a hundred and fifty thousand copies of the book at a guinea, and I had written the largest cheque I ever wrote in my life—£17,500 in favour of Norman Mailer—and André Deutsch had left us to found the firm of his name, we brought out a cheap edition at ten shillings, and we put in that very advertisement. Not a whole page, but big enough to cost a fortune:

I AM OVER TWENTY-ONE. PLEASE SEND ME A COPY OF THE NAKED AND THE DEAD. I ENCLOSE 10/–d.

The next morning nine taxis came in convoy down Beauchamp Place, piled high with sacks of ten-shilling notes. We spent the rest of the day counting them. Nine thousand the first day. We sold two hundred thousand copies of that edition. That makes three hundred and fifty thousand. A year later I sold the paper-back rights to Panther for three thousand five hundred pounds. I believe they have sold something like four hundred thousand copies to date.

Another book André had was the story of the valet who borrowed his sleeping ambassador's keys, photographed the contents of the ambassadorial safe, and sold the negatives to the Germans for vast numbers of £5 and £10 notes which turned out to be forgeries. We called it *Operation Cicero* and had a great deal of fun with it, including tea, somewhere near Canterbury, with Sir Hughe Knatchbull-Hugessen, who was the ambassador in question and submitted to our impudent researches with no loss of dignity.

We plastered the tube stations with posters of a headless man saying 'Who is Cicero?' and were about to rain them down on the rooftops of London from a peripatetic helicopter until an ex-R.A.F. pilot discovered that this would be breaking some law.

But I want to get on to Charles Fry.

[3]

When André, who was a man full of publishing enthusiasm, departed to inaugurate André Deutsch Ltd, I found myself in the menacing position of owning a majority holding in a publishing firm, and a flaw in my character which makes it quite impossible for me to run my own business.

I am not, I believe, unintelligent. In fact, if I may lower the mask for one moment, I have, beneath the dross, one of the most mighty of brains. My understanding of the full implication of $E = MC^2$ is surpassed only by that of the Creator. I know exactly where Darwin and Julian Huxley go off the rails in the matter of natural selection. I know that both Gamow and Fred Hoyle are completely at sea in their contrasting theories of the creation of matter, because they have both been led astray by the Red Shift. I am perfectly prepared to explain about the 'adaptability mechanism' in the individual cell, to define time as 'relative movement', to prove that time, therefore, is an essential constituent of matter, and that a hundred and eighty-six thousand miles a second, squared, is the 'wavelength', to use the wrong word, of our cosmos. But if I tell somebody I expect them to turn up at the office not later than a quarter to ten in the morning, or to draw up a contract with an author giving him a royalty of ten per cent up to three thousand, or to pop over and bring me some sandwiches from the pub, they don't do it. They don't laugh in my face. They just fail to respond.

Charles Fry arrived most opportunely in the firm.

He had been sent off by the established firm of Batsford, with its strong architectural tendencies, to open a branch in New York. Charles literally went to town. He bought a freehold house just round the corner from Fifth Avenue, and flew out Aubusson carpets to lay on the floors. When Batsfords received a bill for something in the region of fifty-seven thousand pounds, they gave him a handshake of two thousand pounds. André got him for Wingate's; I made him joint managing director with myself after André left.

Charles Fry was, in most ways, the most civilized man I have ever known. His knowledge of architecture, painting, history, writing, food, character, motive and the intricacies of royal bastardy was inexhaustible. His manners were on the 'grand' side. He knew everybody, and Christian-named them all, from Willy Maugham to Tom Eliot, John Betjeman, Bob Boothby, Dylan Thomas, Gerald Hamilton, and Gerry (the Duke of) Wellington. Fortunately, to balance my disability, he had flaming red hair, and when he began to rap on the table at a mounting tempo, which meant that an explosion was imminent, people ran at the double to execute his lightest request.

He was also a confirmed alcoholic.

As a confirmed smoker myself I can understand and sympathize with the taking of a drug which becomes essential to life. I can no more do without cigarettes than I could do without air. Charles could not live without alcohol. This is pardonable. But I never ceased to be amazed at the quantity which he found essential.

When he first arrived at the office in the morning he trembled so much that the ash tray would set up a sympathetic vibration on the table. There was, and still is, a pub immediately opposite in Beauchamp Place. As eleven o'clock came and went, Charles's eyes would flit towards its bolted door. At eleven-thirty, humming a little ditty, he would slip from the room, cross the road with irritable gestures at the traffic, enter The Grove, remain within for perhaps eighty-seven seconds, and return, restored to urbanity.

I have no idea how much he drank in a couple of quick swallows. My guess would be three double gins.

At twelve-forty-five one or other of us would suggest lunch.

Charles had discovered a marvellous place called The Belfry, just off Belgrave Square, where the chef was an *émigré* from the Imperial Palace at St Petersburg. The food was amazing. So was the place, which was in the only 'failed' church I know.

A quick one at the pub to stay him during the short taxi ride would take Charles to his table and two large dry martinis. Bottles of wine would follow, and so would several glasses of Armagnac. At this stage of the proceedings Charles was not in the slightest degree 'drunk'. His conversation was enormously amusing and—I can only repeat the word—civilized. Authors loved it.

Round about four o'clock the table in the office would begin to shake again. In the office I always insisted on Lapsang Souchong at four. Charles's cup wilted, untasted. By five the ashtrays were dancing. At five-fifteen Charles was on the pavement outside The Grove, looking at his watch, peering through the window, rattling the letter-box. At five-thirty to the second Charles went in with the opening door.

'Large whisky, please.'

'Good evening, Mr Fry.'

'Large whisky, please.'

The glass scarcely touched the bar.

'Thanks, Richard. Another large whisky, please.'

From that moment, until he went to bed, the large whiskies followed at fifteen-minute intervals. That would add up to about twenty. He did not eat again. I can remember a thousand evenings in that place with people like Peter de Polnay and Lord Killanin and Dylan Thomas, and that man from the B.B.C. René Cutforth who told the story of the Queen of Spain who entered into things with a little too much bravura and danced with a little too much abandon at

186

a Buckingham Palace Ball, so that in a moment of unforced gaiety, one of her breasts became exposed.

Dylan Thomas considered this gravely.

'Would that,' he asked, 'have been the long one or the short one?'

Dylan Thomas was one of the people always to be relied upon for company at Charles's elevenses.

In those days he was completely unknown except to the most esoteric inner circle of the cognoscenti. Charles went across to the pub one day and came back in a state of unusual exhilaration. He told me he had offered Dylan a thousand pounds for a radio script he was thinking of offering to the B.B.C., and pressed a pink folder into my hand.

I looked at Charles with horror and foreboding. We didn't pay prices like that, and we didn't publish radio scripts. And the folder was labelled 'Llareggub'. I could see I had a first-class row on my hands.

'Bugger all,' said Charles. 'Spelt backwards. Don't you think it's an awfully amusing idea?'

It didn't strike me as an amusing idea at all. Charles was humming joyfully to himself. To spend a thousand pounds, just like that, when we didn't possess it, mingled with the gin to induce a facial expression of indecent euphoria.

I exploded. I told him to stop looking like the Cheshire Cat, to go straight back to the pub, explain to Thomas that he had made a dreadful mistake, hand him back the manuscript and call off the deal.

Charles's face puckered and two large tears gathered in his eyes. But he put on his camel-hair coat again, and went across like a naughty small boy to do what he was told.

It was I who made the dreadful mistake. Llareggub was the first, working title of *Under Milk Wood*.

Another of the people Charles knew was Guy Burgess.

Towards the finish of the evening Charles's voice would become grander and grander, and then he would break into French, so that one knew the end was near. He would recite, in the manner of Chairman Mao thinking to himself, a few snatches from François Villon and then recommend everybody, still in French and with an air of revealing the ultimate secret of the universe, to read a book by Stendhal called *Les Caves du Vatican*.

That was the signal. The last taxi would be flagged, and kept waiting. Charles would yawn, delicately behind the back of his hand, rise with just a shade too much dignity, embrace the company in a final Chestertonian gesture of farewell, and be heard in the street calling 'Taxair! Taxair!', as if the thing were rushing past at forty miles an hour. The door would slam. 'Nell Gwyn House!' he commanded with distaste, and was driven away in a diminishing crescendo of sound.

At four in the morning he awoke in his little beehive and, he told me, swallowed vast quantities of Vitamin B. It appeared to do the trick. He awoke for the second time, 'absolutely radiant'. In the mornings he always needed more alcohol, not less.

[4]

I assume that everybody knows about the Burgess and Maclean affair? I am always being caught out by this. A book of mine was published the other day with some references to Hore-Belisha. We gave it a launching party, and I thought it would be nice to invite Mrs Hore-Belisha. So I rang up the War Office. No one had ever heard of her. There was also something about D notices in it, and when I told the P.R.O. lady who was handling the affair that Colonel Lohan was the spitting image of Field Marshal von Hindenburg, she replied, 'Who's that?'

If you don't know B. and M. I am too impatient to explain. They had just gone to Russia.

One day a strong American voice came through on the telephone.

'I want to talk,' he said, 'with someone in authority.'

Charles and I looked at each other with apprehension.

The Income Tax authorities? Some American gunman?

'Speaking,' we said in one joint voice over our respective telephones.

'Oh. Well, say, listen. Do you have a Mr Charles Fry around?'

I could feel Charles's spirit sink into his boots.

'Yeah,' I said, reverting to my other language. 'Who wants him?'

'I have a message for Mr Charles Fry. Strictly incognito.'

'Yeah?'

'Yeah.'

'Oh, for God's sake stop saying "yeah" at each other,' said Charles irritably. 'Who are you? What do you want?'

'Is that Mr Fry?'

'Yes, it is! Will you please stop wasting my time?'

'It's from Mr Burgess.'

Charles and I looked at each other. Mr Burgess? Mr *Burgess*?

'D'you mean Mr *Guy* Burgess?'

'You said it.'

A silent minute passed. A message from Guy Burgess? On the other side of the Iron Curtain? What sort of message? Any sort of message was probably worth about £5,000 to a Press who had hunted Burgess with all their best men for weeks. Was this the beginning of the greatest publishing scoop in history?

'Well,' said the voice, 'do I come around?'

'I think you'd better,' I said in English.

He came around in forty-seven seconds. He must have been telephoning across the street.

He was a thin, wiry little man, with a tanned and pock-marked face, and a hairline moustache, a natty tropical suit and intelligent remorseless eyes. One instinctively looked for the bulges in his clothing. They were there.

'That's right,' he agreed, holding out a hand to each of us in turn. 'I come armed. This is kinda outside my line. Normally they use me as the hatchet man. Which of you is Mr Fry?'

189

'He is,' I said hastily.

'Well, don't look so scared the both of you!'

'I'm not in the least scared as you call it.'

The deadly eyes twinkled and the hairline moustache curled into a catlike grin.

'Do I sit down then?'

Charles waved him to a chair and remained standing.

The little man sat down and crossed his legs, taking a great deal of trouble with his thumbs and forefingers to dispose of his trouser creases.

'You can call me Mr Farinetti.'

'But isn't that your name?'

'What do *you* think?'

'I don't think anything,' I told him, 'except that you seem to be an American.'

'I've lived in the States, but I'm Italian. Born in Naples. I told you, Farinetti.'

'Very well, Mr Farinetti,' said Charles. 'Perhaps you could explain yourself in somewhat greater detail.'

'Surely. Well—I work for a little organization. An international organization. We perform—you might say "services".'

Charles and I thought of it together. Bumping off.

'What sort of services?'

'*Any* kind of services. You want something done? We do it. Nice—clean—easy. No questions asked. I told you.' His thin hand came down in the karate chop. 'Anywhere in the world. No frontiers can stop us. We don't cross frontiers. We pass the instructions across frontiers. Instructions don't need passports. Cuts out all that forged papers stuff. So! We gotta message for Mr Charles Fry from Moss-cow.'

Charles sat down, took out a cigarette, and tried to light it with his gold lighter. It travelled in a half-inch arc.

'And the message?' I asked.

'He wants out.'

'You mean—he wants us to get him out?'

'Crazy. The guy's only been there inside of six weeks.'

This *was* the greatest publishing scoop in history!

190

'I don't see how.'

'Three things,' explained Mr Farinetti, with surprising patience. 'Ten grand deposited in a bank in Switzerland.' He held up one very thin finger. Then another. 'An assurance from your government that he won't be arrested in this country.' A third finger joined the other two. 'We'll undertake the transportation. For a price.'

'What price?'

'Another grand?'

'One grand for the organization?'

'Check.'

'Pounds or dollars?'

Mr Farinetti threw back his head at that. 'Now now!' exclaimed Mr Farinetti. 'Who are you kidding?'

Charles and I looked at one another. We didn't have eleven grand. We didn't even have one grand. You know how it is. But there is a very valuable little custom in publishing whereby an author who demands a heavy advance will always accept the sum in a conveniently split condition, one quarter on signature of the agreement, one quarter on delivery of the MS and so on.

'One quarter down,' I suggested, 'the rest on delivery.'

'Suits me,' Mr Farinetti agreed at once. 'In dirty one-pound notes if you don't mind.'

'Two-fifty advance on commission in dirty one-pound notes?'

'Check.'

'Just a minute,' said Charles. 'Before any actual money passes, how do you know you can do what you say?'

Mr Farinetti grinned at me, vulpine. 'Your friend's kinda hard to convince, ain't he? O.K. Okay fellers, tell you what! You send your friend in Moscow a message. Send him a trick message. Something no one else will understand. Fold it up very small. If we bring back the right answer it's a deal. Howzat?'

We nodded at him.

'Fine, fine and dandy.'

'And how do we get in touch with you?'

'You don't. I contact you.'

'And the name's Farinetti?'

'Like I said,' Mr Farinetti agreed briskly. 'Oh, just one thing. Don't start checking. It won't get you anywhere. And don't tell nobody. *Nobody*, understand? Especially the police, otherwise . . .' He patted one of his bulges.

We swallowed and rose to our corporate feet.

'I'll call you,' said Mr Farinetti. 'At eleven-fifteen tomorrow.' He rose to his full height of four feet eleven. He held out a sinewy hand. 'Mr Fry. Mr Gay-ubs.' He turned cockily on his heel. In the gangster film Charles and I would have fired instantly, once each. The door closed behind him.

I stared at Charles.

'James,' said Charles suddenly.

'James?'

'James Pope-Hennessy.'

'I don't understand.' We had published a charming little book by Pope-Hennessy, all about the West Indian islands. He was a delicate, sensitive writer, the younger son of the redoubtable Dame Una.

Charles banged the table irritably with his fists. 'Do I have to spell everything out? James was collaborating with Guy, just when he disappeared, on a life of Lady Gwendoline Cecil!'

'I still don't get it.'

'The message, you ass! Some reference to something in the book!'

I slammed my desk shut, locked it, and put the key in my pocket.

'Come on!' I said.

He already had his camel-hair coat on and was at the door, humming an impatient little song.

James Pope-Hennessy lived in Ladbroke Grove. There were trees and respectable Victorian Houses and a steep hill leading up. He had the upstairs part of a corner shop. A red telephone box stood just outside. It was very peaceful. It almost slumbered.

192

I drove Charles in the old Rolls and we parked immediately outside with that wonderfully firm and positive click of the ratchet.

James received us politely and proffered sherry.

Charles snorted a bit at the sherry, and together we spilled the story over him. He was extremely amused and excited. The dirty one-pound notes struck him as particularly fruitful in its implications. When we got on to Farinetti's bulges and his phrase about the hatchet man, I thought he became rather less enthusiastic.

In fact he began to refuse to have anything to do with it. He said something about 'the family' and his brother's position at the Victoria and Albert Museum.

'Oh, come on, James!' we cried. 'It's terribly funny. Come on, for goodness' sake!'

Rather reluctantly he rose from his seat and went to his typewriter. 'A small piece, I think you said!'

'That's right.'

He tapped out two lines, tore off the paper carefully and handed it to us.

'DEAR GUY, ARE YOU STILL INTERESTED IN THE SECOND VOLUME OF LADY GWENDOLINE? JAMES.'

We hugged ourselves. This was real cloak-and-dagger stuff.

I folded the missive over about eight times so that it made a tight little packet about an inch square and put it in my wallet.

'You don't think anyone in Moss-cow could possibly know who Lady Gwendoline was?'

'I should think it highly improbable. Have *you* ever heard of Lady Gwendoline?'

'Never!'

'Well, then!'

'Supposing the answer comes back "Dear James, Yes I am. Guy"?'

'Then we know it's a forgery. Isn't that right, Charles?'

'Could I have some more of your ghastly sherry?'

'Help yourself.'

'Ugh!' said Charles, doing so. '*Sherry!*'

'There's just one thing,' said Pope-Hennessy. 'I think you ought to inform the police.'

We looked at him aghast. 'And spoil the biggest publishing scoop of the century?'

'And risk the hatchet man?'

'Don't be so craven!' said Charles. 'Really!'

'I'm not being craven. I'm being patriotic.'

'If you do that,' Charles assured him with terrible emphasis, 'I shall never speak to you again!'

There was a battle of eyes. Charles was always a bit exophthalmic, especially after two glasses of sherry. He also, when roused, blew himself up and reddened like a turkey cock.

'Very well,' yielded Pope-Hennessy, precisely.

All the way back to Beauchamp Place in the Rolls I was subjected to an irritating little French *chanson*. I dropped him at the pub and went to park the car. When I got back the first thing I heard was his voice.

'Large whisky, please.'

'You know, Charles, I believe we could sell this thing to Sam Campbell for five thousand pounds.' Sam Campbell was the editor of *The People*.

'Isn't it too soon?'

'No, I think now.'

'Supposing we don't get an answer?'

'That's why I say "now".'

'Five grand?'

'Five grand. Shall I try?'

'What about "don't tell nobody"?'

'Damn it, he expects us to publish.'

He put his glass on the bar.

'Ten grand,' said Charles. 'Large whisky please.'

[5]

That afternoon I went to see Sam.

He lived in a small glass case in one corner of a vast, girdered, ink-smelling room, crowded with men in shirt-sleeves banging away at typewriters. Hannan Swaffer was always there, his tie twisted twice round his collar like a character out of Dickens. So was Gilbert Harding, near to tears.

'Dear boy, dear boy,' said Sam. 'What can I do for you?'

He was a cheerful, friendly man. We lunched sometimes at The Ivy. He looked as if he wore a wig, but after years of covert inspection I am not sure that he did.

Without a word I took the little wad out of my wallet and handed it to him.

He opened it as though it contained pearls. He read it, and his eyes flashed. He was a pretty good journalist, was Sam.

'Guy?' he whispered.

'Guy Burgess,' I whispered back.

'Phew!' said Sam. 'You're on to something this time.'

'That's what I thought.'

'What's the story?'

I told him. The little Italian. The organization passing things over frontiers. The message to Charles Fry. Burgess wanting to get out. The ten grand in Switzerland. The test message. The hatchet man. The police.

Sam was bouncing in his chair.

'My God!' he kept saying. 'My God! This is stupendous! This is fantastic! This is a world beater! Can I meet this little man? What's his name?'

'You can *call* him Mr Farinetti. But I don't think you can.'

'Look, dear boy!' He seized both my shoulders. 'You've got to let me in on this! You've got to play it absolutely with me! This is much too big for you. You'll get into trouble. You'll get bumped off.'

'I promised I wouldn't tell.'

'Laddie!' said Sam reasonably. 'You're too small. You're tiny. You haven't the resources.'

'Resources?'

'Legal departments. Publicity. Influence. Crime reporters. People don't bump off newspapers, they get found out!'

'If you start publishing the story now, the whole thing will fall flat in our faces. We shall never get an answer.'

'Oh, my dear simple-minded fellow!'

I laughed.

'Be serious, laddie! For God's sake, be serious! I want to meet this little man. I want to be in on this right from the beginning. I know how to handle a story. And remember, old boy, *resources*!' He paused. 'Have *you* got ten grand to deposit in Switzerland?'

'No,' I said, 'we haven't.'

He spread his hands. The point was won.

'I was rather hoping to sell you the serial rights.'

He leaned back in his swivel chair with a helpless squeak of springs.

'Of course you're trying to sell me the serial rights! I'm trying to buy them!'

I sighed. 'All right,' I said. 'How much would you pay?'

He eyed me.

'If we get an answer.'

'If you get an answer.'

'That's right.'

He got up from the swivel chair and walked once round to the glass case. Then he sat down again.

'Ten grand if you get an answer.'

'And if we get him out?'

'A hundred thousand pounds?' suggested Sam.

[6]

Punctually at eleven-fifteen the next morning the telephone girl came in, much flustered.

'It's that same man again,' she said. 'Wants to speak to someone in authority.'

Thirty-seven seconds later Mr Farinetti was at the door.

Without a word he went to the armchair he had occupied before, sat down, arranged his creases, crossed his legs, pulled the wrinkles out of his socks, and held out one hand.

I took the wallet out of my pocket, found the Pope-Hennessy message and put it in his hand.

He opened his coat, took out a wallet, put it inside and replaced it.

'Never use a hip pocket,' he said. 'Let's see. Today's Toosday. Say fifty-six hours. And another fifty-six. That's one hundred twelve. Say five days. Sunday. Or don't you guys work Sunday?'

'Not usually.'

'I know. English gentlemen.'

'On an occasion of this sort—'

Mr Farinetti held up his hand.

'No!' he said. 'No! We gotta observe the customs of the country. Regulations!'

Charles began tapping the table. 'My dear Mr Farinetti—'

He was interrupted firmly. 'Cops! They know. Has Mr Fry or Mr Gay-ubs ever visited his office on a Sunday? Then how come he's visiting now? Must be sump'n up. Say, didn't we see a little guy going in there last Toosday? Maybe there's some connection? Say, he had a muss-tache on his face, but he was kinda like that little runt Farinetti, alias—well alias.'

'And did you?' I asked.

'The muss-tache you mean?'

'Yes.'

'Sure. Specially for the occasion! How d'you like it?'

'It suits you.'

'As a matter of interest,' Charles said, 'where do you telephone from?'

Mr Farinetti grinned, and his index finger pointed vertically downwards.

We both stared at it, nonplussed.

'Down below?'

'Yup.'

'Our basement, you mean?'

'Hell, you don't expect me to pay my own telephone calls?'

Mr Farinetti was making fun of us. He took pity.

'Cops don't notice basements. Down eight or nine steps and you're in. But start banging around on front doors and chatting up receptionists and would you wait in there please, and brother . . . But you won't see me here again.'

'Oh?' we said.

'Twice is twice too many. Now don't write this down. And don't make mistakes.' Mr Farinetti was suddenly serious. 'Monday, 11 a.m. Check?'

'Check.'

'Three four three Soho Place. Check?'

'Where's that?'

'You'll find it. Check?'

'Check.'

'No taxis nearer'n Piccadilly Circus. Then walk. Check?'

'Check.'

'Three four three,' said Charles to me. 'Can you remember that?'

'You'd better,' said Mr Farinetti grimly. 'Walk right in. Second floor. I guess you call it first floor. One floor above ground level. Check?'

'Check.'

'Door on left. Open it. Go right in. Check?'

'I wish you'd stop saying "check",' cried Charles. 'You sound like a gangster.'

'I *am* a gangster, Mr Fry.' He put his hand where the wallet was and showed the blue butt of a weapon which looked as if it could decimate a regiment. '*Check!*'

'Oh, all right,' grumbled Charles. 'Check.'

198

'That's better. Two hundred and fifty, soiled, one-pound notes. In a valise for easy carrying. Check?'

Charles waved feebly.

'Check,' I said.

'What's the number again?'

'Three four three.'

'Fine, got a good memory. Remember one other thing?'

'I know. The cops.'

'Say!' exclaimed Mr Farinetti. 'You're catching on! And when you're walking, don't trust *anybody*. Not with all that money. People in the street, guys with handcarts—watch it.'

'There's just one other small point. Can we bring someone else?'

Mr Farinetti's eyes went steely, like the barrels of twin revolvers.

'He's a newspaper editor.'

The steel pupils narrowed to a sharper focus.

'I know we weren't supposed to tell a soul, but we *are* publishers, and you must have known—you must have intended—that we should publish the story. Otherwise, why the eleven grand?'

'This had better be good.'

'We don't have the eleven grand. So I sold the story to a newspaper.'

'How much for?'

'I'm not going to tell you. Sorry!'

Mr Farinetti considered this for about three minutes. Then his eyes changed and he laughed suddenly. It was a sort of cackle. He rose to his feet.

'Oh, well,' he said. 'What's the odds? Two stiffs? Three stiffs?'

He gave us a nod and went.

[7]

That afternoon I went around to the Midland Bank in Sloane Street with a brief case in my hand and laid a cheque on the counter.

'Pay self. Two hundred and fifty pounds.'

'Could you cash that, please?'

'Certainly, sir.'

A few whispered conversations took place. There was one of those embarrassing pauses. Somebody came back and whispered a reassurance.

'Certainly, Mr Gibbs. How would you like it?'

'Could I have it in dirty one-pound notes, please?'

The man didn't bat an eyelid. He stooped down behind the counter, opened a drawer, produced twenty-five packets and began counting them with that satisfying little flick of each note. I stuffed them in my briefcase, thanked him very much, flung it into the Rolls and drove down to Peaslake.

Six days after Toosday I drove back again to town. We had arranged to meet Sam Campbell outside the Windmill Theatre fifteen minutes before the witching hour, and as we got out of the taxi, there he was.

'Dear boys, dear boys,' he said. 'Is this safe, I wonder?'

I wondered too. I didn't really believe in that answer from Moscow. I thought it far more probable that we should go through some door, get slugged from behind, and lose a briefcase full of notes.

'Can anybody remember the number?'

'Three four three. D'you know where it is?'

'That sort of open-air market just off Denmark Street.'

'Shall we chuck it?' asked Charles.

'Not on your life, dear boy.'

'Let's chuck it.'

We looked at one another. We very nearly chucked it. But somehow we started walking. I had the briefcase. We walked very slowly among the unattractive crowds of Shaftesbury Avenue. All the women looked like tarts and all the men like Mr Farinetti. We turned into the maze. The place reeked of rich cooking and rancid coconut butter. Cabbage leaves littered the road. Vegetable stalls and indecent publication stalls. There was an organ-grinder. He was grinding away opposite a house with the number 343 on a window above the door. Sam stopped. I had an odd sensation of being watched. I got ready to let go of the briefcase, fast. Then I caught the organ-grinder's eye, and it seemed to me there was recognition in it.

'It's empty,' said Sam. 'It's an empty house.'

'Well let's get the bloody thing over with.'

Charles was already half across the street. Taking great care not to look over our shoulders, we kept pace with him. Sam Campbell pushed the door. It opened with a dilapidated creak. The place was deserted, silent and dirty. Charles was humming. Our footsteps echoed on the stairs.

'First on the left.'

Charles kicked open the door violently.

'After you,' he said.

Sam Campbell walked in. We followed.

'No one here,' said Sam. 'D'you think——?'

'You guys nervous?' asked the voice of Mr Farinetti. We spun round. He came out grinning from behind the door where Charles's kick had imprisoned him. I experienced a second's wonder at his foreknowledge. He must have been waiting in exactly that place for exactly that to happen. Mr Farinetti was enjoying himself. His hair-line muss-tache was unashamedly sadistic.

'Not in the least nervous,' Charles declared. 'Merely slightly ridiculous. Rather disinclined to continue with this charade.'

'Got the dough, I see,' Mr Farinetti pointed out.

'It's full of newspapers,' I told him.

Mr Farinetti tut-tutted. 'Introduce me.'

'Ah, yes. Mr Farinetti, you can call him that. Mr Campbell, Editor of *The People*.'

'Glad to know you, *sir*.'

'Got the message?' Charles asked.

With a due sense of the drama involved, Mr Farinetti searched in his pockets and finally discovered a small folded piece of blue paper. He unfolded it slowly, smoothed it, and held it out. We grabbed it and huddled round.

It was written, in blue ink, on a badly registering portable typewriter:

DEAR JAMES, I AM VERY INTERESTED IN THE PLAIN. GUY.

It looked extraordinarily genuine. There was something about that irregular line of type which immediately evoked the picture of Burgess, sitting in some hotel room, tapping it out on an old and battered English machine.

'I don't understand what it means. "I am very interested in the plain". It doesn't make sense.'

'Very interested in the plain.'

'What plain?'

'Any ideas, Mr Farinetti?' Sam asked.

'Me, I'm illiterate,' said Mr Farinetti.

'Is there a telephone?' Charles asked.

'Help yourself,' said Mr Farinetti, pointing. There was one, sitting on the floor in the corner, with a few scraps of paper.

Charles picked it up with distaste and dialled. The burr-burr echoed in the empty room. A click.

'James?'

'Who's that?'

'It's me.'

'Oh, is that you, Charles?'

'We've er—we've had an answer.'

Silence.

'I say, we've had an answer. Are you there?'

'Of course I'm here.'

'I'll read it to you: "Dear James, I am very interested in the plain. Guy."'

Silence.

'Well?'

There came a torrent of words with only the last two audible. 'Utterly convincing.'

'What's it mean? We don't know what it means.'

'Victorian joke,' came the tinny sound of Pope-Hennessy.

'Lady Gwendoline Cecil. The ugly daughter of Lord Salisbury. Known to her contemporaries as "Salisbury Plain".'

Charles put the receiver back with a clonk. Then he put the machine back and wiped his fingers with a handkerchief.

'Did you hear?'

'Yes,' we said.

We stood in a little group, still staring at that piece of paper. No Russian, no Italian, could possibly have faked that Victorian joke.

'Satisfied, gentlemen?'

I pushed the briefcase towards Mr Farinetti with my foot.

'Got the numbers?'

'No.'

'Okay. Now! I have a verbal message. The guy who wants to get out. He has a speaking engagement in Yugoslavia three weeks on Friday. He has another four days later. So he has four days. Yugoslavia's easy, compared with Moss-cow. All he has to do is rent a small boat—'

'Look,' Sam interrupted him, 'can we possibly discuss all this in my office, dear boy, where we can sit down in comfort and make notes?'

Mr Farinetti blenched.

'We've gone through your comic rigmarole. You've got your money. We're convinced of the genuiness of the message. For heaven's sake let's behave like grown men. Either you come to my office, or we don't go a step further.'

Mr Farinetti seemed to dissolve round the edges. He licked his lips. They were white.

'I can get taken for a ride too, you know.'

'Taken for a ride?'

'Sure. Bumped off somewhere. I ain't the boss. I'm the hatchet. And I ain't the only hatchet man.'

'Damn it,' said Sam. 'This is London, not Chicago.'

'You don't know the half of it!'

'Well, I'm sorry. This is an ultimatum. We've trusted you. Now you trust us. If you want your money, that is.'

'No—no cops?'

'Cross my heart. No cops.'

Mr Farinetti sighed. 'If you say so.'

'Good. Good boy! Stout fellow!'

Mr Farinetti opened the door. There seemed to be quite a lot of people suddenly outside. He jerked his head at the briefcase. One of them picked it up.

'I'll be out for a while,' said Mr Farinetti.

We got into a taxi. On the way Mr Farinetti revived somewhat. I cannot explain any of this. I merely record. We arrived at *The People* offices. A great many heads turned as we filed through. Sam sent for extra chairs and coffee. Mr Farinetti became almost human. I wondered whether he was experiencing a sense of safety, temporarily removed from his gang.

'Now,' said Sam, taking a piece of paper. 'You want ten thousand pounds at a bank in Zurich?'

'Check.'

'In whose name?'

'Mr Burgess.'

'Mr Burgess?'

'Sure. You didn't think that was for the organization? We don't operate that way.'

'Very commendable. Right, dear boy. I'll fix that. What else?'

'The organization in Yugoslavia will put Mr Burgess on a boat. Would you three gentlemen be prepared to meet Mr Burgess in mid-Adriatic?'

'You bet we would!'

'You might have to—persuade him a little. He's kinda scared.'

'We'll risk that.'

'You might have to persuade the crew a little.'

'Persuade?'

'Well,' said Mr Farinetti, 'you know how it is.'

'Money?'

'Maybe money.'

'Guns?'

204

'Could be,' said Mr Farinetti.

Sam Campbell put down his pencil, and took it up again. He wrote the word 'guns'.

'Anything else?'

'Sure. The French organization has a bullet-proof car garaged in Nice. If you three gentlemen—'

'A bullet-proof car? What the hell for?'

'Don't under-estimate the Iron Curtain, fellahs. Could be quite handy. It's an Opel Kapitan.'

'Good God. Well, go on.'

'The French organization will pick you three gentlemen up in Nice at midnight on the fifteenth, cross the Italian border in the mountains and hand you over to the Italian organization who will drive you to Ravenna. In Ravenna there's a bar, run by an Englishman. Name of Randall. He knows about us. You should be there around five in the afternoon. Go to the bar and stay inside until midnight on the sixteenth. Mr Randall has a boat. He'll take you out to meet Mr Burgess. If you get him, you'll drive to Switzerland. Mr Burgess will stay in Switzerland until he has a categorical assurance that the British Foreign Office won't order an arrest if he arrives in this country. Check?'

'Check,' we said faintly.

XII

Five days later the Wingate telephone girl buzzed. We had a new buzzer. It amplified all calls so that we could listen and speak from any part of the room.

'There's a gentleman,' she said, 'who wishes to speak with somebody in authority.'

'Oh, no!' Charles cried. 'Not again!'

'Better show him in.'

We fastened our eyes about half-way up the door, expecting Mr Farinetti. Instead an enormous man appeared with his head very near the ceiling. He had a moustache, quite unlike Mr Farinetti's. A euphonium player, I thought.

'Good afternoon, gentlemen!'

'Good afternoon,' we chorused with a rising note of enquiry.

'I'm an Inspector from Scotland Yard.'

It didn't seem possible to be faced by a real inspector from Scotland Yard, straight out of detective fiction. All the same we scrambled to our feet.

'I understand that you've been in touch with Guy Burgess.'

I knew what Charles was thinking. I was thinking it, too. The hatchet man would have his hatchet out.

'Whoever told you that?' I asked innocently.

'No names no pack-drill,' murmured the inspector.

'I never know what that means. Is it something out of Kipling?'

'It means I'm not telling. It's true though, isn't it?'

Charles was oddly silent.

'I'm not going to tell you a thing,' I said.

206

'It's extraordinary,' continued the inspector. 'Shameful in a way. Here's the entire police force trying to get in touch with that man, and a couple of civilians, apparently respectable people, beat us to it. You are respectable people, aren't you?'

'Extremely,' I said.

'You're the son of Sir Philip Gibbs. You, Mr Fry, are the nephew of Admiral Lord Fisher. And Mr Pope-Hennessy is the son of Dame Una Pope-Hennessy. It would be hard to find three *more* respectable people.'

Charles was silent. Suddenly I knew why he was silent. He had told somebody. After the twelfth double whisky. What's more, I knew whom he had told.

'Well,' the inspector encouraged us genially, 'are we going to have it?'

The conversation seemed to have devolved upon me. I decided to make him a speech.

'I'm awfully sorry, I'm not going to tell you a thing.'

'So there is a thing?'

'It's faintly possible that we may be in touch with Guy Burgess. Personally I'm not at all convinced. The whole thing could probably be a hoax. But we're publishers. And if it isn't a hoax it's the greatest publishing scoop of all time. We aren't breaking any laws. And I'm not going to share it with the police.'

He turned to Charles Fry.

'Do you agree with that?'

'Absolutely.'

'Very well then,' said the Inspector sadly. 'We'll have to find out the hard way.'

'The hard way?'

'Telephone tapping. Following you about. It's not nice, you know. Not for respectable people. What beats me is, how you *managed* it!' He shook his head. 'Poor old police force. Still, I expect we'll ferret it all out. I'll be discreet, of course. We'll put a chap on this building. Not in uniform. And there'll be a chap in the pub, which I believe you frequent? And d'you mind a chap or two in uniform, just looking into shop windows?'

'Not at all.'

'Sure you won't tell?'

I shook my head.

'Ah, well. We'll probably meet again, in some court or other.'

'Are you presuming to threaten me?' demanded Charles in his grandest manner.

'No, no. Not threaten, no. Just a glimpse of the obvious.' He slapped a hand on each knee and rose. The bowler went back on his head. 'I'm sorry, gentlemen. We always like a little co-operation—in a little matter like the apprehending of traitors.'

He tipped the bowler sarcastically, and left.

I went straight to the telephone and took it off its gadget.

'My God,' Charles said, 'that's torn it.'

'You *bloody* fool!'

'Why?'

'You told somebody. I know who it was, too.'

'I never told a soul.'

'Yes you did.'

'Who?'

'That chap Tompkins or whatever his name is. You know bloody well he's M.I.5.'

'Oh my God.'

'He probably suffers from patriotism.'

'Well what do we do now?'

'Just get butchered, I imagine. By the organization.'

'Can we stop them finding out?'

'Not for long.'

'Perhaps we'd better warn them.'

'How? We haven't any address.'

'Three four three?'

'It's empty.'

'Oh dear. Look!'

He jerked his head at the window. Two policemen in

uniform were looking in the windows of the little shops. A faceless character in a sports jacket loitered near the pub.

Charles took up the telephone.

'What are you going to do?'

'Ring Sam.'

'Don't be an absolute madman!' I grabbed the thing out of his hand. 'Didn't you hear what he said?'

Charles sighed.

'We're besieged,' he said.

'Thank goodness I don't live in this place. I'm getting out of here.'

I left him. He was almost in tears. Sometimes he looked exactly like a little boy. A petulant, bad-tempered little boy. You had to be sorry for him.

I walked down Beauchamp Place. The policeman viewed me with total unconcern. I found the car in Lennox Gardens and drove down the Kingston by-pass at seventy miles an hour. No one followed me.

When I got home I decided to ring the local garage. They were friends of mine and I thought they would answer frankly about any unusual police activity in the village.

Our telephone then was—and still is thank goodness—of the old sort where you have to ask for the number.

The moment I lifted it a tremulous voice said, 'Is that Mr Gibbs?'

'Yes, why?'

'Well I ought not to be saying this, but we've known each other so long, just on the telephone.'

'Yes?'

'He's out of the room for the moment. Just be careful what you say, that's all. I can't tell you any more. Just be careful.'

The siege had spread to Peaslake.

[2]

Somehow or other we had to lie very low, it seemed to me, if we were going to get aboard the Opel Kapitan without interference. The situation, as I saw it, was not that the police would prevent us. They just wanted to be there. And my mind raised pictures of the four of us surging through the night behind our bullet-proof windows, with three British Wolseleys and five French Citroens in hot pursuit. In those circumstances the windows were not going to be of very much use. The shots would be coming from inside the car. I decided to take the day off from the office.

Left alone with a suspect telephone, I couldn't resist exploring the situation. I rang up the garage and listened to an unusual amount of heavy breathing, and asked if I could come in for a grease. When I got down there, our Mr Hutchins, who is one of the best mechanics in this country, asked me, 'Is your telephone all right?'

'Fairly all right,' I said. 'Why?'

'Funny thing. We don't seem to be getting through to anyone properly. Sort of clicking and interference.'

'Heavy breathing?'

'Yes, that's right.'

'It's a policeman.'

'Cor!' said Hutchins, his eyes narrowing. 'What have you been doing?'

'Nothing.'

'You sure?'

'Absolutely sure. Can I use your telephone?'

'I don't see what good that does.'

'I just want to see how the net spreads.'

So I rang up my father, in Shamley Green.

'Hullo,' I said. 'My telephone's being tapped.'

My father was alarmed beyond words.

'I wish you wouldn't do these things! Can't you publish some decent novels? How d'you know it's being tapped?'

'There's the poor bloody policeman. If you listen hard you can hear his breathing.'

The breathing stopped.

'It's a damned outrage.'

'He'll have to breathe again soon.'

'I should complain.'

'Who to?'

'Ring up the telephone manager in Guildford,'

'That's the hell of a good idea. I will.'

I hung up. In those days one did hang up. Then I deman
ded the telephone manager.

'Telephone manager's office.'

I put on my grandest voice, almost as grand as Charles's.

'Oh, this is Mr Anthony Gibbs speaking—Spurfold
House, Peaslake. Abinger 233. Could you tell me if my
telephone's being tapped?'

'Just a moment, please.'

I waited for some time. Then a new voice spoke.

'Hullo?'

'Hullo. Am I expected to say this all over again?'

'If you wouldn't mind.'

'I'm Mr Anthony Gibbs, of Spurfold House, Peaslake,
Abinger 233.'

'Abinger 233?'

'Yes. Could you tell me if you've had orders to tap my
telephone?'

'Oh—er—h'm. That's a nasty one.'

'You mean, you have?'

'I don't know that—er—h'm. Not on any orders from
this department, anyway.'

'Well,' said I, 'I wish to complain, and I hope the officer
records my words correctly. I regard this as an intolerable
invasion of my privacy, and a revolting disregard for the
rights of the citizen. I doubt whether it has any justification
whatever. Having said which, I should be greatly obliged to
you if you would now give orders to have me untapped, and
certainly not extend your activities to tapping every number
I ring up. I'm not even speaking on my own telephone. If I
ring up half the people in Surrey, are you going to tap half
the people in Surrey?'

'You've made my position very difficult, Mr Gibbs.'

'Okay,' I said, letting the grand manner drop. 'I'll start

ringing. I'll see you damned soon run out of policemen!'

I did too. I went home and rang up everybody respectable I could think of, my in-laws in Cambridge, some people in Farnham with a baronetcy in the family, Dame Harriette Chick in Branscombe, South Devon, my cousin at the legation in Salisbury, Rhodesia, and, running out of distance and distinction, every shop I could think of. I ordered more cigarettes from Morland's in Grosvenor Street, more note-paper from *The Times*, films from Wallace Heaton, still more cigarettes from Fribourg and Treyer, booked a table for lunch at the R.A.C. and another at Speranza in Beau-champ Place. In two hours of solid telephoning I made thirty or forty calls, and in the days before the tape recorder, the scurrying of policemen with notebooks and a knowledge of shorthand must have been a sight for sore eyes. Having got that off my chest I felt sorry for Charles, and drove up to town.

He was not alone.

There was a plain clothes man in the doorway. A man in uniform stood at the doors of the pub, doing the full knees bend. Two other policemen sauntered in the street. In our room on the first floor was the Detective-Inspector from Scotland Yard. He seemed amused.

'Been doing a bit of telephoning, eh?'

'Yes,' I said, 'how did you make out?'

'Not too badly. Kept us on the hop all right, didn't you?' He grinned. 'Not a bad dodge at that!'

'I'm glad you think so.'

'And how is everbody? It seems to me I see one or two pale faces in the office?'

He was absolutely right. Charles was white as a ghost. So had been the girl in the guichet and the sales manager on the stairs.

'Care to come clean?'

I shook my head.

'Well, we'll just keep up the good work then.' He trundled out, as menacingly as he could.

Charles and I sat down, and lit shaking cigarettes.

'The ten thousand's in Switzerland,' he told me.
'How d'you know? Not on the telephone?'
'Chap with a note from Sam.'
'A *hundred—thousand—pounds*!'
'Shall we ever get it?'
'Posthumously.'
'I need a drink.'
I looked at my watch. 'Hour and a half to wait.'
'There's a chap in the pub.'
'Does he drink?'
'Sips beer.'
'That makes five.'
'I don't think they know about *The People* yet.'
'Why not tell 'em?'
'What for?'
'Why don't we ring Sam after all? Put him in the con-
centric circles. Might make them a bit more careful. National
newspaper.'
Charles hummed.
'D'you think Farinetti knows?'
'He soon will.'
'Well I'm going to ring up Scotland Yard and ask for
police protection.'
'No, don't do that.'
'Why not?'
'You might as well ring Farinetti.'
'I believe Farinetti's probably as frightened as we are.'
'Of the police?'
'Of the organization!'
It was about ten minutes past four. We went on talking
like this. The hands of time crept slowly by. Every now and
then we went to the windows to watch the police through our
brave show of red geraniums. Apart from the man in our
front hall whom we couldn't see there still seemed to be four,
one standing outside the pub, the other plain clothes man
on the bench filing his nails, and two more common-or-
garden bobbies looking in the shops.

213

'They must know those corsets by now,' said Charles. 'What's the time?'

'Twenty-three minutes past four . . .'

At five o'clock we had worried ourselves into a condition of palsey.

Charles sat, taking his gold lighter to pieces and putting it back together again. I was drawing motor-cars, something which Burgess used to do.

'What's the time now?'

'Quarter past five. Can't you look at your own blasted watch?'

'Well, I'm going over. To hell with the police. I shall go and sit on that bench and wait for the place to open.' He got up from the table.

'Just a moment,' I said.

'What?'

'That taxi.'

He swung round to the window. A very ancient taxi, not of the sort currently in use in London, was chugging across the road on to the wrong side. It was sagging on its springs. It had to wait for some cars to pass, and then it staggered up to the kerb immediately opposite, and sat down. Both doors opened, and about fifteen Italians poured out of it and formed a cluster on the pavement. Wiry, sallow, black-haired, alert.

'Christ,' whispered Charles. 'There's going to be a machine-gun battle in Beauchamp Place.'

I couldn't think of anything to say.

The staff began to leave. Archie Savory pushed into the pub, blissfully unconscious of danger. The plain clothes chap followed him in. The front door kept swinging shut on its spring. Presently we were alone. Peter de Polnay came down the pavement, stepped into the street to avoid the Italians, and met Archie coming out. They both looked up at our windows in surprise and went away.

We stayed there till nine o'clock, scarcely daring to breathe. It was quite dark. The office must have looked very shut. The front door clicked on a Yale latch. There was no light in any of the windows. The pub, of course, was ablaze.

'I suppose we can't climb over the roofs?' I whispered.

'Of course we can't.'

'Or over the gardens?'

'You can do that, if you like. I'm going across to the pub.'

'Don't be a fool, Charles!'

'I'm not going to stay here all night. *I need a drink.*' He felt his way past several loose chairs and began groping into his camel-haired coat.

I couldn't let him go alone. I struggled into my own over-coat, got my hat, my rolled umbrella, and followed Charles's tiptoeing down the stairs.

'I *must* visit the ladies!'

'I'll follow you. Don't pull anything.'

We were very silent.

'Ready?'

'Come on!'

'We'll go together.'

We crossed the road at the double. The Italians watched us with slit eyes.

'Working late this evening?' Richard asked from behind the bar.

'Mild and bitter, please,' said the policeman.

[3]

It was quite obvious that this couldn't go on. During a completely sleepless night I decided that in the morning the whole thing had got to be called off, and that I had better lobby James Pope-Hennessy first, in case there was any division of opinion.

James had been secretly enjoying the whole thing in a removed, dilettante way. I think he obtained a certain amount of quiet amusement from watching the puppet antics of Charles and myself quite as much as the palpable absurdities of 'the organization'.

At ten o'clock I rang him from Peaslake.

'James?'

'Oh, hello.'

'Can I come and see you?'

'Of course.'

'I'll be with you in exactly one hour.'

'I'll have tea ready.'

In exactly one hour the ancient but honourable Rolls drew up beside the corner shop. Two large Wolseleys were there, ostentatiously labelled 'police'.

I marched up the stairs and rang his bell. He opened the door, showing just the right amount of shirt cuff.

'There are five police cars outside,' he said.

'*Five?*'

He drew aside the net curtain. The two Wolseleys were obvious. There was also a small laundry van with a name painted on it and a very large aerial on the roof.

'The laundry van?'

'All five cars,' said James.

He was quite right. A Ford, a Morris, and the laundry van all had giant transmitting aerials jutting from them.

'And there's a man permanently in the telephone box.'

So there was, looking up at the window.

'Well, I'm fed up. I'm going to call off the whole thing. I'm then going to spend at least two weeks in the most respectable place I can think of. Bournemouth.'

'*Boorn*-mouth, *please*!' said James.

'All right. Boorn-mouth.'

'Aren't you enjoying it? Five police cars wherever you go? By the way, how did they know when to expect you?'

'I telephoned you.'

'Oh, dear,' said James.

I told him about the Battle of Beauchamp Place. I told him he might find the whole thing was quite tolerable, indeed amusing, except that I didn't want to die for the sake of a good joke. And I reminded him of the family name, Dame Una, the Victoria and Albert and all that.

216

He agreed, provided me with a chaste cup of Earl Grey, and promised he would be watching from the window.

I emerged into the street and was observed. The man in the telephone box began telephoning. I got into the car. Five starters whirred in unison. The Rolls, of course, didn't whirr. You started it just by switching on. I put the car in motion. The two Wolseleys surged up the hill at eighty miles an hour and disappeared. I travelled two yards, stopped, put out a flipper, reversed into a side turning, put out the flipper the other way, and crept forward. The two Wolseleys had discovered their mistake and were bearing down the hill again, flat out, only to skid all over the road with yelps from their tyres when they found I was in exactly the same place, but pointing in the opposite direction.

I decided that if the police wanted a chase, I was going to give them the most peculiar chase they had ever had in their lives. The whole thing was going to take place at exactly eight miles an hour.

I stuck my head out and looked up. James was laughing his head off at the window. I waved to him and moved almost imperceptibly forward towards the Shepherds Bush road. It was the three 'Q' cars this time which shot across both lines of traffic and disappeared into Holland Park. The two Wolseleys had learned their lesson and took up station behind.

Right flipper up, I kept them waiting for four minutes. They began sounding their horns. I was really waiting for exactly the right gap in two long lines of traffic which would just permit one car to zip over, but not two. I did it beautifully. That car had the lithest and quietest leap from a standstill, probably in the history of motoring. In two seconds I was across, and the traffic was solid again, with the two Wolseleys still vibrating violently in Ladbroke Grove. So I waited for them on the corner, leaving insufficient room for them to stop behind me. When they got over I waved them past.

They went past but pulled into the kerb in front, and an

irate policeman got out and stuck his head through my
window.

'What's up with you?' he demanded.

'Nothing. Why?'

'Well, why don't you get a move on?'

'I'm in no particular hurry.'

'Disgusting!' he muttered, got back into his car, and waved
me past.

At that moment a laundry van and two other small cars
revealed themselves flashing over a crossing just ahead, in
opposite directions. So far we had travelled about a hundred
and twenty feet.

I didn't want to rile our magnificent police force too much,
so I did in fact move forward at exactly eight miles an hour,
taking as many turns as I could, and punctiliously putting up
flippers at every turn. I never saw the Morris, the Ford or
the laundry van again. I don't know what happened to them.
The two Wolseleys crept along behind, in funeral procession.
Somewhere in the region of Camden Hill one of them
passed me and flagged me to a halt. It was a different
policeman. He came over.

'Look here! Where are you going?'

'Where am I going?'

'Yes! Where are you going?'

'To Beauchamp Place of course.'

'Why of course?'

'Because that's where my office is.'

'You're not going anywhere else?'

'No. Why should I?'

He swallowed.

'O.K.,' he said, sickly. 'Carry on.'

I carried on. The Wolseleys did not move. I drove to the
office, at a reasonable speed, had a word with Charles, rang
up the Inspector and told him we were going to call the
whole thing off.

'Word of honour?'

'Word of honour.'

218

'The whole thing?'

'The whole thing. Now would you kindly do the same?'

'It'll be a pleasure.'

Now why did he say that? I thought they wanted to catch Burgess. By lunch time the policemen had disappeared.

At three o'clock Mr Farinetti walked in.

'No police?'

'They've gone,' Charles said.

Mr Farinetti expelled a great deal of air, sat in the armchair and produced a packet of American cigarettes.

'Jesus, that's a load off my mind.'

'Ours, too.'

'You don't understand. I *trusted* you guys. And if anything goes wrong, *I* get the rap!' He shook his head. 'Jesus, that was a close call.'

'Mr Farinetti for the high jump.'

'You can say that again!'

He blew smoke rings. 'Who told the cops?'

'Not me.'

'Not me.'

'They just seemed to find out.'

'The telephone?'

Mr Farinetti wagged his head.

'You guys are too damned innocent. It's a shame to bump you off.'

'You're not going to do that?'

'I don't know. Regulations. I gotta think this thing out.'

He began thinking it out, inhaling the cigarette and blowing the smoke out like the letter F.

'Did they get on to you? Did they find out anything? Have they picked anyone up?'

'Nope.'

'Well, then.'

'Just let me think, willya?'

We let him think. Charles's ashtray was ringing like an electric bell.

'Don't be so tense!' cried Mr Farinetti. 'Re-*lax*!'

'How can anyone possibly relax,' Charles demanded, 'with an assassin in the next chair?'

'Now, now! Assassin! That's a nasty word.'

'Death is nasty too.'

'Sure,' Mr Farinetti agreed, generously. 'But will you guys pipe down and let me think?'

'After all,' Charles said, 'I'm in the prime of life.'

'Oh shut up, Charles! Let the blessed little man think.'

'Oh, very well.'

Mr Farinetti finished his cigarette, and stubbed it out.

'How did you get rid of 'em?'

'Called the whole thing off.'

'You did, huh?'

'And how did you know they'd gone?'

'Me? Oh, I've been here right along.'

'Here? Where?'

Mr Farinetti's index finger pointed vertically downwards. 'In the b-b-b-'

'In the b-b-basement?'

Mr Farinetti began to laugh. It was very extraordinary. He began to cackle and to shake. He flung back his head, making the most evil sounds, and his Adam's apple, which could have done with a shave, was in violent movement.

Charles and I watched him with horror and dismay.

Mr Farinetti slapped the arms of his chair, slapped his knees and laughed till he cried. Then gradually the paroxysm was brought under control.

'O.K., fellas, you can live!'

He got up, still with the occasional hiccup, went to the door, and came in again with my briefcase.

'With the compliments of the organization,' said Mr Farinetti. 'We thought you might be needing it back.'

He exploded a handful of fingers at the temple in salute and disappeared.

'Is it possible?' Charles whispered.

'The whole thing was—'

'Was a hoax?'
'I can't believe it! The Salisbury Plain.'
'Open the brief case!'
I opened it. Inside were two hundred and fifty dirty one-pound notes.

XIII

[1]

It was a great pity about that hundred thousand pounds, for there came a time when something was obviously wrong with Wingate's.

Publishing seems to be peculiarly susceptible to the deflationary zeal of recurring Chancellors of the Exchequer. The names of these gentlemen have long since eluded me. Who was Chancellor in 1952? Not that puritan man Sir Stafford Cripps?

Whoever it was, he nearly ruined us. The temptation, when this happens, is always to take in directors who are 'prepared to make a small capital investment'. London is populated with people who want to be publishers, and who are quite anxious to invest a thousand or two for the sake of a genteel position and a salary of £1,500 a year.

We took in several, including a splendid lady called Mrs Rowell, whose name I only mention because she makes a later appearance in this narrative. We had a good staff.

One member was given the responsibility of arranging the covers. We were about to publish a very good novel by Upton Sinclair, who was a great personal friend of Professor Einstein from whom we had obtained a useful quote as follows: 'One of the most remarkable novels I have read.'

Our staff went to work. Some months later we issued a not terribly distinguished thriller by a terribly distinguished author called Anthony Heckstall-Smith, who I'm sure will forgive me if I say that his book was deliberately beamed at the popular market. The title was *The Man with Yellow Shoes*, and this very light prose work went out to all the reviewers and the book shops, bearing in enormous

222

letters the legend, 'One of the most remarkable novels I have read. Albert Einstein.'

However, we survived. Not so in 1957.

Between 1952 and 1957 we had a rich and expansive period. We had a trick up our sleeve, which was to follow through with similar books whenever we struck a bestseller.

Thus the *Naked and the Dead* was followed by a whole series of grim and outspoken war books, of which *Battle Cry*, by Leon Uris, was a bestseller in its own right. Another great success was Neville Duke's reminiscences of a famous test pilot. Those were the days when British aviation led the world, and all the world flocked to Farnborough to watch those god-like characters crash the sound barrier.

We used to be invited down to the pilots' tent at Farnborough, where we met all those test pilots, who were the most charming and civilized men, particularly poor Mike Lithgow, whose book was a great success. These apparently ordinary and modest men thought nothing of flying about fifty feet up past the grandstand at exactly the speed of sound, so that the whole plane shimmered into near invisibility, upside down.

My son and I went down one year, on Mike's invitation, to watch John Derry produce the first sonic boom on the De Havilland 110. Martin had acquired an improbable motor-cycle and volunteered to take me on the pillion. As a permissive father I agreed to this, and when we got to Farnborough he steered into an enclosure labelled 'Motor-bicycle car park 5/–'.

This seemed an immense distance from where we wanted to go, and I persuaded him to turn round and park his machine near the administration buildings, one of which was the pilots' tent.

Derry's plan was to fly from Hatfield at a great height and then dive down over the packed multitudes through the sound barrier, making as much noise as possible. I imagine that in those days you had to go into a steep dive to build up the necessary speed.

223

Presently the commentator announced his arrival and we saw him like a little dot in the sky, hurling himself towards the earth. Two tiny white clouds appeared suddenly behind him, and a moment later the double crack of the sonic boom whipped our ears.

Down he came. You could see the shape of the plane now with its twin fuselages and its twin jets and its twin vapour trails. When he was five hundred feet or so above the multitude he pulled out into level flight and a right-angle turn to make his run past the stands, and at that moment both wings became shapeless and absurd, like an umbrella turning inside out, and the whole thing gently disintegrated before our eyes. The wings flew away. The cockpit with Derry inside it fell like a stone. But the two engines flew on. With deadly momentum and no loss of speed they zoomed across the runway, straight towards the faces of the crowd. One of them hurled itself at the feet of the people with a mighty thud. The other, flying slightly higher, plunged straight into the motor-cycle car park where it indulged in massacre before it became still.

In addition to test pilots, we had the George Mikes books: *How to be an Alien*; *How to Scrape Skies*. How to this and how to that. A charming little Hungarian, he had an inexhaustible fund of humour, and an equally inexhaustible ability to write books about his fellow human beings. And he claimed, when visiting Florence, to be the first man to do the four-minute Ufizzi.

He wrote another book called *Eight Humorists* in which he was not very appreciative of P. G. Wodehouse. P.G., whom I knew, wrote me a letter saying: 'Tell that little Hungarian I shall come over personally and kick him in his decaying teeth.'

We also 'discovered' Maurice Edelman who wrote, and sometimes looked, like a modern Lord Beaconsfield. *Who Goes Home?* was a brilliant parliamentary novel. In some ways I think his transcriptions of his books for television were even more brilliant than the books themselves, in that

224

when the characters said one thing they were doing something else, and obviously thinking of a third.

So publishing had its moments. In 1957, however (would that name have been Selwyn Lloyd?), once again our balance of payments was awry, the pound was in danger, inflation was rampant, and the thumbscrews began to turn.

The way in which this affected us was not so much that people stopped buying books. They didn't. What happened was that all the banks began calling in overdrafts, so that people who owed us money couldn't pay, and the other people, like printers, began screaming for their money.

We were in the middle of a sandwich, but there was also something the matter with our own house. Far too many people were living on Wingate's. We had two managing directors, both with expensive tastes, and five other directors. We spent between three and four thousand a year on advertising, and five thousand a year on lunches. Captain Maxwell's Simpkin Marshall, a distributing organization, went bankrupt in our faces, owing us quite a number of thousands, and making serious inroads in our sales.

Once a situation develops in this way, it is surprising how quickly the horizon darkens and begins closing in. The actual facts of the situation were that we had a gap of seventeen thousand pounds. That is to say that we owed, say, forty-four thousand pounds to our suppliers and our bank, and we were only owed twenty-seven thousand from the sale of books. In a period of normal credit this might have been quite supportable, by the simple process of yelling for *our* money and keeping our creditors waiting for a couple of months longer than they liked. With the government clamps on, this was outside the range of possibility, and the situation began to look very menacing indeed.

It became obvious to all of us that something rather drastic had to be done, and all of us knew in our hearts what that something was. As the principal shareholder it fell to me to try to put that something into effect.

225

My son Martin had astonished us all by showing an unexpected and inexplicable head for figures, and was now a chartered accountant. We put our heads together and evolved a scheme for the salvation of Wingate's. This meant passing the hat round the family. Five of us, Martin, his wife Jessica, my father, my wife and I all managed to beg, borrow or steal two thousand pounds apiece, and were going to put the money in, in the name of a separate company, on conditions that certain alterations were made. So we founded a £100 company called Publishing Investments Ltd and the money was all placed on loan with a promise that it would be repaid on demand. When the Augean Stables were cleaned the cash would go into Wingate's on debenture.

'Alterations' is a mild word indeed. It meant no more advertising, no more lunches, a ruthless selling off of all the books in stock—and that most of the directors had to go, including the man who had made Wingate's what it was, Charles Fry.

This, I think, was really the most unpleasant thing I have ever had to do in my whole life.

I am extremely bad at long knives. But after months of nerving myself to what was obviously inevitable, I went to Charles, armed with a mass of figures from our accounts, and asked him if he thought he could find another job.

He was perfectly civilized about it, as indeed I hope I was. He agreed at once.

'D'you think I shall get one?'

'I'm sure you will, if you try now. If you wait till the crash it may be more difficult.'

'How long have I got?'

'As long as you like.'

'A pity,' said Charles. 'We got on so well together.'

'I know. It's frightful.'

'Goodman will help.'

'I'm sure he will. There's a chap called Howard Samuel. He's just bought McGibbon & Kee. He's buying others.'

'O.K.,' said Charles. 'If that's the way you want it.'

226

It wasn't the way I wanted it; but there was a man downstairs from the Gas Board refusing to go till he was paid his money. We were owed something like twenty-seven thousand pounds, and couldn't pay the gas bill.

I went round the other directors. They were incredibly good about it. They went down like friendly ninepins. My position was highly unattractive, and the whole thing made me feel like the worst sort of tycoon, which is not really my character at all. At the end of that day I found it difficult to look my fellow humans in the face. The trouble is that in these abominable moments one is faced with a terrible choice, between people one likes enormously, and the people one loves. The Gibbs family now had exactly thirty-eight thousand pounds involved.

The main difficulty was Charles. Three-thousand-pounds-a-year jobs do not grow on trees. Goodman—not yet ennobled—was pressing hard with that Howard Samuel who had made a million pounds in no time at all out of house property, and after some months of negotiation I came to the office one morning and found Charles in a state of astonishing euphoria.

'Hello, Charles,' I said. 'What's happened to you?'

'My dear Tony, when I woke up this morning I was absolutely radiant!'

I laughed. Always the master of phrase was old Charles.

'You were radiant, were you?'

'Everything's settled. Last night. Samuel came through. Three thousand a year. He's going to buy Cresset Press and put me in as managing director.'

'Oh *thank God*!' I said. 'That's marvellous.'

'He wants to meet you.'

'Meet *me*?'

'I've got a message. He wants you to lunch with him at the Ritz to meet Aneurin Bevan. Today.'

'Whatever for?'

'You've got to go, my dear fellow. It's a royal command.'

'But what's it all about?'

'I really don't know,' said Charles, beginning to hum; 'it's about time for my elevenses.'

Humming happily to himself he went across to the pub.

That was the last time I ever saw Charles.

[2]

I turned up at the Ritz. The fountain was splashing on the Golden Maiden. All I knew of Howard Samuel was Charles's description of him, 'Neat and rather grim', but Nye Bevan's puff ball of white hair shone magnificently among the pattern of sleek heads. He was talking to a neat and rather grim little man. I approached delicately.

'Howard Samuel?'

'Oh, hullo,' he said. 'What will everyone drink?'

'Introduce us first,' said Bevan.

'Oh, yes,' said Samuel, doing so. 'What would everyone like to drink?'

'Something with gin?' suggested Bevan.

'All right with you, Gibbs?'

I said thanks very much that was perfectly all right with me.

Three bottles of gin were put on the table.

Samuel opened his bottle, poured out a third of a glass, drank it, poured out another third and raised it.

'Cheers,' he said.

This looked as if it were going to be quite a party.

Bevan and I exchanged shy glances and poured out modest tots.

'Cheers.'

'Um—cheers.' Bevan had the slightest of stutters. There was a pause.

'You're just back from Russia,' I said, making conversation. There had been a lot about it in the papers.

'Y—yes,' said Bevan.

'Before we all get tight,' Samuel interrupted, 'I must tell you the reason for this lunch. I understand from Goodman

228

that you're in rather a bad way. I'm prepared to make you an offer for Wingate's. A generous offer. Of course, I should want control. My wife is a very dedicated Socialist, I should want Wingate's to concentrate very largely on left-wing books, supporting the general policy and philosophy of Nye here. Are you left-wing?'

'No,' I said. 'I can't honestly say I am.'

He looked surprised and slightly amazed. 'Well you'll have to talk that over with Nye. I want your decision by this evening.'

He drank some gin. We all drank some gin.

I looked at Nye, who was showing signs of embarrassment. I decided that he was a nice man.

'You'll have to tell me your philosophy!'

'It's very complicated,' he said diffidently.

The gin was working. 'Too complicated for me to understand?'

'Much too complicated on an um—empty stomach. Howard, could we eat?'

'Yes, yes, of course.' He finished his glass and rose.

I stole a look at his bottle. A third of it was gone. The level of the other two had dropped smartly, though not perhaps so dramatically. To leave those three bottles seemed an awful waste of gin. We followed a waiter into the restaurant, so charmingly Edwardian with its pink shaded lights and trellis work. It was agreeably hazy and there was a smell of lobster. We sat down.

'What,' asked Samuel, 'would everyone like to drink?'

Nye Bevan tucked a napkin round his knees. 'Well, since I am just back from Russia—'

Three bottles of vodka were put on the table.

We all had a bit of this. I have no doubt we also had a bit of fish and a bit of meat, but I only deduce this from the passage of some hock and some red wine across the pages of memory. When this degree of intoxication assails me, it does so ocularly. I can only see what is immediately in front of my face.

229

In this case Nye Bevan's face was in front of my face, pink, full lipped, alight with intelligence beneath an explosion of white hair. I had no idea what had happened to Mr Samuel. He was not within my field of vision.

'Come on, Nye. Can I call you Nye? You haven't told me about Russia.'

'It was um–horrible.'

'Horrible?'

'Ants.'

'Ants?'

'Only a corporate intelligence. No individual thought allowed or even possible. A form—a form—a formicarium.'

'But, don't you like that?'

'Christ in heaven, no!'

'The purest form of Socialism.'

'Um–horrible!'

'But what price left-wing books?'

'Listen.'

'I am listening.'

'Listen! I believe in the dignity of the individual human soul. I believe in the majesty of the individual intelligence. I believe the state should wither and die. I believe in the highest form of indiscipline. I believe the world's troubles stem entirely from the organization of society. I believe nations are hell, and monarchs are hell, and presidents are hell, and parliaments are hell, and police courts are hell. I don't *want* any potatoes.'

'Yes, I'll have some.'

'My God,' I said, 'this sounds like one of my election speeches.'

'But you didn't get in.'

'No, I didn't.'

'There you are, you see.'

'I don't know what you mean.'

'You didn't take the teleological view!'

I started searching among my Greek roots. It was the first time I had heard the word. We didn't have syndromes, either.

Telescope. Telephone. Logos, the idea. The science of distance.

'The end justifies the means?'

He shrugged.

We both had some red wine or some white wine or some vodka or something.

'What you're telling me,' I announced with an air of discovery, 'is that you aren't a Socialist at all!'

He closed one eye slowly. At least I think he did.

'Shall I tell you what you are?'

'Would it be better if I told you?'

'It would be an appalling indiscretion. You're an anarchist!'

He sighed and put down his glass. He had an air of complete exposure.

'A benevolent anarchist,' I amended, rubbing it in.

'That's right. It *must* be benevolent.'

'And how do you get that?'

'You don't yet. But it's um—worth um—working for.'

'Generations and generations?'

'Probably.'

'In the Labour Party?'

'Damn it, dear boy, you don't expect to get it in the *Conservative* Party?'

'But this is so cynical!'

'Not cynical at all. My family were miners. Everyone was miners. Except the Berry Brothers. I was supposed to go down the pit. We were organized that way. But I was a weakling. And I had ideas. And I could speak. How else?'

'No,' I said. 'Good for you.'

'These things have to come up from below. How else do you come up from below except through the Labour Party?'

'I hope Attlee isn't listening.'

'Don't be bathetic.'

'Sorry. What do I do about this chap, Samuel?'

'Do whatever you like.'

'The teleological view?'

231

'It's your decision.'

'What would you do? Books on steel nationalization? Books about trade unionism?'

'Would anybody,' said Mr Samuel suddenly, who must have heard his name mentioned, 'care for a brandy?'

We looked round. There were coffee cups on the table. I thought Bevan was the best man I had met for years. We said we'd love a little brandy.

Three bottles of brandy were placed on the table.

A waiter brought a bill. I managed to catch sight of it. Forty-seven pounds. For three gentlemen lunching alone that must surely be a record. I must buy the Guinness book. We got to our feet in zero gravity and floated past the golden maiden and down some stairs. The commissionaire produced a taxi. Bevan said he wanted to go to the dentist. I said I wanted to go to Beauchamp Place. Samuel didn't say where he wanted to go, missed the strapontin which sprang shut with a snap and sat on the floor.

The commissionaire lifted him up by the armpits, lowered him gently, and said 'Thank you, Sir.'

At about five-fifteen I stirred heavily in my seat and woke up in the library of the R.A.C.

I went down to the telephone room. I told myself something idiotic about selling my soul. I rang up Samuel and told him I wouldn't do it. He sounded angry.

It was a Friday night and I drove down to Peaslake in the Rolls.

The next day was Saturday. The day after was a Sunday. On Monday I went up to the office. No Charles.

I didn't bother much. I thought he probably had a cold. Or was talking to Samuel. I got on with the usual business, reading manuscripts, staving off creditors. The next day was a Tuesday.

Still no Charles.

On Wednesday I didn't go to the office. I had to go down to the city to see various people.

About five o'clock when I turned up, I found the place

full of police. My first thought was that Guy Burgess had been arrested.

'Mr Gibbs?'

'Yes?'

'Would you be so good, Sir, as to identify the body?'

I didn't know what on earth he was talking about.

It was Clifford Simmons, our company secretary, who told me simply. He had to speak rather clearly to get through.

'Tony!'

'Yes? What? What's happened?'

'Charles is dead,' he said.

[3]

They drove me down to a place in Fulham Palace Road, near Putney Bridge. The policeman was talkative.

'Not a very pleasant sight, I'm afraid, Sir. Been there for some days. Central heating and all that. Surprising how quickly they go.'

I couldn't say anything. We slid expertly down the King's Road.

'Found two empty bottles of gin, an empty bottle of whisky and an empty box of pheno-barbitone. Made a proper job of it.'

I grunted.

'How many days?' I managed at last.

'Saturday night, Sir.'

'How do you know?'

'Left a note, Sir. Very well expressed. You *are* Mr Anthony Gibbs?'

'That's right.'

'And would you know a Mr Brian Cook-Batsford?'

'Yes, Brian Batsford. Batsfords the publishers. Mr Fry used to work for them.'

'Ah.'

'What do you mean?'

'Something in the note, Sir. Something like "If you wish

to enquire further into the reasons for my action, I suggest you get in touch with Brian Cook-Batsford and Mr Anthony Gibbs".'

'Oh, my God.'

'Don't you worry, Sir. They always say something like that. Business troubles, was it?'

'I suppose so, in a way.'

'Would there be much publicity attached to this? Awkwardness for the company?'

'I should think quite a lot. He knew a great many people.'

'We're quite used to that, Sir. We'll get the coroner to hear the case at eight o'clock in the morning. It'll be all over before the Press gets to hear of it.'

We threaded our way by Parsons Green.

'The fool!' I kept saying to myself. 'What a damn silly, useless, idiotic, over-dramatic, fatuous, unnecessary thing to do!'

I am all for suicide in the proper circumstances. It seems to me that the one unarguable right of intelligent man is the right to take his own life if he so decides. But this!

'You fool, Charles!' I said, almost as if he were still alive. 'You bloody fool!'

'Rather a nasty little chore for you, Sir. I'm afraid. Hope you won't mind. It is behind glass.'

We were stumbling along a very dark passage in a ramshackle building. I hadn't noticed our arrival.

'This way, Sir.'

There was a sort of interior window in the wall, about three feet off the ground, six feet long and three feet high. We stopped before it.

'Ready, Sir?'

'Do I look through here?'

He flicked a switch, and there on a slab on the other side of a glass was the illuminated Charles.

He was unrecognizable. He lay with his face turned sideways. He was bloated and blotched and three little runnels of dried blood ran from his nostrils and one corner of his lips. His hair was snow white. I stared in growing disbelief.

'Do you identify the body, Sir?'

'No, I don't.'

'You *don't*, Sir?'

'No, I don't.'

'But—'

'I'm sorry, but that's not the Mr Fry I knew. For one thing his hair was bright red.'

'He had white hair, Sir.'

'Well I never saw him with white hair. And I don't recognize him. He never looked like that. I certainly don't identify him. You'll have to get somebody else.'

'There isn't anybody else.'

'Of course there is. Who found him? And will you switch off that damned light?'

'The cleaning woman, Sir. She failed to gain entry, and finally went to the manager of the place. They sent for us, we broke in, and that's how we found him.'

'Well there you are, then. Get the cleaning woman. She probably knew him better than I did. She may have seen him with white hair. I'm sorry. I'm not going to do it. Certainly not on oath at a coroner's inquest.'

Sadly he switched Charles back into the darkness. His manner to me let me know clearly that I was not co-operating with the police.'

'Well, I suppose we *could*—'

'You do that. And let me out of this place!'

He let me out. I caught a bus at Putney Bridge.

The verdict at the inquest was 'died by his own hand'. I was glad of that, thinking that the phrase 'While of unsound mind' is the crowning humiliation.

They set fire to him at Kensal Green.

235

XIV

[1]

A year went by.

To be precise, a year and four days went by. I had been thinking about Charles. I imagine we all had on the anniversary of his death. Mrs Rowell, who was a good Catholic, told me she had burnt some candles at the Oratory.

We had managed to get two extremely good books off the ground, and I remember thinking that if Charles were with us he might have been glad. One was *Exodus* by that same Leon Uris whose *Battle Cry* had been a bestseller. This one was about Palestine and the formation of the state of Israel. There were some very anti-British passages in it, deservedly so in my opinion. We had been given the Mandate for Palestine by the old League of Nations, and at a time when hundreds of thousands of Jews who had survived the tortures of the concentration camps were flocking to what they believed to be the Jewish National Home, the British Navy was occupied in preventing the refugees from disembarking from their ships.

The other was *The Desert Generals*, by a remarkable young man called Corelli Barnett who was still in his twenties and who, with the utmost seriousness and no sense of impudence whatever, clinically examined the strategy of men like Wavell, Auchinleck and Montgomery, and in many respects tore their legends to shreds.

That night, with the sense of a day well used, I went to bed at about eleven-fifteen, smoked a last cigarette as is my bad habit, took a swig out of a bottle labelled Carpano, which the Speranza had recommended, pushed the bottle back among my shoes in the cupboard and went to sleep.

236

At about half past one I was woken up by a sensation of overpowering malevolence. It was worse than malevolence. It was like two hands at the throat, and I reacted with strong physical symptoms. My heart was pounding. I broke into a violent sweat. I tried by will-power, since there was really nothing there, to get those hands off my windpipe.

Suddenly an intense conviction took hold of me.

'Is that you, Charles?' I said.

The answer was immediate.

'I could kill you, you know.'

'Well don't. For God's sake don't do that. That's not going to do anybody any good!'

I could feel him pause. After about ten seconds the malevolence was turned off. It took a short time to dissipate, like a fog of poison gas. Gradually I began to breathe again. My heart settled and I struggled to rise.

'Let me get out of this bed, will you?'

'What do you want to get out of bed for?'

'Damn it. I want to get up. I want to turn on the light. I want to smoke a cigarette.'

'Oh, all right,' said Charles.

I switched on the bedside light, swung my feet out of the bed and sat with my head between my knees. Then I lit a cigarette.

'I thought I should get through to you all right,' Charles said. 'We were always pretty telepathic in the office.'

'Well, I wish you hadn't,' I said irritably.

He was surprised. 'Why not?'

'I don't like all this stuff. I can't bear the occult. I find the whole thing unpleasant and distressing.'

'That's ridiculous.'

'It isn't ridiculous at all. It upsets one's idea of rationality. I mean if I'm to believe this sort of thing I might as well believe in everything—visitors from beyond the grave and all that stuff. Why didn't you leave me alone?'

'Oh,' said Charles, mollified. 'I'm sorry.'

Then I was sorry. 'Now *I'm* sorry. Sorry, Charles.'

237

'That's all right. I hadn't anything particular to do.'

I became interested. 'By the way, where are you?'

'Oh, just a place . . .'

'What sort of place?'

'Just a place.'

'Can't you be more specific?'

'You wouldn't understand. It's just a place.'

'Is there anybody else there?'

'There are some people who look after me.'

'People?'

'Well, people. Things. I don't know.' There was a hint of shame in his voice, if you could call it a voice, for it was entirely inside my head.

'You mean—guards?' I asked him. 'Wardens?'

'I wish to God you'd stop cross-questioning me! I shouldn't have come!'

'Sorry! I'm interested.'

'I'm not allowed to explain it.'

'Oh, well. Pity.'

There was an awkward pause.

'You wouldn't like a cigarette, I suppose?'

'Don't be absurd!'

'Well *I* don't know what you can do and what you can't do.' I lit another for myself.

'Charles—'

'What?'

'What made you do that damn silly thing? It wasn't my fault you know.'

'Indirectly it was your fault.'

'I wish you hadn't left that note.'

'I was angry.'

'But you were all fixed up.'

'No I wasn't.'

I was amazed. It didn't seem necessary to say anything to register my amazement.

'Samuel rang up, said Charles.'

'Good Lord, I didn't know that. When?'

238

'Saturday.'

I waited for the rest.

'Said he'd bought the Press, but wasn't going to put me in charge. Said he'd had bad reports.'

'Oh, Lord help us. That wasn't my doing, anyway!'

'No, I know you didn't.'

'Can you find out things backwards, then?'

'Within limits.'

'And forwards?'

'Within a limit of about four—' He broke off suddenly. 'I'm not supposed to say that.'

'So that's why you're four days late?'

'Am I? I didn't know. I'm not supposed to say.'

'How extraordinary! Sort of time flux.'

'Afterwards it gets greater. That's what they say. Anyway, could we *possibly* get down to the main purpose of my visit?'

A little of the malevolence returned. Just a very little. About as much as I used to experience almost daily in the office.

'O.K., Charles. Shoot.'

'I want you to say you're sorry.'

'I am sorry.'

'I want you to apologize. Properly. A formal apology.'

'All right, Charles. What d'you want me to say?'

'I want you to say "Charles this would never have happened if I hadn't kicked you out of Wingate's. To that extent I admit that I was personally responsible. And I apologize and would like to make restitution".'

I had the odd feeling that this was for the purposes of documentation, of setting the record straight for some extra-terrestrial officialdom.

'All of that?'

'Every word of it.'

'I'll try. "Charles, I agree this would never have happened if I hadn't kicked you out of Wingate's. To that extent I admit I was personally responsible. I apologize and am quite prepared to make restitution." Is that all right?'

I could feel him sigh with relief.

'That's very much better. Now you can drink my health.'

'D'you mean actually, physically, drink your health?'

'That's right. You've got a bottle in the cupboard.'

'So I have. See through doors, too, can you?'

'Of course I can! Go on. Get it out.'

I got to my feet, bent down and opened the sliding door, very gently so as not to waken my wife, who was sleeping in the next room. I scrabbled away the shoes and came up with the Carpano.'

'Filthy stuff,' said Charles.

'Francesco made me buy it at the Speranza.'

'Well, pour it out.'

I poured out one finger.

'No, No! That's no good. Fill it up. I want my health drunk properly.'

'A whole glassful?'

'Go on!'

I was horrified. 'I shall have the most appalling hangover in the morning.'

'So you will. It will be a sort of punishment for you. You were always po-faced about my drinking.'

With great reluctance I poured out a full tumbler and put it to my lips.

'Do it properly!'

'Eh?'

'Raise the glass and say "Cheers".'

I supposed I had to agree. It seemed an absurd thing to do in a perfectly empty room. I raised my glass.

'Cheers,' I said. I drank it in about four swallows. I must say that, for the moment, it felt rather good.

'H'm. I fear the worst. You made me say something funny about restitution.'

'Oh, that's right. I almost forgot. I think you ought to put some flowers on my grave.'

'That's an easy one. Yes, of course.'

'With a card saying "To Charles from Tony in great affection".'

'Yes, of course.'

'Five pounds' worth of flowers.'

'Have a heart Charles! Five *pounds*?'

'Damn it, man, you can put it down at Harrods. You don't have to pay.'

I was amused. There spoke the true Charles.

'Anything else?'

'Not really.'

'I suppose you couldn't buzz off now?'

'D'you want me to go?'

'I've got to get a bit of sleep some time.'

'I don't know where to go,' he said miserably.

'Now you're being ridiculous! Go and see someone else. Go and pretend to strangle Howard Samuel.'

'No, I'm saving that one.'

'Well, go and see Mrs Rowell!'

I could sense his delight at the idea.

'D'you think she'd mind?' he asked boyishly.

'Of course not. She'd be tickled to death.'

'All right,' he said. 'I will.' Suddenly the room was empty. I looked at my watch. It was exactly three o'clock.

[2]

I was right about the hangover.

I woke up in the morning with a tongue like leprosy and a steam-engine in my head. The glass was by the bedside, with a little brown liquid at the bottom. The bottle was behind the jerry. There were four cigarette-ends in the tray.

I had imagined the whole thing of course. A guilt syndrome! I have a very powerful imagination and, as a professional writer, I would have had no difficulty in composing the most authentic dialogue for a man with whom I had shared a room five days a week for years.

I was worried about the cigarettes and the bottle, though.

Quite clearly I had been awake. This was no dream. And I had smoked four cigarettes, drunk a whole glass of Carpano, given myself a hangover, and looked at my watch.

I gave the whole thing up for future pondering, and got myself off to London. It was very late when I got there. The first person I met on the steps was Mrs Rowell. She had a dead white face.

'Hello, Mrs Rowell.'

'Oh, hello.'

'You don't look awfully well.'

'I feel frightful,' she said. 'I had an absolutely frightful night.'

'Oh dear.'

'I very nearly didn't come.'

'Why did you?'

She walked ahead of me through the door, past the guichet where the telephone girl sat, and turned to face me at the foot of the stairs. She dropped her voice.

'I had a frightful experience in the middle of the night. It was exactly as though someone was making desperate efforts to get through to me. There was an angry sort of struggle about this. But it wasn't my fault. I couldn't do it. No matter how hard he tried.'

'He?' I said.

'You know it's just about a year since—well, since Charles . . .'

She was in tears. 'So when he gave up I went downstairs and drank masses of gin.' She cried without shame.

'What time was this?'

She didn't hear me.

'Mrs Rowell! What time was this?'

'Three o'clock,' she said, turned, ran ahead of me up the stairs, and slammed her door.

I went to my own room, and rang up Harrods.

The difficulty was that I had no idea where they had buried him.

I explained this very apologetically to the lady at the other end of the telephone. I told her I knew that he'd been cremated, but whether they had put him in Kensal Green or Golders Green, or any of the other Greens, I really didn't know. I gave her the date and the name. 'Mr Charles Fry.' Was there any sort of list, or anything, in which she could look it up?

She was uncertain, but promised to do her best. How much did I want to spend?

'Five pounds,' I said.

I could hear that she was impressed.

That was all the time I could give to it because, as Mrs Rowell would have said, the most frightful things were happening at Wingate's.

There was a printers' strike.

We had done a formidable job of selling *Exodus* and *The Desert Generals*. In advance of publication we had sold twenty-one thousand copies of the first, and nine thousand of the second. Since they were both thirty-shilling books and a publisher always sells to the bookshops at two-thirds of the published price, this meant that exactly thirty thousand pounds would flow into our coffers the moment the printers would agree to load those books on to lorries. And that was simply the pre-publication sale. We could reasonably rely on twice that again, once the books were on the market.

I tried everything. I even offered to drive down to Exeter at the head of a fleet of vans and help load the books myself.

The situation was not really alarming at all. Obviously the printers, to whom we owed at any given moment large sums of money on a long-term credit arrangement, were not going to press for payment when it was their own wretched strike which was running us out of funds. The gas-man, it is true, was threatening to wind us up. So was the Income Tax man. But there was a great fund of goodwill among our suppliers, our printers, our blockmakers, our artists, our authors, and all the other people whose future was linked with ours.

I wish I could tell you what it was that led me to take the decision which I have been convinced, ever since, was the greatest mistake of my life.

I remember standing in a half-rebuilt City street, with new skyscrapers sprouting from ugly bomb-sites, and a view of the old Roman wall. It was raining.

We stood under umbrellas. There were people there of whom I was very fond, and others who represented people to whom I owed all that really matters in life.

They put the arguments to me. I argued back. I said that Wingate's was *saved*, that all we needed now was strong nerves for a week or two, and a splendid future was before us. I am sure this was true. If I had been a tycoon I would have over-ruled them. But I am not that sort of man, particularly when the family is involved. So I gave in.

'O.K.,' I said. 'Wind up.'

They rushed away from me with happy faces.

Four days later I woke in the night. It was Charles again.

I was suddenly aware of him in the room, and, this time, it was I who was angry. My nerves had been too stretched. I couldn't face the post-mortem. This time I spoke to the guards—or wardens:

'Look,' I said, 'I'm terribly sorry, but could you stop that man coming? I don't want this to become a habit. And I dislike this whole business. I don't want anything to do with the spirit world, or whatever it is. It upsets me. To be honest I'd much rather not *know*. So if you would be very kind and just take him away I'd be really grateful. I don't want to hurt anybody's feelings, but I'm sure you understand.'

There was a ten-second pause, during which I got the odd sensation of intelligences—rather surprised intelligences—digesting what I'd said. Then came the unmistakable impression of old Charles being hustled away. He seemed to call over his shoulder, with the Doppler effect of hurried removal.

244

'There's something I wanted to say! I just wanted to say . . .'

I got a strong sensation of struggle, and even of reluctance as if the guards were soft-hearted and turned to me for some sign of relenting.

I wouldn't relent, and his words came to me, very clearly, in a tiny shout, as he was finally led away, camel-hair coat, exophthalmia and all, 'Thanks for the flowers!'